Passage
to
Promise
Land

Passage
to
Promise
Land

Voices of Chinese Immigrant Women to Canada

VIVIENNE POY

McGill-Queen's University Press

Montreal & Kingston · London · Ithaca

ISBN 978-0-7735-4149-8

Legal deposit second quarter 2013
Bibliothèque nationale du Québec

Printed in Canada on acid-free paper that is 100% ancient forest free
(100% post-consumer recycled), processed chlorine free

McGill-Queen's University Press acknowledges the support of the
Canada Council for the Arts for our publishing program. We also
acknowledge the financial support of the Government of Canada
through the Canada Book Fund for our publishing activities.

Library and Archives Canada Cataloguing in Publication

Poy, Vivienne, 1941–
Passage to promise land : voices of Chinese immigrant
women to Canada / Vivienne Poy.

Includes bibliographical references and index.
ISBN 978-0-7735-4149-8

1. Chinese Canadian women–Interviews. 2. Chinese
Canadian women–Social conditions–20th century. 3. Women
immigrants–Canada–Interviews. 4. Women immigrants–
Canada–Social conditions–20th century. I. Title.

FC106.C5P69 2013   305.48'4120971   C2012-908373-9

This book was designed and typeset by studio oneonone
in Minion 10.6/14

To Beverley

This book is dedicated to all

Chinese immigrant women in Canada

with best wishes

Vivienne
Feb 13

Contents

Preface

This volume might be described as a panorama of the twentieth century – on two sides of the world. Canada went through two world wars and developed from a narrowly Eurocentred semi-colonial outpost into a nation that embraced a multicultural identity and gained respect for its independent foreign policy and initiatives in peacekeeping. China went through those same world wars, followed by a Communist revolution in 1949 and thirty years of political movements that led to great suffering for many of its citizens. Following Deng Xiaoping's accession to power in 1978 and the decision to open up to "modernization, the world and the future," China's economic progress changed the face of the nation and its role in the world. The tiny outpost of Hong Kong on the South China coast, a British colony from 1842 to 1997 and a dynamic city, also changed dramatically over the twentieth century. Its role as a way station for refugees from China who found their way to Canada in the years after the Second World War, along with the special relationship it developed with Canada in the years leading up to its return to China in 1997, give it a prominent place in the unfolding story.

The focus on Chinese women who moved between China, Hong Kong, and Canada gives this story its unique character, providing unusual insights into the historical change process. Their lives were often caught up in restrictions imposed by China's patriarchal traditions and in disadvantages arising from discrimination and bias in Canadian immigration policy. Nevertheless, they exerted a remarkable degree of agency in the decisions they made and in their contributions to "Promise Land," the name given to their newly adopted country in the early years. The framework drawn from feminist analysis and understanding is introduced delicately, non-dogmatically, and in ways that shed new light on many well-known junctures in Canadian history.

In chapters 2 to 9 of this volume, we are treated to the vivid narratives of twenty-eight women who emigrated to Canada between 1950 and 1989 – years of political, economic, and social change in China, Hong Kong, and Canada. They tell the stories of their childhood in China or Hong Kong and the conditions that led to their immigration to Canada. This was largely a matter of family reunion or pre-arranged marriage in the early years; later, higher education became a main attraction, and ultimately it was the diverse professional and business opportunities that opened up. For most of these women, the opportunity to tell their stories was welcomed, and in some cases they felt it had been a healing and affirming experience. Follow-up interviews with many of them in 2010 has enabled us to observe their progress into the first decade of the twenty-first century.

Chapter 1 provides a historical background that explains the highly discriminatory immigration policies that had barred entry to Chinese women, with a few exceptions, up to the late 1940s. The role of the early immigrants, including such outstanding activists and political organizers as Jean Lumb and Douglas Jung, in demanding equal citizenship rights and fair immigration policies, gradually led to a more equitable playing field. Finally, Hong Kong's prosperity and Canada's policies of encouraging an investor category of immigration created a situation that was favourable to Chinese immigrants, and the stories of professional women and business leaders coming in this later period are riveting. Sadly, it did not mean the end of discrimination, since new causes for social prejudice arose from an envy inspired by the educational and economic success of many Chinese Canadians. Chapter 10 ties all the threads of the stories together in a thoughtful analysis of the interconnected historical causes lying behind the dramatic changes that unfolded between the 1950s and the first decade of the twenty-first century.

Generally, this is an uplifting story, with compelling evidence of the greatly increased agency and possibility for Chinese women over the decades, and a remarkable degree of agreement among those interviewed that their lives had been transformed in positive ways by the opportunity to settle in Canada. By the same token, they have made remarkable contributions to Canadian society as teachers, university administrators, artists, community organizer, and multinational businesswomen. All of this, of course, rested on their equally important roles as homemakers and as the heart and soul of Chinese Canadian communities. In some cases, Chinese women have excelled in important social and political leadership roles, reflecting the increasingly prominent role women have played in Hong Kong's social history.

Nevertheless, readers should not view this as a book narrowly focused on the experience of Chinese women. Rather, it is a breathtaking overview of Canadian history seen from the perspective of women immigrants who have contributed in important ways to that history. A rich array of historical sources, from scholarly texts to archival material, newspapers, and the records of parliamentary debates, have been drawn upon to give a critical account of changing immigration policies over more than a century. Given the importance of immigration in Canada's history and the composition of the Canadian population, it is also a book about Canadian identity. Insightful analysis is given into the interconnection between the reform of immigration policy and Canada's efforts to improve its international image in the 1960s. The slow unfolding of a policy of multiculturalism is also presented, beginning in the early 1970s and culminating in the passage of the Multiculturalism Act of 1988. There is further analysis of how Canada has navigated the difficult waters of globalization since the end of the Cold War in 1991 and how it has benefited from the input of a privileged and mobile international capitalist class of people.

Most of all, this is a very human book – connecting readers to successive generations of immigrants, their parents and grandparents, their children and grandchildren, their joys, anxieties, efforts, and achievements. It is a book that calls upon readers to interrogate themselves and reflect on where they have been over these years and how they have contributed to, or possibly resisted, the social transformations that are described. It is also a book that calls for much comparative reflection – across different time periods and among different groups of immigrants and citizens in Canada's cultural mosaic.

I would like to bring this preface to a close by sharing with readers a little about the remarkable author of this book. She came to Canada from Hong Kong for university studies in 1959, and thus her life experience has some parallels with the women whom she profiled in chapter

6. Subsequently she has had a highly distinguished career. Not satisfied with her university qualifications, she later studied in a community college and became a successful fashion designer. In 1998 she was appointed to the Senate of Canada, the first Asian woman to hold such a role, and in 2003 she was elected chancellor of the University of Toronto. Over these demanding years she also pursued a doctoral degree in history at the University of Toronto under the guidance of the renowned scholar of Chinese religion and philosophy, Professor Julia Ching. When Julia passed away in the autumn of 2001, I was privileged to take over as chair of her doctoral thesis committee and saw her through to a successful defence in July 2003.

She was thus conferred a doctoral degree in history and inaugurated as chancellor of the University of Toronto at one and the same graduation ceremony in November 2003. This was the celebration of a remarkable combination of dedicated scholarly effort and outstanding community leadership. Most recently, in May 2010, she was recognized as one of Canada's Top 25 Immigrants, a people's choice award based on a wide popular vote. The publication of this book stands as further testimony to her remarkable ability to combine academic scholarship with service to the community and nation. It is based on a large amount of documentary research and repeat interviews with many of her research subjects during the years since the defence of the doctoral thesis. It has built on the findings and analysis of the thesis in ways that enable the reader to engage with current and emerging issues of Canadian identity at the end of the first decade of the twenty-first century.

Professor Ruth Hayhoe
Ontario Institute for Studies in Education
University of Toronto

Acknowledgments

I have been very fortunate to have the assistance of Irene Brown, Paul Chan, Carol Irving, Carole Lefebvre, Peggy Ku, Carol Reichert, and Peter Yeung, as well as staff at Citizenship and Immigration Canada, Library of Parliament, the Library and Archives Canada, and the Richard Charles Lee Canada–Hong Kong Library (formerly a resource centre), whose help has been invaluable to me, and to all of them I say thank-you.

Friends in the Chinese Canadian communities have been most helpful: Jean Lumb, *tusheng* community activist, who told me about her life; Howe Lee, president of the Chinese Canadian Military Museum Society, who gave me information and documentation on Chinese Canadian veterans; and Trevor Sam, who generously shared his research on a biography of his father, Douglas Sam. To these friends, I wish to express my greatest gratitude.

I am grateful to Dr Jessica Li, who assisted me with updating my research to 2010, to Professor Bernard Luk, who helped me through the historical background of China, Hong Kong, and Canada, and to Professor Eric Fong, who gave me the perspective of seeing through the eyes of a sociologist. I thank my husband, Dr Neville Poy, for providing some of the photographs and for converting and preparing the map and all the photographs to make them ready for publication.

I wish to thank all my interviewees who so generously gave me their time, and who offered the information central to this book. Some interviews could not have proceeded without the assistance of Paul Chan and Yew Lee with translation from the Szeyup dialect. Thank you.

Last but not least, I owe my most sincere thanks to Professor Ruth Hayhoe and Professor Emeritus David Lai, who so generously offered to read my manuscript and gave me their guidance and opinions.

Vivienne Poy

Official opening of the first Chinese cemetery in Canada,
Harling Point, Victoria, BC, 8 April 2001. Courtesy of
Neville Poy.

Mary Mah holding her head tax certificate.
Courtesy of May Truong.

Establishment of the Chinese Canadian Heritage Fund,
19 February 2000. Courtesy of SFU Chinese Canadian
Heritage Fund.

Alberta Network of Immigrant Women, 4 May 2001.
Courtesy of Neville Poy.

Mon Sheong Foundation annual Fun Run, Mother's Day,
2000. Courtesy of Anjelina Kwong.

Grand Opening, Chinese Cultural Centre of Greater
Toronto, 2 May 1998. Courtesy of CCC of Greater Toronto.

Centre for Information and Community Services' launch of
Information Hotline, 18 April 2001. Courtesy of CICS.

Demonstration of CCCO against W5.
Courtesy of Irene Chu.

Carefirst Community Services, 31 October 2002.
Courtesy of CCS.

"Race in Media and Higher Education," OISE Town Hall
meeting, University of Toronto, 15 February 2011.
Courtesy of Yeong-Tong Chia.

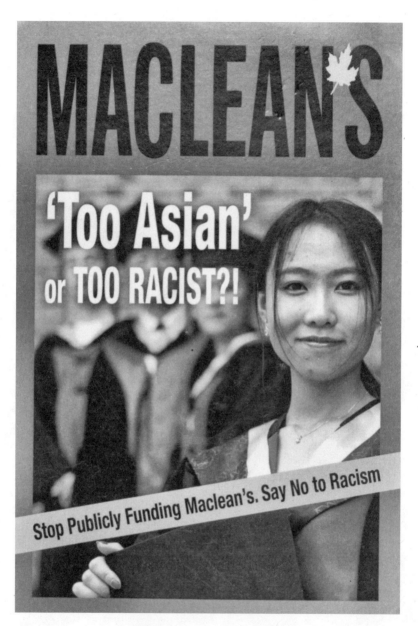

"Too Asian" postcard. Courtesy of Jenn Kuo, Graphics
Coordinator, Ryerson Students Union.

Safe Driving campaign for the Chinese community,
13 May 1999. Courtesy of Neville Poy.

Federal government's celebration of Asian Heritage Month,
Ottawa, 14 May 2003. Courtesy of Neville Poy.

Passage
to
Promise
Land

Hunan

Jiangxi

Fujian

Guangxi

Guangdong

Bei Jiang (North River)

Dong Jiang (East River)

Zhu Jiang (Pearl River)

Xi Jiang (West River)

●Guangzhou

Hoiping

Sunwui

Yunping

Toisan

Hong Kong

Macao

South China Sea

China

Map of South China

Hainan

■

Guangdong Province

Chapter 1

Introduction

The eighth of August 2008 was an auspicious day for Chinese Canadian communities. There was a grand celebration in Victoria, British Columbia, which in 1858 had been the first Canadian city to establish a Chinatown; the ceremonies marked the 150th anniversary of recorded Chinese settlement in Canada. There was a whole weekend of celebration, with participation by the federal, provincial, and municipal governments. The mayor of Victoria at the time was Allan Lowe, of Chinese descent. Chinese Canadians across the country received awards for their contributions to the community. This recognition of the success of many Chinese Canadians – despite severe institutional discrimination in the past – and of the present strength of the entire community in Canada was of great significance.

A great deal had happened over those 150 years. Canada had become a country, aided in no small way by Chinese labourers, who helped to open up British Columbia by building roads and working in mines, forestry, and canneries. It was their labour in building the most dangerous section of the Canadian Pacific Railway that had made it possible to link British Columbia to the rest of the country. No one could have imagined at Confederation that the mayor of Victoria would one day be of Chinese origin.

The Canadian government's attitude towards Chinese settlement in Canada has evolved from one of tolerance to exclusion to welcome. What happened? Through the voices of immigrant women, we will learn how the Chinese community has evolved and the role women played in building successful communities.

In the middle of the nineteenth century, a number of Chinese came to the colony of British Columbia, and many more were brought in during the early 1880s as labourers on the Canadian Pacific Railway. The Chinese constituted the first major group of non-European migrants to enter British Columbia. At the time, there was no official restriction on the entry of any racial group. Since the immigration policy of British North America was traditionally influenced by the constitutional and political links with Britain, the Chinese immigrants had the same rights, liberties, and privileges as other immigrants.[1]

Nonetheless, until the latter part of the twentieth century, because Canada's immigration and citizenship policy reflected its relationship with the source countries and because its economic agenda required a search for cheap labour, racism characterized the treatment of the majority of the Chinese who migrated to Canada.[2] For this reason, when the Canadian Pacific Railway was nearing completion in 1885, the dominion government imposed a head tax on the Chinese as a deterrent to their entry, and this was subsequently increased twice. However, the tax did not in fact deter their entry. Only when a Chinese exclusion act was passed into law in 1923 was Chinese immigration halted.

The head tax mainly affected the entry of men and adolescent boys. Until 1949, the Chinese communities in Canada consisted mostly of men who worked to send money home to support their families in China; they were bachelor societies. Few women migrated with their men because of the Chinese tradition of keeping the women back home to look after the in-laws, the children, and the graves of the ancestors. This occurred despite the fact that since women are the bearers of children, they should be an inseparable part of the men's lives.

The few Chinese women in Canada came mainly as dependants of the men, as wives, daughters, and servants, though some women brought to Canada were forced to work as prostitutes. The men who brought the women were mostly merchants, though some were ministers of the church and some were teachers. Despite their small numbers, these women played an integral part in the economic survival of the Chinese Canadian communities. In this connection, it is important to note that despite Chinese women's historical lack of equal rights in the family and lack of opportunity to participate in politics and society, they had contributed significantly to social, cultural, and economic production throughout Imperial China.[3]

After the Second World War, political turmoil in China became the impetus for family members left behind in China to leave the country. Meanwhile, the Canadian government at last made it possible for them to enter Canada. Canada's involvement in the Second World War had influenced Canadian policy makers in respect to immigration because of the fight against Nazism and Fascism. At the same time, Chinese Canadian veterans as well as other human rights activists had lobbied the federal government for the right of citizenship for the Chinese residing in Canada. This would enable them to sponsor their family members in China to come to Canada. On the other side of the Pacific, China was in the throes of a civil war, which ended with the establishment of the People's Republic of China in 1949. This became the push factor for emigration from China. All of this marked the beginning of the end of the bachelor society and the formation of family life for the Chinese in Canada. As the law changed, more women came, but it was not until the 1970s that their numbers approached those of the men.[4]

While there was some loosening of immigration policy in the 1940s and 1950s, Canada had a "white" immigration policy until the 1960s. Immigration restriction on account of race was not uniquely anti-Chinese, since similar restrictions were imposed on other non-European groups, based on the supposition that they were inassimilable because of race, customs, and religion. What was unique in the case of the Chinese was that they were the only group ever targeted by legislation to limit their entry into Canada. Today, the Chinese Canadian communities across the country are flourishing, and it is because of the arrival of the women. Women, together with their children, build communities because mothers want a better future for their children. At the same time, the men no longer need to send their earnings back to China; their families are with them and can contribute to the economic and social well-being of Canada.

This book tells the stories of women who immigrated to Canada in the second half of the twentieth century and made the country their home. The stories are told in their own words, through interviews I conducted between 2000 and 2003. The book focuses on women's agency, their experiences with patriarchy in Chinese culture, and how they dealt with different forms of discrimination in China and Canada. Through their voices, we hear of their immigration and settlement experiences after the repeal of Chinese exclusion.[5] I use gender for historical analysis because women have a different perspective from men on events and on society in general. We learn of the evolution of the Chinese community because of changes in Canadian immigration legislation and regulations, and we hear why the immigration of Chinese families became a norm in the 1970s and why some women were able to apply as heads of household.

Historically, all Chinese who migrated to North America in the nineteenth and most of the twentieth centuries were from the southern coastal region of China, and their port of departure was usually the British colony of Hong Kong. They spoke Cantonese as well as their own village dialects, and the better educated also spoke English. Thus, the interviews were conducted in Cantonese, Szeyup, and English.[6]

Mandarin speakers were not part of this study because having arrived recently either directly from the People's Republic of China or from Taiwan, their life experiences would be very different from those of the original Chinese settlers in Canada, as well as those in the large migration from Hong Kong since the 1980s.[7] Even in terms of their use of written Chinese, those who immigrated in the 1990s from the People's Republic of China were educated in simplified Chinese characters (*jiantizi*), which are different from the traditional Chinese writing (*fantizi*) used by the Chinese from Hong Kong, Taiwan, and most established overseas Chinese communities.

My interviewees were chosen at random, covering the period of immigration from 1950 to 1990. In the interviews, we can see the evolution of the different types of immigrant Chinese women, beginning with those who came direct from the villages of South China and those who migrated from cosmopolitan Hong Kong. The interviews tell of their status in their home societies, the locales from which they came, their level of education, how they entered Canada, and their settlement experiences. I follow the life course of each woman, hearing how her life was constructed, organized, and defined by patriarchy in her home society and how it was redefined by the Canadian immigration system. I explore how, in the course of her immigration and settlement into life in a new country, she made choices and exercised her own agency within the constraints of patriarchy, the immigration system, and the laws of Canada. As the laws and regulations in Canada changed, Chinese women were able to immigrate to Canada under different categories instead of only as dependants of men. Their stories provide a woman's perspective on Canadian immigration policy and also illustrate the changing status of women in the Chinese Canadian communities.

The year 1950 was chosen as a starting point because that was the beginning of family reunification for Chinese Canadian families when the men could at last bring their dependants to Canada. This was also the year when one of my two ninety-year-old informants immigrated with her children to join her husband in Canada; she was the earliest immigrant among my group of informants. When I was updating the research for this book, some of the original interviewees agreed to be interviewed again, so we are able to have a sense of their lives up to 2010. Unfortunately, I was not able to locate everyone, and a few have passed away.

I interviewed twenty-eight Chinese immigrant women of different ages, the oldest two being ninety and the youngest in her late thirties. The former represented the original Chinese women immigrants after the Second World War. Their experiences during the Sino-Japanese War and the civil war in China, as well as their lives under the Communists soon after the establishment of the People's Republic of China, were very different from those of the women who came to Canada at a later date.

The interviews were carried out in Ontario and British Columbia, the two provinces with the largest ethnic Chinese populations. I was fortunate to be able to conduct many of my interviews in Victoria in the historic Chinese Consolidated Benevolent Association (CCBA), thanks to the kind assistance of Paul Chan, former president of the CCBA. The rest were conducted in Ottawa and Toronto as well as by telephone. Some of the older informants spoke only the Szeyup dialect, since they had spent a large part of their adult lives in the villages in South China. When they arrived in Canada, their social circles were in Chinatown, where most residents spoke the same dialect, since they all came from the same region. Paul Chan, as well as the son of one of my informants in Ottawa, very kindly helped with translations into Cantonese or English, since I know only a smattering of the Szeyup dialect.

As an immigrant Chinese woman myself who came from Hong Kong and whose ancestors originated in the Pearl River Delta, like many of the women I interviewed, I felt very comfortable with my informants. Furthermore, the fact that I have participated in functions held by various Szeyup associations in different parts of Canada helped my informants feel that they could speak to me in confidence, knowing that I would understand their immigration experiences.[8] In fact, some of them referred to me as their village cousin, telling me they were familiar with my ancestral villages in China.[9]

I had some initial difficulties in obtaining interviews with Chinese businesswomen who immigrated to Canada as independent entrepreneurs and investors, since many were in partnership with their husbands, which automatically disqualified them as interviewees. However, I was successful in finding an informant who immigrated to Canada in the investor category and also a businesswoman who came as the head of household in the entrepreneur category. My group did not include any women who immigrated as dependants in "astronaut" families in the 1980s.[10]

It is normal for women to talk to one another about experiences in our lives, good or bad, and we like to be heard. For some of my informants, it was a chance to have their stories recorded, and I had a sense of being able to give voice to the voiceless. In listening to the stories, it became apparent that the notions of victimization and agency were not clear-cut. In fact, even those who were seen to be victimized by the Canadian immigration system had actually proved capable of manipulating the system to their own advantage. When women immigrated to Canada, because their labour was needed for the survival of the family, their agency became more obvious. This is evident even with the less-educated women. Agency is, after all, partly a matter of circumstances and partly a matter of personality.

Some of the women brought supporting documents to show me. One brought a copy of her husband's head tax certificate and a photograph of the family when they first settled in Canada. Another brought a copy of her passport containing the official stamp she received when she was first approved by Canadian Immigration. I sensed that these women were happy that someone wanted to hear their life stories, and I believed what I was doing was important and should be recorded.

During the interviews I uncovered events that were known to immigrants but never recorded. Some interviewees expressed relief in being able to tell their stories. One actually said that it was a healing process for her, because she had never before told her story to anyone, and she felt so much better afterwards. Another gave me what I considered very confidential information and insisted that I should put it on paper. It was her way of asserting herself.

The names used for the informants are fictitious in order to protect their identities. In some of the interviews, readers may find some information that might identify the speakers, but I have been careful to include only information of this nature which the person herself insisted should be there and which is important in the context of this book.

Readers will note that all my interviewees have done reasonably well in Canada, despite the fact that they came from very different economic and educational backgrounds. On their arrival, many experienced great economic hardship, as well as difficulty with language and cultural adjustment, but with perseverance, they overcame their difficulties. Whatever crises some had to face in the past are over now, and they no longer mind talking about them. This in itself is a built-in limitation to my research, because I have interviewed the survivors of the Canadian immigration system. What happened to the others? I believe a comparison study needs to be done on women who have fared poorly in Canada.

It became obvious in my interviews that when they had a choice, many of the women from the villages of South China chose to immigrate with their husbands. The life of the early migrants is illustrated in greater detail in the life stories of Chow and Kan. These women became pregnant each time their husbands visited China – once every few years for as long as they could afford it, though some husbands stayed for as long as the Canadian immigration law would allow without penalty.[11] The wives left in China would ask letter writers to send messages reminding their husbands how difficult it was for them to perform the duties of wives and daughters-in-law without foreign remittances. Keeping in mind that marriages were arranged in traditional China, as in the stories of Chow and Kan, romantic love did not exist. As Chow kept repeating in her interview, her marriage was "blind." In choosing partners for their sons, parents often chose daughters-in-law for themselves, since the young women would be living with them.

Chow talked about the importance of the remittances, not only from her husband but also from his brothers, who were overseas too; the entire family in China depended on them. During the Second World War, families that had been receiving overseas remittances suffered greatly because of the disruption of communications. The act of sending remittances was not only a necessity; it had become ritualized and in-stitutionalized within the overseas Chinese communities.[12]

Being tied to one's home and ancestral village had always been very strong in Chinese culture. I believe that after the Second World War, if China had been peaceful and prosperous, the story of the immigration of Chinese women to Canada would have been very different. One can only guess what the Chinese Canadian community would have been like today.

The introduction of the points system into the immigration regula-tions in 1967 had a great influence because it allowed individuals to im-migrate on the basis of their education, skills, and entrepreneurship and, in the 1980s, on the basis of their investments as well. Of great signifi-cance for Chinese women has been the freedom to immigrate as indi-viduals and as heads of households when an entire family immigrates. Among the later Chinese immigrant women, many were well educated, and many others came to Canada for higher education. Because of their educational background in Hong Kong, their English-language skills, and their adaptation to the Canadian culture of rights, freedom, and equality, they expected to be treated as equals in their adopted country.

From the 1980s on, immigrants of Chinese heritage have been by far the largest group entering Canada.[13] By the turn of the twenty-first cen-tury, Chinese had become the third most-spoken language in Canada after the two official languages of French and English.[14] And despite the fact that Chinese women did not immigrate to Canada in large numbers until the 1970s, over the years there have been numerous outstanding leaders: political figures such as MPs Sophia Leung and Olivia Chow, successful entrepreneurs such as Cindy Lee of T&T, and community leaders such as MLA Teresa Woo-Paw of Calgary, as well as numerous outstanding women in the professions and academia.

The journey, from the first mention of immigration of Chinese women in the Canadian parliament in 1879, referring to them as "slaves" and "prostitutes," to the end of the twentieth century, when an immi-grant Chinese woman was appointed to the Senate of Canada and an-other was appointed as governor general of Canada, is a very long one.[15] This book details the important events along this journey through the voices of the women.

Chapter 2

Reuniting Families

The Second World War marked the turning point for Chinese Canadians, both in China and in Canada. In 1945 the civil war in China, which ended with the establishment of the People's Republic of China in 1949, changed the relationship between the Chinese Canadian communities and their Chinese homeland. At the time, there were more than six million dependants of overseas Chinese (*qiaojuan*) in Guangdong Province, mainly in the rural areas of eastern Guangdong, the Pearl River Delta, and the adjacent four counties (Szeyup).[1] Members of the overseas households made up one-fifth of the total population of Guangdong Province, and many of them were family members of Chinese Canadians.[2]

The Chinese Communist policy towards investment in China by Chinese living overseas fluctuated between encouragement and condemnation. This brought about a collision between efforts at socialist transformation and domestic policy regarding overseas relations, and resulted in ideological and bureaucratic confusion. The promotion of class division and class struggle in the villages ran directly against the intractable realities of the lives of those who depended on foreign remittances: their lack of labour power; the preponderance of the elderly, women, and children in their populations; and their inability and unwillingness to engage in agricultural production.[3]

Since 1949, there had been numerous contradictory views about the overseas Chinese expressed within the Communist Party, from seeing them as ethnic loyalists who could be made to join a patriotic united front, to regarding them as a subversive fifth column for capitalism in China; and from regarding them as being within the broad ranks of the labouring people to seeing them as anti-Communist and enemies of the people. For example, in 1954 a policy of special privileges was aimed at this group in order to mobilize the financial resources of domestic overseas Chinese for development purposes. However, during the Cultural Revolution of the 1960s this group was regarded as contemptible, if not treasonous.[4]

Following the Second World War, the Cold War served to block or discourage overseas Chinese remittances. With the land reform in China in the early 1950s, together with the socialization of the Chinese economy, the traditional lineage system was destroyed, and a most important avenue of investment for Chinese Canadians in the homeland was blocked. Also during this period of land reform, many families of overseas Chinese were branded as landlords and persecuted, and travelling back and forth between Canada and China ended.[5]

On the Canadian side, Canadian immigration policy was going through changes because of Canada's international involvement with refugees, its role in the Commonwealth, the postwar economic conditions, and a labour shortage. As Prime Minister Mackenzie King said in the House of Commons on 1 May 1947, "The government has also extended admissibility to persons who are suitable for employment in the primary industries. As hon. members are aware, Canada's primary industries are experiencing an acute shortage of manpower."[6]

Policy makers in Ottawa were also concerned about emigration from Canada and as the low rate of population growth. In his speech in the House of Commons, Mackenzie King said, "The policy of the government is to foster the growth of the population of Canada by the encouragement of immigration ... The population of Canada at present is about 12,000,000. By 1951, in the absence of immigration, it is estimated that our population would be less than 13,000,000 and that by 1971, without immigration, the population would be approximately 14,600,000 ... In a world of shrinking distances and international insecurity, we cannot ignore the danger that lies in a small population attempting to hold so great a heritage as ours."[7]

Besides economic interests, issues of race and ethnicity had influenced the Canadian agenda. Fighting a war against Fascism and racism helped the Canadian government realize the undemocratic aspect of the country's immigration policy. In 1946 an Act Respecting Citizenship, Nationality, Naturalization and Status of Aliens (also known as the Canadian Citizenship Act) was passed.[8]

After the passage of the act and the repeal of Order-in-Council 1378, which had prevented Chinese residents in Canada from becoming naturalized citizens, more than 22,000 Chinese residents became naturalized.[9] Furthermore, some Chinese Canadian veterans, as well as civil rights groups, led by people such as E.C. Mark of Toronto and Foon Sien of Vancouver, lobbied Ottawa for the repeal of the Chinese exclusion act, as well as for the right of ethnic Chinese to vote as Canadian citizens.[10]

The general world trend towards decolonization and human rights helped the cause of the Committee for the Repeal of the Chinese Immigration Act, which was formed at the end of November 1946. The committee was based in Toronto and closely associated with the United Church of Canada.[11] It included seventy-nine prominent Canadians of whom 80 percent were non-Chinese.[12] Their legal adviser was Toronto attorney Irving Himel. The committee had support from Chinese and non-Chinese organizations across Canada, including the Protestant and Catholic churches, the Council of Women, several members of Parliament, the Canadian Labour Congress, and the Toronto Trades and Labour Councils.[13] The committee sent a statement to the minister of mines and resources, whose department was responsible for immigration at the time, setting out the reasons why the Chinese Immigration Act of 1923 should be repealed. Following a successful campaign, the franchise was granted to the Chinese at all levels.[14]

Despite the act's repeal and the government's approval of limited postwar immigration designed to recruit labour in Europe, Mackenzie King mirrored the wishes of the majority of the nation by proclaiming that it was not the intention of the government to change the social composition of the country. While sustained prosperity and a slowly widening circle of racial and ethnic tolerance gradually eroded barriers against eastern and southern Europeans, as well as against Jews who were displaced by the war, the barriers remained concerning immigrants from Asia.[15] In the immigration act passed in 1947, many discriminatory clauses and regulations were retained. "Any considerable oriental immigration would, moreover, be certain to give rise to social and economic problems of a character that might lead to serious difficulties in the field of international relations," said Mackenzie King in the House in May 1947. "The government, therefore, has no thought of making any change in immigration regulations which would have consequences of the kind."[16]

The act stated that "the Chinese Immigration Act, Chapter ninety-five of the Revised Statute of Canada, 1927, is repealed."[17] From that time on, Chinese immigrants came under the regulation governing other Asian immigrants, PC 2115: "From and after the 16th August, 1930, and until otherwise ordered, the landing in Canada of any immigrant of any Asiatic race is hereby prohibited, except as hereinafter provided: the wife or unmarried child under 18 years of age, of any Canadian citizen legally admitted to and resident in Canada, who is in a position to receive and care for his dependants."[18] This applied to all Asian immigrants who had obtained Canadian citizenship, including Chinese.

Although the Canadian Citizenship Act had been passed in 1946 and the Chinese Immigration [Exclusion] Act was repealed in 1947, it was not until April 1948 that the machinery was set up to accept applications from the dependants of Chinese Canadians. The new legislation continued to imply restrictions on Chinese families. Instead of allowing any Chinese resident in Canada to bring in his dependants, (as was the case for other immigrants), the government allowed only those who were Canadian citizens to bring their wives and minor children.[19] Despite this, there were immediate changes in the Chinese communities in which families could be reunited. Up to that point a very small proportion of the Chinese had secured naturalization.[20] When the Chinese exclusion act was repealed, naturalization took on new significance because it meant that one could sponsor one's dependants.[21]

The legal procedure to obtain citizenship papers was slow and could take anywhere up to two years. This explains the small number of citizenship papers granted initially. Soon after the certificates of naturalization were granted, citizens could register with the National Employment Services of the Department of Labour and Immigration Services, recording their desire to bring their dependants to Canada. Because of the normal lapse of time involved between receiving the certificates of citizenship and the registration by Chinese Canadians with the National Employment Services, the number who arrived in Canada were very small at first.

Table 1
Certificates of citizenship granted

Year	No.
1947 (calendar year)	34
1948 (calendar year)	276
1949 (calendar year)	570
1949–50 (fiscal year)	1,460
1950–51 (fiscal year)	3,145

Source: Based on the 1947–49 annual teport of the Department of Mines and Resources, and the 1949–51 annual report of the Department of Citizenship and Immigration, cited in Davidson, "Analysis of the Significant Factors," 16

Table 2
Dependants arriving in Canada

Year	No.
1946–47	7
1947–48	24
1948–49	111
1949–50	1,028
1950–51	2,178

Source: Based on the 1946–49 annual reports of the Department of Mines and Resources and the 1949–51 annual reports of the Department of Citizenship and Immigration, cited in Davidson, "Analysis of the Significant Factors," 17

Throughout the 1950s and the beginning of the 1960s, selection based on geographic lines was another way of selecting immigrants according to race and culture.[22] The preference for immigrants from Europe remained. However, in 1955, immigration regulations towards dependants in China changed to admit some children up to the age of twenty-five years on compassionate grounds. This exception had already been applied to some Chinese Canadian citizens since 1950.

Despite the restrictions, Chinese immigration increased dramatically.[23] Between 1946 and 1955, fourteen thousand entered Canada, and by 1960 another ten thousand had landed. Spouses sent for by the older settlers made up one-quarter of the new immigrants in the early 1950s, many being wives who had been left in China with their children. In 1957 the right of immigration sponsorship for Asians was extended to include landed immigrants; this enabled Chinese who had immigrated to Canada after 1950 to sponsor their immediate dependants.[24]

The years from 1947 to the late 1950s were anxious ones for Chinese Canadian men and their family members in China. We learn about these years of anxiety from the experiences of three Chinese immigrant women, Chow, Kan, and May. First is the story of Chow, who immigrated in 1950. Chow was ninety years old when she was interviewed in Ottawa in the fall of 2001. Due to years of working on her feet, washing dishes and helping in their restaurants, her feet were swollen and she is now confined to a wheelchair. Her interview was delayed because she had not been well, and was staying in Sudbury, where her daughter lives.

At the time of the interview, Chow got out of her wheelchair and sat in an armchair before we started. She was accompanied by her son, who acted as translator from her Szeyup dialect into English. Chow spoke with a very strong voice, dotted with a smattering of English words, in an accent that was sometimes difficult to decipher. They brought with them a copy of her husband's head tax certificate and copies of newspapers about the head tax redress issue, as well as some family photographs. She began:

❖ I was born in a village in the district of Hoiping in 1911, into
a merchant family of two girls and seven boys. My family was
in the import-export business and was established in Changsha,
Hong Kong, and Guangzhou. Because we were well off, I got
to go to school in the village. As a young girl, I also had the
experience of helping as a cashier in one of the family businesses
in Changsha.

My husband came to Canada in 1913, paying a head tax of five
hundred dollars. He was also from Hoiping. When we got married in 1930, he was thirty-eight and I was nineteen. He was
handsome and good-natured. My parents thought that since he
was from *Gum San*, he must have been well off, and age was of

no importance to them. It was an arranged marriage. After the wedding, my husband returned to Canada.

My husband had many siblings. Some brothers were in the United States and one in Mexico. All the sons contributed to the family income. We were always short of money because of the bad business venture of the brother in Mexico. I lived with my in-laws in China, all the women and the children together, while the men were working abroad. My husband would return to China for visits, and each time I would get pregnant with another child.

The age difference between Chow and her husband was of no importance to her parents as long as he was a Gold Mountain *Gum San* guest. It was a common myth in China that those from *Gum San* (or Gold Mountain, as Canada was known) were all rich. Like many daughters-in-law in South China, Chow lived with her mother-in-law, to whom remittances were sent by all the men in the family who were working abroad, and the money was then shared by all members of the family.

❖ During the Sino-Japanese War, communications were cut off between the family in China and the men overseas. We had great difficulties during that period. I was able to buy some land to farm to grow vegetables. Some family members worked by cutting grasses, dried them, and sold them. Others went to cut firewood. We grew turnips and cooked them with shrimp paste. When we had extra turnips, we would dry them and keep them for food. It was a very hard life for me because I had never laboured before. I never had the choice in marrying into this family.

Throughout the interview, Chow stressed the fact that she was from a well-off family, so life was very hard during the war years: "In 1947 Chinese exclusion ended, and when my husband received his Canadian citizenship he came back to China with the intention of staying, but when he saw the civil war raging, he decided that it would be best to bring all of us to Canada." The civil war in China and the establishment of the People's Republic of China in 1949 were defining factors in the decision of many Chinese Canadian men to move their families to Canada. Traditionally, it had been common for Chinese men to save enough money abroad so that they could return to China, buy land, and attain the status they could not otherwise have had.

❖ In 1949, the small piece of land I bought to feed the family during the war was confiscated by the Communist government. I was glad to leave. Around that time, I gave birth to another child.

In 1950, when I was thirty-nine years old, our entire family came to Canada. We opened a restaurant in Sudbury, close to a big arena and near the railway station. Because I didn't know any English, I washed dishes, day in and day out. My feet became very swollen and I couldn't continue. I then made myself learn some English words so that I could work behind the cash register. My husband didn't think I could manage, but I did it very well.

Chow was hard-working and took great pride in her ability to adapt to the Canadian way of life and help to make a good living for the entire family. Although she did not know English, she had good business acumen and performed well as a cashier at her father's business: "You know, I memorized the English words by their sounds, including the names of the cigarettes I sold behind the counter. I'm very good in math and knew what things cost and what they should be sold for. I managed well even during lunch hours when I sold hundreds of lunches."

Chow's son interjected to explain how a restaurant managed to have so much business during the lunch hour. It was because much of its business was from miners who came to have their lunch pails filled. They were mostly single men with meal tickets to pay for their food, and they looked to Chinese restaurants as a centre of their social life where they could meet one another. There were thirty thousand miners in Sudbury in its heyday and only six restaurants in the area.

❖ Business was so good that we opened another restaurant. My husband looked after one, and I looked after the other. My husband worked until the day he died at the age of seventy-two from a concussion on the head. I suspected foul play, but there was never any proof. After my husband died, my older children didn't want to run the restaurants, so I sold part of the interest to my son-in-law and bought income properties in Sudbury, while my younger children went to school in Ottawa.

The properties I bought in Sudbury aren't worth much anymore. I really should have bought properties in Ottawa when my children were going to school there.

Chow's son explained that in the early 1980s, with forty thousand people laid off, the boom in Sudbury came to an end. Despite her age, Chow sounded the businesswoman that she was.

Chow reminisced about her difficult life. She said she spent her early years struggling to raise her children by herself in China, and later on she had to raise her teenage children on her own as a widow in Canada. She expressed her feelings in no uncertain terms, seeing herself as a victim of patriarchy because she did not have a choice in her marriage partner, who was twice her age. She did say that she was fond of her husband, who had been handsome, but she believed that she was definitely smarter than he, even though he was the one who could speak English. She believed that if it had not been for her, their business would not have prospered as it did during the boom period in Sudbury.

Chow did not mention whether she had a choice to immigrate to Canada, but for a woman from a village in South China during that period, the choice would not have been hers anyway. However, she did say that she had been glad to leave Communist China. She repeated the words "blind marriage" with reference to herself a few times, and she obviously felt victimized by it. What other choices she might have had, we will never know. Chow's Chinese education and her intelligence had made it easier for her to adapt in Canada, and together with her husband, she had been able to make quite a lot of money in Sudbury during its boom years. It helped that she had a good business head, as she told me.

Chow was a victim not only of patriarchy but also of the Second World War and the Chinese civil war that followed. I noticed that she did not mention once that she was fortunate not to have suffered great hardship under the Communists in China, even though they took away her land. But she had had the opportunity to immigrate to Canada with her children. What was important to her was her victimization by her blind marriage and by the head tax her husband had to pay to come to

Canada. In fact, she was very active in the redress movement to seek compensation from the government.

At the end of 2010, Chow, almost one hundred years old, was in a seniors' home and, according to her son, still feisty. She had received $20,000 from the federal government for the head tax redress that was paid to head-tax payers or their surviving spouses at the time of the apology made by the Canadian government.[25]

According to her son, Chow often reminisces about the good old days in China, the land and orchards her family used to own, and how prosperous they were. Her father also had made his money in *Gum San*. Being a daughter, she had been left behind in China and had never met her father, so her marriage to a "Gold Mountain guest" was not unexpected. Perhaps her objection to a blind marriage was a result of her observations in Canada.

In the case of the head tax, it should be remembered that it did not deter migration from China, even at $500 per person by 1903. Annual immigration reached four thousand in the last two years of the First World War, culminating in a total population of forty thousand ethnic Chinese by the end of the war, mostly men and adolescent boys. Sponsorship was always for male family members, and even extended male family members had priority over immediate female family members. So Chow would not have had the chance to go to Canada with her husband when they were married anyway.

Female members of the family were very seldom sponsored. Like Chow, female members of different generations lived together with their children and depended on the money, sent by their male relatives overseas. If one member of the family lost money the entire family suffered. That was the reason Chow complained about her brother-in-law in Mexico. The fact that her immediate family had immigrated to Canada and run their own business was in itself an assertion of freedom. Chow did have some agency in her life. She had the trust of her husband, and she was capable in managing the business. She was able to raise her children well and to look after her investments after her husband passed away. The death of her husband and the subsequent economic slump in Sudbury were unfortunate incidents over which she had no control.

The following is another story of a wife separated from her husband until after the Second World War. Kan's interview in Victoria had to be rescheduled twice because she had a busy social life. The interview took place in the spring of 2001 in the Chinese Consolidated Benevolent Association (CCBA) office in Victoria, with Paul Chan, former president of the CCBA, acting as translator because Kan only spoke the Szeyup dialect.

Kan was ninety years old at the time of the interview. She spoke confidently in a firm voice. Thinking that I could understand her perfectly, she rambled on, and all of a sudden I would be lost and Paul Chan would have to step in to translate.

❖ I was born in 1911 in a village in Toisan County, where my family leased land to farm. We were poor, and I was fortunate to have had three years of schooling.

My husband was sent to Canada at the age of thirteen or fourteen as a student, just before the passage of the exclusion act. At that time, Chinese students were allowed to enter Canada under the age of fourteen. Many Chinese boys entered as students and stayed as students for just long enough to fulfill the immigration requirements. After he left, two more ships brought Chinese to Canada, and then exclusion came into effect.

When my husband was eighteen, he came back to China to get married [1928]. I was then seventeen. He stayed for about four months and then returned to Canada. Three years later he came back to China again, and this time I became pregnant with our first son. When our son was a year old, he went back to Canada.

Kan's husband's family was able to manipulate the immigration act of 1903 to his advantage, and the fact that he had entered Canada before Chinese exclusion and did not have to pay the head tax was, to her, fortunate.[26] As she said, after leaving for Canada, he did not return to China for three years. Paul Chan explained to me that staying away for three years was normal for Chinese men working in North America; few could afford to make the trip back to China and then stay for months without earning. The only exceptions were those who worked in fish canneries because the work was seasonal and the pay was quite high.[27] However, these were known as suicidal jobs because the men had to work "like machines." Many of the cannery workers went back to China every year during the off-season when the plant was closed, and they helped with the farm work in the villages back home.

> ❖ During the Second World War, my husband was not able to visit me in China, and since communications were cut off, he couldn't even remit money to me, so I had to support my son and myself. I bought used clothes to sell, carrying them in baskets on a bamboo pole, and went from village to village. I sometimes travelled for days, and my son had to look after himself. This was normal for children whose poor parents had to work away from home. They helped each other to prepare meals. Once he told me that an aunt asked him to give his rice to feed her cat, and I told him not to do it again because we couldn't afford it.

Kan did not mention living with in-laws, as was the custom in the villages in China. But as she had been married at the age of seventeen, she would not have been left on her own. She never mentioned whether her husband had any siblings. Maybe she did not consider other family members important to her life story. The "aunt" who asked her son for rice for her cat could have been an unrelated person in her village, since in the Chinese tradition it is polite to call every female "aunt."

A woman like Kan had to be very resilient to survive. Her description of how she managed was heart-wrenching, but she was proud of her own capabilities, and being from a poor peasant background meant that she was used to hard work.

> ❖ After the war, in 1948, my husband came back to China, and this time our daughter was born. At that time he was not preparing to bring us to Canada; he thought it was fine for us to stay in China since the war was over. Soon after the birth of our daughter, he returned to Canada. In the meantime his uncle had taken our son to Hong Kong for schooling and to work.
>
> After the Communists won the civil war in China, my husband applied for me and my daughter to come to Canada. In 1953 [age 42] we immigrated, and I was relieved that the family could be together in Canada. I believe that we were allowed out of China because we were poor, since only the landowners in the countryside were targeted by the Communists.

After the war, Kan's husband was quite prepared to leave her and their daughter in China because both were women. Meanwhile, her son had moved to Hong Kong to stay with a great uncle. According to Chinese tradition, he would be the first in line to immigrate to Canada. However, with the establishment of the People's Republic of China in 1949, old traditions no longer applied. As with Chow, the push factor for immigration was the political situation in China. Noting that they left China in 1953, Kan was correct in saying that it was fortunate that they were poor because they were allowed to leave.

❖ I had to work so hard when I arrived in Canada, partly because we had to support my son and his family while they were in Hong Kong, waiting for immigration to Canada. We were anxious that he might start a business, which he had planned to do. In 1955 our son and his family immigrated to Canada. It was so nice that the entire family was reunited in Canada.

My husband worked as a waiter in Chinatown. Until I retired, I worked at different jobs. I was willing to do any kind of work. I worked in greenhouses, in outdoor farming, in the Maplewood factory slaughtering chickens, as well as cleaning streets. I did that kind of work in China anyway, so doing the same in Canada didn't make any difference.

We are glad to be in Canada because in China, no matter how hard you work, you could still go hungry, and sometimes when you wanted to work you couldn't find any.

Our children have good opportunities in Canada. My son worked for B.C. Ferries and is now retired. My daughter is a schoolteacher. Life has been good in Canada.

Kan was a victim of patriarchy in an arranged marriage, victim of the Sino-Japanese War, and victim of poverty in China. However, she and her entire family benefited from immigration to Canada, and she was grateful that Canada had given her children opportunities which they would not have had if they had remained in China. In making the choice to continue to work hard in Canada, Kan was able to have the greatest joy of her life, which was to be reunited with her entire family.

The above are life stories of two ninety-year-old women who were married in China during the exclusion period, which meant that immigrating to Canada was out of the question. At the same time, Chinese tradition dictated that they stay with their in-laws in China, and they were not expected to immigrate with their husbands.

Both Chow and Kan struggled through the war years. Their resilience and survival prepared them well for their new lives in Canada after 1947, when their husbands sponsored them. In fact, conditions in China were so bad that the Canadian government made special allowance to admit children of Chinese Canadian men up to the age of twenty-five. In a sense, Chow and Kan were victims of Chinese tradition and the political situation in China more than they were victims of Canadian exclusion. If the political situation had been different in China after the war, they probably would have remained in there. However, by being in Canada, where there were educational opportunities for their children, both women had their own agency in bringing up a new generation of Chinese Canadians who were totally immersed in Canadian culture, though this was not so much their own doing as a result of the educational system in Canada.

Neither of the women discussed their intergenerational relationship with their children, but from our conversations it was clear that they were able to retain parent-children ties – this despite their children's assimilation, which could have created a deep division between them, both linguistically and culturally. I suspect they had anticipated a cultural gap to arise as a matter of course and did not think about the matter as consciously as some of my other interviewees who were better educated and immigrated to Canada later.

By the beginning of the 1950s, because of the political situation in China, the majority of the South China immigrants had to go to Hong Kong as a first step. Their stay there gave them an urban experience that helped them with their integration into Canadian society.

Another interviewee, May, provides an example of family reunification that involves, not an older wife with children in tow but a young wife without children. I interviewed her in the CCBA office in Victoria in the spring of 2001. She had a pleasant demeanour and spoke entirely in Cantonese.

❖ I was born in a village in the district of Hoiping in 1929 and attended the village school. My family farmed the lineage land, and we always had enough to eat, even during the Sino-Japanese War.

My husband was born in Canada. In the 1920s, because of the tough economic times in Canada, his mother, while pregnant, brought him and his siblings back to China because life was easier there. She then left the older children in the village in the care of a woman the family hired, and she returned to Canada with the youngest two.

When the Second World War broke out, communications were cut between China and Canada. After the war, my husband's father wanted his son [my husband] to get married in China before he returned to Canada. In 1947 we were married [age 18[. We knew each other, being from neighbouring villages. Instead of bringing me back with him, he left me in China and he returned to Canada. In the meantime, I stayed in his village and lived with the woman who brought him up. I called her Foster Mother, and over the years we developed a close relationship.

In 1954, my husband asked me to go to Hong Kong as a first step to get to Canada.

The problem at that time was no longer immigration to Canada for family reunification; it was that those living in Mainland China had great difficulty leaving the country. It was to the advantage of the Communist government to keep family members of overseas Chinese in China so that it could use their financial remittances for the country's development.[28]

❖ I was fortunate that I had kept my status in my own family, which was that of landless peasant, and had not adopted that of my husband's family, the status of wealthy peasant. As a landless peasant, even though I lived in my husband's village, the village cadres – after Liberation in 1949 – allowed me to join the youth groups and participate in their activities, as well as attending school. It seemed that the authorities didn't have the record that I was already married, so when I applied to go to Hong Kong, I applied to go there to get married because my fiancé was returning from Canada for the wedding.[29]

According to May's description, the political situation in China was the main reason her husband wanted her to immigrate to Canada. Since his family had the status of wealthy peasant, she would be targeted sooner or later by the Communist cadres. Here again, it was the political situation in China that was the push factor in the wife's immigration.

❖ I was relieved to be given permission to go to Hong Kong for three months, along with my foster mother. We stayed in Hong Kong for three years, rented a room to live in while being supported by my husband and my father-in-law. I had to wait for three years before immigrating to Canada because my husband said he didn't have enough money, and he felt life would be too hard for me in Canada. In 1958 [age 29] I immigrated to Canada. I didn't mind moving twice, because that was the only way I could be with my husband.

When I first arrived in Victoria, because I knew little English I worked as a dishwasher at Oak Bay Marina for one dollar an hour. The chef liked me and asked me whether I would like to learn to make salads for one dollar and ten cents an hour. I did this for ten months, but then the restaurant's business didn't go well, and I was laid off.

A friend recommended that I apply to the Empress Hotel because they were hiring. I worked at the Empress as a salad maker for twenty-eight years, making hundreds of salads every day, working from 6 AM to 2:30 PM. I was the only ethnic Chinese there and the only woman in the kitchen until later years.

The fact that May was young and had stayed in Hong Kong from 1954 to 1958 helped her adapt to life in Canada fairly easily. During those four years, she would have been exposed to the English language and to Western food, such as salads.

❖ When I worked as a dishwasher, I worked only until I was pregnant. I stopped working when I had two children. When the youngest was six, I sponsored my husband's foster mother to come to live with us to help with the children so that I could go back to work. I felt very close to this woman, who had treated my husband as a son, and I want to look after her in her old age.[30] One of my nephews blamed me for not sponsoring my own mother, but my mother had other children who would look after her in China, and this foster mother didn't have any family. We were the only family she had.

My husband worked at a sawmill for over thirty years. We were content with our lives. I was urged by my husband and my children to retire at age sixty, and I have a good pension from the Empress Hotel. I really liked working at the hotel. I never experienced any discrimination in Canada, even though I always worked for white Canadians.

I like living in Canada because I'm free to do or say anything I want. In China, if you have a little more than others, people will be jealous of you, and if you have less, they will look down on you. I'm happy for the opportunities my children have in Canada, both in education and in job opportunities. Both my son and daughter are doing well. My son works in Vancouver, and my daughter works as a nurse in the Middle East. I am happy now that I'm retired and have the freedom to travel all over the world.

May's was another immigrant success story. Like Chow and Kan, she was glad to be out of China. She was thankful for the opportunities Canada gave her children, both in education and in job opportunities. It is difficult to know whether May would have immigrated to Canada if conditions in China had been different. She did not suffer under the Communists, though she probably would have, because of her marriage into the wealthy peasant class; and if she had remained in China, her husband would not have been able to visit her because of restrictions by the Chinese government. Her immigration was the obvious choice.

The three women interviewed did not have unrealistic expectations of their immigration to Canada. They continued to work hard and were able to feel fulfilled and happy. After 1949, and especially after the Korean War broke out, it became increasingly difficult for the families of Chinese Canadians to leave China. As May mentioned, she had to get to Hong Kong by deception first.[31] And on the Canadian side, throughout the 1950s the barriers against non-white immigration remained, with certain exceptions.[32] However, despite the difficulties both in leaving China and in entering Canada, between the end of the war and the mid-1950s more than 12,000 Chinese relatives of Chinese Canadian citizens had been admitted.[33]

The Chinese Canadian communities enjoyed a renewal through this family reunification. The new immigrants were culturally very different from their relatives who had lived in Canada for a very long time or had been born in Canada (*tusheng*), so conflict was bound to occur. However, it was the *tusheng* who lobbied the federal government and helped the entire community in changing the immigration law with respect to ethnic Chinese. The details are recounted in the following chapter.

Chapter 3

The Formation of Chinese Canadian Identity

After the Chinese [exclusion] Immigration Act was passed in 1923, the Chinese community was expected to wither. The young Chinese who grew up during the exclusion era attended English-language schools and worked in businesses that were open to non-Chinese customers. Yet despite the declining population, a new era emerged, characterized by increasing involvement in the social and political activities of the country and resulting in the formation of a distinct Chinese Canadian culture.[1]

By 1931, because of Chinese exclusion and the consequent lack of new blood, 75 percent of the Chinese Canadian teenagers were Canadian-born, and this helped to increase the English-language literacy rate to 83 percent. This period also saw an increase in naturalization, the highest rate of which was in Ontario. Over the next two decades, the most striking development was the greater participation of Chinese women in the white sector of the economy.[2]

On the eve of the Second World War, politicians were concerned that the Chinese would demand the vote if they were called up for duty. In the minds of many Chinese Canadians of military age, compulsory service was indeed intrinsically linked to obtaining this right. From 1940 on, the government would not call up Chinese Canadians for military training. There was never an official public announcement of the ban, but there were numerous stories of people of Chinese heritage being turned away, since "Orientals" were not accepted.[3]

However, the Canadian Armed Forces often overlooked official policy because of the government's contradictory statements and the insistence on secrecy in decision making. As a result, in the eastern provinces, not only did Chinese Canadians volunteer, but they were called up under the National Resources Mobilization Act (NRMA). British Columbia, however, remained strongly opposed to Asian involvement in the war effort.[4] The Royal Canadian Air Force accepted Chinese Canadians for aircrew from 1 October 1942 on, and this acceptance never became entangled in definitions of whether the applicants were British or ethnic Chinese, unlike the Canadian army, which lumped all categories together as "Allied Aliens."[5]

In 1944, the British High Command was looking for Chinese Canadians to serve with its Special Operations Executive (SOE), dubbed Force 136, to work behind enemy lines in Burma, Malaya, and the Dutch East Indies. Accordingly, in March it presented Canada with a request for Chinese Canadians "wanted for dangerous duties."[6] The SOE trained its agents in sabotage, subversion, and guerrilla warfare for service in Asia.[7] All of a sudden, it became an advantage not only to look Chinese but also to be able to speak the language.[8] Some resented being called up to fight for a country that denied them their rights as citizens, but the majority were glad to take this opportunity in order to demand full citizenship after the war.

No sooner had the enlistment begun than a few *tusheng* – who were not timid about pointing out to the Canadian government that its policies were wrong according to its own laws – took action to seek redress for their inferior constitutional status. To this end, they set up the Chinese Canadian Association in Vancouver, and in February 1945 the association petitioned the B.C. government "for the granting of franchise to all Canadians of Chinese descent in the province." The document decried the range of political and economic restrictions imposed on Canadian-born Chinese and referred with pride to their efforts at acculturation and assimilation, as well as their manifold contributions to the Canadian war effort. The petition argued passionately that since the Chinese Canadians bore – and bore gladly – full citizenship responsibilities, they should be entitled to all citizenship rights. Since the petition yielded no immediate result, at the end of the war the returning Chinese Canadian soldiers organized themselves into the Army, Navy, and Air Force Veterans of Canada, Unit 280, with its headquarters in Vancouver, to continue the lobbying effort.[9]

The membership of Unit 280 commanded respect from both inside and outside the ethnic group. However, after the successful conclusion of enfranchisement and the repeal of Chinese exclusion, it lost its raison d'être and became a low-key social club on Pender Street. Nevertheless, during the 1950s and the early 1960s, the *tusheng*, people such as Douglas Jung and Jean Lumb, presented themselves as heroes who had struggled for and achieved historical changes that benefited all ethnic Chinese.[10]

It was partly because of the *tusheng* lobbying for the reunification of Chinese families after the Second World War that an increasing number of women and children arrived from China, as described in the last chapter, and this in turn brought about the renewal of Chinese Canadian communities across the country. In 1956 the policy of Order-in-Council PC 2115 was finally abandoned, in part because of the pressure of the annual visits to Ottawa by the Chinese Benevolent Association's leader, Foon Sien, and no doubt also because of the Canadian need for labour at the time.[11] Thus, by the mid-1950s, the Chinese communities had managed to have the Canadian government remove the most crushing restrictions of Chinese immigration laws in Canada.

From the end of exclusion to 1956, the majority of the Chinese immigrants to Canada were the wives who had been left in China with their unmarried young children, women such as Chow and Kan, whose stories were told in the last chapter. When the rules were changed again in 1954, parents of Canadian citizens of Chinese descent were also admitted, and immigration became more of an extended family affair. By 1957, the group also included young wives whose husbands were post-1947 arrivals, because Chinese who were landed immigrants could now sponsor their families.[12] Not only were families reunited, but new families were formed with the arrival of young brides of Chinese Canadian men who preferred to marry girls from China rather than those born in Canada.

The later group of young brides was generally better educated, for many of them came from Hong Kong, Macao, or indirectly from Guangzhou, having had to stay in Hong Kong as a first migration out of China. Thus, they had urban experience, and because of their youth they were likely to adapt easily to the Canadian cultural environment. The story of Gina will illustrate this.

Gina was interviewed in the CCBA office in Victoria in the spring of 2001.[13] She came to the office with her husband and granddaughter as part of a family outing. During the interview, her husband and grand-daughter waited outside in the sitting room. She was composed and spoke entirely in Cantonese.

❖ I was born in a village in Hoiping County in 1943. I was the only child and lived with my mother. My father worked in the Philippines, and my mother didn't want to go there. I don't know my father at all, except that he sent money to support us. My father had another family in the Philippines. My family was well off, and we lived in a very nice house. My mother's family also owned land.

I went to school in Guangzhou, and I remember school was a lot of fun. One day in 1955, my mother came from the village to see me and then left for Hong Kong. She was only allowed to leave by herself, because the Chinese government believed that if she left me in China, she would always come back.

Gina talked about how difficult it was for Chinese citizens to leave China in the 1950s. For that reason, her mother, who belonged to the landlord class, did not want to live under Communism. She chose to leave China first, and expected her daughter to follow when an opportunity arose. At that time, Chinese citizens had to make false pretenses to leave the country, as mentioned in the story of May in the last chapter. Hong Kong was the first stop because it was culturally and linguistically Cantonese, like South China. Many of the immigrants had relatives and close friends there with whom they could stay.

❖ In 1958, when I was fifteen, I applied from Guangzhou for a student pass to visit relatives in Hong Kong. It would have been too difficult to apply from the village. I had to buy a return ticket to indicate that I would return to school at the end of the summer. The line-up for the train in Shenzhen was so long that my uncle advised me to go via Macao.

In Macao, I had to get an ID card before I could get to Hong Kong, and the wait was six months. Since I was not at school, I was going out all the time, and one day I met a distant relative who asked me to join them and be smuggled by boat to Hong

Kong. The cost was two hundred dollars, and of course I didn't have the money. She said my mother could pay for my trip when I arrived.

We started at night and got onto a boat. It was a very secretive and frightening, experience because we were stopped by a Hong Kong police boat. However, I'm sure it was all arranged between the smugglers and the police, so it was just a routine check. The boat landed in Aberdeen, where we were met by someone who took us by bus to the Southorn Playground.[14] From there, I was led by another person to my mother's address. My mother was out, and the man would not leave until she returned to pay him. Was my mother surprised when she saw me! After she paid this person twenty dollars for bringing me, he left. [The two hundred dollars was paid separately to the smugglers.] My mother was horrified to hear how I got to Hong Kong but was happy to see that I was safe.

Gina's story of how she arrived in Hong Kong during the 1950s was not unusual. The political situation had made it difficult for anyone to leave China, and the diplomatic relationship between China and Britain was such that it was not easy for Chinese nationals to get into Hong Kong. Many arrived illegally and were absorbed into the local community.

❖ While in Hong Kong, I went to night school in Wanchai for three years, every night from 7 to 9 PM. It was too difficult to get into a day school [1958] because there were too many students for the number of schools in Hong Kong. I learnt some English, but I'm no good at it. Also, I liked to help my mother, who worked in a factory. Sometimes she brought work to do at home, such as beading shoes. Toisan people like to work whether they need to or not!

Gina's difficulty in getting into a day school in Hong Kong was because of the sudden increase in population, legal and illegal, for which the schools were not prepared. The only practical way to deal with the situation was for the schools to have three sessions – morning, afternoon, and evening – thereby tripling the number of students enrolled.

❖ One day, when I returned home from a movie with a friend, I met an old friend of my mother's who had a granddaughter who married a Chinese man from Montreal. This friend asked Mother if I would like to go to Canada, because there was a very nice young man back in Hong Kong looking for a wife. My mother said that I was only seventeen, but if I liked this young man, she would give her blessing since it would happen sooner or later anyway. I met him and we went out together for two months. We liked each other, and everything went well. We were married in Hong Kong in 1961. My husband returned to Canada first, and I arrived by boat in time for Christmas.

The fact that Gina had been able to learn some English and gain some exposure to Western culture helped her integrate into Canadian society. Her education and background were probably also deciding factors in her marriage to her white-collar husband.

❖ My husband's grandfather came to Canada to build the railroad, and my husband's father paid the head tax to come to Canada. My husband was born in China, and when he was thirteen [1951], his father sponsored him to come to Canada. My husband owned a store in Victoria in partnership with his sister. When we got married, his sister had just had a baby, so he had to rush back to mind the business. After we were married, I helped in the store for three years until it was sold.

I was very lucky, because, when I arrived, I had a new house to live in. After the store was sold, my husband worked for the Royal Bank. Since my mother-in-law was helping to look after the children, I wanted to continue working. I got a job in a restaurant making sandwiches and salads.

Gina's story illustrates clearly the generations of Chinese men and boys who went overseas to make a living, leaving behind their women and the children who were conceived in China.

❖ I felt very fortunate because, unlike many Chinese immigrant women who didn't have much formal education, I didn't have to wash dishes. I worked in the restaurant for a few years, and then my husband decided to buy a gas station and tore it down to build a Chinese restaurant, which we ran.

The restaurant is now sold. Since then, my husband took a computer course. He now works as a self-employed accountant and I am retired. We travel back to Hong Kong and China frequently. We have two sons and two granddaughters.

I never met my father, and the only communication we had was through photographs that we sent each other. I never had any wish to visit him in the Philippines. He passed away a few years ago.

I'm not religious, but we practise ancestral worship.

In relating her life growing up, Gina revealed that her father, like her husband, had gone abroad to make a living, as was common among men from South China. If Gina had been a boy, her father would have sent for her to join him in the Philippines even if her mother had refused to go. But since she was a girl, she remained in China.

Gina believed it was her luck that had been the deciding factor in her life, which she compared favourably to other Chinese immigrant women at that time. She did not seem to have any settlement difficulties, being educated and having a knowledge of English. In her case, she did have agency in her choice of a husband. From meeting her husband and speaking to him briefly, I sensed a good marriage of a Chinese man who had found a wife of his choice and a Chinese woman who thought she was lucky, both to be married to a good man and to live in Canada. It was for these reasons that many such men returned to China and Hong Kong to look for marriage partners. They became the dream of many young Chinese women who wanted the chance of a life in *Gum San*. Similar types of marriage arrangements continued to be very common into the 1960s.

The influx of the new Chinese immigrants into Canada led to prejudice and conflict between them and the *tusheng*. The newcomers used their inflated cultural pride and self-assured Chineseness partly as self-defence against cultural dislocation in migration. It was also a reaction to the claim of the *tusheng* that their acculturation and identification with Canada had put them in a position to lead the way for the ethnic Chinese.

The best-known *tusheng* woman activist was Jean Lumb, who worked tirelessly for the reunification of families.[15] Lumb's passion for politics was a result of her father's influence.[16] After the Chinese were given the vote in 1947, her father was proud to be able to vote twice before his death, for he knew the power of the ballot and its effects on his community. He would have been very proud of the achievements of his daughter.[17]

In 1955 the Canadian government issued Order-in-Council PC 1955-1551, which allowed Asians who were landed immigrants to sponsor their immediate family members. This was very important to the Chinese because many who had immigrated after 1950 had not yet acquired citizenship. In 1957 Lumb was part of a delegation of about twenty representatives from Chinese Canadian communities across Canada who met Prime Minister John Diefenbaker in Ottawa to request further change in the immigration law that separated Chinese families. Being the only female in the delegation, Lumb was asked to sit next to the prime minister on his left, while a Mr Wong, another delegate, was seated on his right. When Mr Wong was making his presentation, the prime minister kept asking Lumb what he was saying. Since Lumb knew the speech by heart and was seen speaking the most to the prime minister, she became the spokeswoman for the entire delegation. "The change in the immigration laws was my greatest accomplishment," she said.[18] Later she commented, laughing, "I was just lucky to be sitting on the side of the prime minister's good ear. He was deaf on the other side."[19]

In March 1962, Lumb represented the Chinese Benevolent Association at an immigration forum at which she made three requests to the government: to set rules for the education and skill levels of immigrants; to allow students to apply for landed immigrant status after graduation; and to be able to sponsor family members as other immigrant groups could.[20] The *Shing Wah Daily News* frequently reported the open discussions on Chinese immigration. Such English-language media as the *Toronto Star* and *Globe and Mail* also exposed the unfairness of the Canadian government.[21] The English media helped to move public opinion – and hence the politicians – to advance the changes in immigration legislation. Meanwhile, Jean Lumb continued to press her cause. She made friends with the prime minister and the immigration minister, and invited them to her restaurant, Kwong Chow, in Toronto. Then she questioned them about why it took so long for Chinese immigrants to come to Canada.[22]

By the 1950s, the Chinese Canadian community's outspokenness had made it into a political force that could no longer be ignored by politicians. Despite their small numbers, the fact that their members could speak English fluently and could influence the English media, besides the fact that they had the vote, were important reasons for politicians to start paying attention. Their community's ability to speak out was partly due to the educational achievements of the *tusheng*.

In the Chinese Canadian communities, prolonged marital separation and deprivation of a family life had adverse social, psychological, and economic consequences for the bachelor husbands. They lacked motivation to make economic investments in Canada; they suffered from an imbalance between work and leisure, from isolation, loneliness, and alienation in an ethnic ghetto; and some succumbed to alcoholism and heavy smoking. They took up illicit activities such as gambling, prostitution, and opium smoking. Many were in poor physical and mental health as they approached old age and perhaps serious infirmities. Their fear of dying alone in a foreign land prompted many of these men to send for their wives and children.

The older immigrant women had a history of hard work and devotion to husband and children. They were strong and self-sufficient, and had played an integral, indispensable role in holding the family together, both in China and in Canada. Their hardiness may have buffered them from the direct onslaught of the stresses of life. They brought with them to Canada their deep sense of devotion and dedication to work, as well as their frugality, which was a source of strength and enabled them to have considerable agency.

Leaving Communist China was a big step towards freedom for the women, even though many remained isolated in Chinatown for the rest of their lives because of their lack of knowledge of one of the official languages and their unfamiliarity with the culture of Canada. But they were happy to be able to live in a free society where there were opportunities for education and jobs for their children. Unfortunately, however, many of the elderly wives were brought to Canada literally to nurse their ailing husbands, who then passed away within a few years of the family reunion.[23] Upon their arrival in Canada, many such women were shocked to find a poor, ill, aging, and dependent husband (although this was not the experience of those who immigrated in the early fifties whom I interviewed).[24] These women continued to work to support their husbands and children, mainly as dishwashers or manual labourers in Chinese restaurants and food-processing companies, until they were eligible for their old age pensions.[25]

As time went on, those who were widowed seemed to become stronger and happier, because finally they were rid of their roles as wives, daughters-in-law, and mothers – and their former role as workers when they were pensioned. In China they would have become matriarchs and enjoyed power over younger members of the family. But in Canada they had more freedom and independence rather than power over others.

Since these women were frugal, the pensions they received were enough for them to live comfortably. Some, perhaps for the first time in their lives, found that they had autonomy. Many enjoyed themselves in the comfort and protection of their peers within the ethnic neighbourhood by staying in rooming houses, separate from their children and grandchildren, living a life of leisure, participating in community events and social visits, all of which had been unknown to them for much of their lives.[26] Some are still enjoying themselves despite their advanced age. Kan, for instance, who was profiled in the last chapter, had plenty of leisure time for playing mahjong with her friends and for travelling.

As the old settlers celebrated the arrival of their family members, the arrival of thousands of young men drew the most controversy in Chinatown. It was a shock to many sons who joined their fathers to find them working long hours in a two-by-four "grease joint" (laundry). These were the same men who had been sending money home and writing about Gold Mountain, giving the impression to relatives in China that it was a great land and that they had great jobs.[27] The older generation expected respect and submission from the youths, perhaps through participation as junior members in the native place and surname associations. This turned out to be wishful thinking. The young newcomers complied at first but soon made known their objections to and repudiation of the norms and practices in Chinatown. The result was ambivalence and often tension between the two generations.[28]

The latent tension was more than a matter of different expectations and lifestyles; it was a struggle by the newcomers for social space and autonomy. This period also marked the gradual transition of the community from being one of immigrants from the Pearl River Delta in South China to one mostly consisting of those who came from or through Hong Kong.

The elderly immigrants in charge of the existing organizations were certainly not accustomed to serving the needs of teenagers and young adults. The cultural, emotional, and generational gaps between them and the new arrivals were considerable. The youths usually had a better Chinese education, as well as some ability in English before their arrival; they had more urban experience from their time in China and Hong Kong, and higher expectations concerning their future in Canada.

In the mid-1950s, these youths emerged as the most severe internal critics of the Chinese Canadian minority. Since this was also the time of the Cold War, it became popular for the old settlers to label these youngsters as "Commie kids."[29] Many youth societies that were set up by the newcomers were short-lived, but a few enjoyed a fairly long existence. Their activism represented a competitive claim on social space, resources, and power within the ethnic group, and their agenda spoke constructively of new visions of Chinese identity and community.[30]

Thus, during the 1950s, we have three different groups in the Chinese Canadian communities – the older generation from the Pearl River Delta, a younger group of new immigrants directly or indirectly from Hong Kong, and the *tusheng* who were born in Canada – each jostling for leadership, and each trying to define the meaning of Chineseness. This was most apparent in Vancouver, since it had the largest population of those of Chinese heritage. However, the controversy over illegal immigration at the end of the fifties brought solidarity to the community as a whole. In public relations with the government, it was the established elders of the community as well as the *tusheng* who helped the new immigrants and who persuaded the government to relax the immigration rules.

In January 1954, a physical fight broke out between the local-born and the new immigrant youth groups in Vancouver's Chinatown. By attributing the event to cultural differences and mutual dislike, the *Chinatown News* held that both sides were responsible.[31] The *tusheng* youths should not have looked down on the newcomers because of their ineptitude in a new cultural environment, nor should the immigrants have ridiculed the *tusheng* for their poor command of Chinese cultural skills.[32]

The 1950s should have been known as an era of reunification for Chinese Canadian families, but unfortunately for the communities and from the standpoint of the Canadian government, they became known as an era of illegal Chinese immigration. It was reported that the deputy minister of immigration worked late into the night trying to unravel the mysteries of Chinese family relations. What fuelled the suspicions was the discovery by American officials of a large and well-organized immigration racket operating out of Hong Kong, specializing in forgery of birth and marriage certificates and passports. This discovery was coupled with the realization that the primarily male Chinese population in Canada was sponsoring the immigration of wives between the ages of twenty and twenty-nine, along with sons and daughters who were not minors. This led to a full-scale investigation by the RCMP in the late 1950s.[33]

On 14 February 1960, RCMP plainclothes officers suddenly launched a search of eight Chinese homes and offices in Vancouver in relation to illegal immigration. Papers and documents were taken and people were brought in for questioning, but there were no arrests.[34] On 24 May, plainclothes RCMP officers launched a cross-Canada raid, lasting up to six hours. They searched immigration agencies, travel agencies, private offices, and homes of Chinese Canadians, seizing documents, typewriters, bank account records, photographs, and even over twenty-year-old bills of sale. Some people had to open their bank safety deposit boxes for the search. In Montreal, even the home of a United Church minister was searched. The president of the Toronto Chinese Benevolent Association (CBA), Wong Wai Ching, and the Chinese consul general in Toronto, Chou T'ien-lu, appeared on CBC-TV to express the misgivings of the Chinese communities over the actions of the government.[35]

Two days later, more raids were carried out in nine cities: Montreal, Toronto, Peterborough, Sarnia, Winnipeg, Brampton, Regina, Edmonton, and Vancouver. They carried on into the night, and people were taken in for questioning.[36] Because of the language problem, the confiscated material took a long time to be translated. Meanwhile, all Chinese Canadians across the country were under suspicion.

From the Chinese Canadian perspective, these illegal activities would not have taken place if the Chinese had been treated like other immigrants. The CBA of Toronto called a cross-Canada meeting for three days, 28–30 May. A group of representatives planned to meet with the minister of immigration at the end of the meeting at the CBA in Ottawa to voice objection to the Canadian government's unfair treatment of Chinese immigrants.[37] However, on 30 May the representatives cancelled the meeting because of the bad treatment given to the entire Chinese community across the country.[38]

The government estimated that it cost between $4,000 and $8,000 to obtain illegal documents to get into Canada. Those who could not repay the cost would be blackmailed and could end up working virtually as indentured labourers. The amount involved in illegal immigration, as well as underground labour, was estimated at $40 million.[39] The illegal immigrants were coming from Hong Kong, Macao, and Mainland China. The RCMP maintained that 11,000 of the 21,000 Chinese immigrants who had entered Canada since 1950 were illegal. The Chinese communities challenged the RCMP to come up with proof and make arrests.[40]

In the House of Commons on 25 May, J.W. Pickersgill said, "I wonder if I could ask the Minister of Justice … whether he could give the House any information on the fantastic story attributed to the Royal Canadian Mounted Police that approximately half the Chinese immigrants to Canada since the war have entered this country illegally."[41] The minister, E.D. Fulton, replied, "I would not care to comment on that … in the absence of the Minister [of Immigration]."[42] The minister of immigration, Ellen L. Fairclough, contended that these numbers were probably exaggerated, and she intimated that a small number of illegal immigrants wanted to come forward. When they did so, she said, they would be treated fairly; they were not the ones the government wanted to target.[43] In the House of Commons she confirmed this: "I have already said that the facilities of the department will be placed at their disposal to try to regularize their entry."[44]

Consul General Chou T'ien-lu, along with Goh Jung Sung, president of the Chinese community organization Hip Tsun Wui, and the Chinese Benevolent Association president and vice-president all accused the Canadian government of discrimination in its immigration policy, which had caused the illegal activities to happen in the first place.[45] Meanwhile, Chinese Canadians accused the immigration office in Hong Kong of corruption and of taking bribes, which had made it impossible for some qualified immigrants to get into the country because they either refused or were not able to pay the bribes.[46] The Chinese community also accused the immigration department of corruption, saying that gifts had to be given to the immigration officers before application papers were dealt with. This was vehemently denied by the minister of immigration.[47]

In June the *Shing Wah Daily* reported that the Immigration Department had ordered the RCMP to question all Chinese Canadians, man, woman, and child.[48] In British Columbia, two hundred bank accounts of Chinese Canadians were investigated. Hundreds of Chinese Canadians were asked to answer a questionnaire sent by the RCMP. They refused until the legality of such a request could be confirmed.[49] The Chinese community charged the Canadian government with targeting the Chinese and ignoring the democratic rights of its citizens. After all, being of Chinese descent should not be the reason for being subjected to investigation. Being Chinese was not equal to being a criminal.[50]

In defence of the Chinese community, Douglas Jung, the member of Parliament for Vancouver Centre, stated in the House of Commons, "I again urge all Canadians not to allow the current investigation into alleged Chinese immigration irregularities to distort or prejudice the status of the Chinese communities in Canada. Much of the irregularity in Chinese immigration has sprung from the desire to rejoin loved ones."[51]

In July a meeting was set up between representatives of the Chinese community, including activist Jean Lumb, with Prime Minister Diefenbaker and Minister of Immigration Fairclough. Both confirmed that the RCMP questionnaire did not have to be answered, and they assured the community that it was illegal for the RCMP to search without a warrant. This meeting was reported to be the longest meeting on record that any group had with a prime minister.

Diefenbaker said that the Chinese community was the most law-abiding of all community groups. He added that he had had a great deal of respect for the Chinese ever since he had been a practising lawyer, when he had done a large amount of work for Chinese immigrants. He assured the community that he wanted to be told if there were any problems, and he confirmed that the RCMP was not authorized to do anything illegal.[52] In the House of Commons he stated: "I want to say this to the hon. member for Vancouver Centre. I want him to convey this message to those of his race. Canadians of Chinese origin are law-abiding, loyal and thrifty. The fact that prosecutions are taking place at the moment does not in any way detract from that fact ... I say to him, and I say to all Canadians of all racial origins that one of the major responsibilities of parliament ... is to provide the assurance that the heritage that is ours shall be maintained undiminished and shall be handed down to generations yet to come."[53]

In July the *Shing Wah Daily* reported that the English media had started to criticize the RCMP for targeting the Chinese community. The media asked whether other groups, such as the Italian community or the German community, would have been targeted in the same way.[54] The prime minister asked MP Douglas Jung to speak to the community to explain the government's position.[55] Some members of the Chinese community wanted to sue the government, but this position was not supported by the community leaders.[56]

The Hong Kong police force, having been co-opted to help the RCMP, was criticized by the Chinese Canadian community for discrimination, particularly against Chinese female immigrants. At the end of July, the *Shing Wah Daily* reported that the justice department had admitted that the Hong Kong police force was getting out of hand in its investigation but this was out of the control of the Canadian government.[57] One week later, the newspaper reported that the Immigration Department had repeated its offer of amnesty to illegal immigrants if they came forward to the RCMP or the Immigration Department. In the case of paper families, their identity would be corrected, which would help with any future sponsorship of their real family members. It was explained that paper families could complicate inheritance when someone with a false identity died. By that time, only a few hundred had come forward. There were those who were threatened by "piggy heads," the agents who sold fake papers and paid off corrupt immigration officers both in Hong Kong and in Canada.[58]

By October it was being reported that there was a tremendous drop in Chinese immigration compared with the previous year. Up to June 1960 there were only 695. In the previous year the number had been 2,561. It was also reported that thirteen people had been arrested, including two from Vancouver, six from Montreal, and three from Toronto.[59] In March 1961 representatives of the Chinese community met with George F. Davidson, deputy minister of immigration. In this meeting, Jean Lumb acted as a representative of Chinese women. The president of the CBA questioned the immigration policy of limiting the age of family members being sponsored. The group also questioned what the RCMP had discovered since the arrest of the thirteen people. The deputy minister replied that the cases were before the courts and could not be made public. In the spring of 1961 the Chinese press encouraged illegal residents to come forward to obtain amnesty.[60]

In the summer of 1961 the *Shing Wah Daily* reported that the *Globe and Mail* had criticized the Canadian government for its methods of conducting searches and was advocating that the government should not discriminate in its immigration policy.[61] An incident in Winnipeg was reported where a Hong Kong policeman was attacked with a knife by the cook in a Chinese restaurant, which was related to alleged bribery in illegal immigration.[62] In September, Douglas Jung stated in the House of Commons that he would like to see the age limit of sponsored family members relaxed, because at that time those between the ages of twenty-one and sixty could not enter Canada.[63]

Reaction to government actions continued. Three Manitoba Chinese organizations petitioned the government against the RCMP raids on the grounds that they implied that all Chinese Canadians were criminals. In any case, the RCMP should not be dealing with immigration; it should be the Immigration Department doing so. Moreover, the involvement of the RCMP went against what the prime minister had said to the Chinese community earlier, and it went against human rights. The immigration minister had no comment, and the Justice Department said it had not received the petition.[64] The leader of the Liberal Party in Manitoba also questioned the legality of the RCMP raids.[65]

The problems described above began with a few Chinese middlemen in Hong Kong and Canada making a small fortune by arranging blind marriages and paper families, topics that will be discussed in the next chapter. The success of the investigation was not nearly as great as the fear it had inspired in the Chinese communities across Canada. In Toronto, only one person was convicted of direct involvement in illegal immigration.[66]

In November 1961 members of the Chinese community were interviewed on the CBC. The economic aspect of discrimination in immigration policy was brought up: if the Chinese immigrants had been treated the same as other European immigrants, the money sent back to China over the past hundred-odd years would have remained in Canada, and this would have been much better for the Canadian economy. In the interview, Jean Lumb advocated family reunification and equal treatment for the Chinese with other immigrants. An appeal was also made on the CBC for illegal immigrants to come forward.[67]

During the federal election in 1957, one of John Diefenbaker's campaign promises had been that a Conservative government would overhaul the immigration act.[68] He proclaimed that Canada must "populate or perish." Yet when his Conservative government had been elected, nothing happened. By 1961, however, the illegal immigration controversy had brought the unfairness of the Chinese situation into the open. Because of the pressure of public opinion and that of the opposition in Parliament, as well as the persistent pressure of the Chinese Canadian community, it was necessary for the government to take action. On 18 January 1962, Immigration Regulation PC 86 was adopted, giving the right of landing to those with the education and skills that Canada had come to need as more and more skilled Canadians emigrated to the United States. At the same time, the family class was expanded to include sons-in-law, daughters-in-law, and unmarried grandchildren under the age of twenty-one.

The new regulations marked the first time in Canada that the major criteria for the admission of independent (unsponsored) immigrants were education, training, skills, and other specialized qualifications. Another radical step was that discrimination in respect to admissible classes of immigrants based on national or ethnic origin was removed. Eligible immigrants were now defined as persons who, by reason of their education, training, skills, or other special qualifications, were likely to be able to establish themselves successfully in Canada; who had sufficient means of support to maintain themselves in Canada until they had so established themselves; and who had arranged placement in employment or to establish a business, trade, profession, or work in agriculture.[69]

These new regulations did retain one privilege for European immigrants over most non-Europeans (including those from Turkey, North, Central, and South America, and the adjacent islands, Egypt, Israel, and Lebanon). This was the privilege of sponsoring a wider range of relatives.[70] Although this aspect of discrimination remained until 1967, the new regulations did mark a significant turning point in Canadian immigration policy. After this, Canada appeared to the world at large as an immigrant-welcoming country. By the 1960s, Canada was competing with countries such as the United States and Australia to attract highly skilled immigrants. Consequently, immigration rules were relaxed, giving immigration officials a great deal of discretion in determining the right applicants for immigration development. This will be illustrated in the interviews in later chapters.

When a Liberal government came to power on 22 April 1963, Immigration Minister Guy Favreau met with representatives of the Chinese communities from major cities across the country and assured them that there would not be any discrimination in his government's policy. He also visited Hong Kong to assess the immigration situation there, and the *Shing Wah Daily* noted that he wanted to speed up the immigration process.[71]

By the summer of 1964, few illegal immigrants in the Chinese community had come forward to ask for amnesty. As a result, the Immigration Department cancelled the deadline of 1 September.[72] The Chinese media suggested that those who came forward should be assured that they would not have to wait for another five years to attain citizenship, that they could sponsor their family members right away with their real identity, and that they should now be treated the same way as European immigrants.[73]

At the end of 1965, the Chinese community was still pressing the government to treat all immigrants equally.[74] There were several attempts made to terminate the Chinese Adjustment Statement Program, so-called because illegal Chinese immigrants could have their status adjusted; its continued usefulness seemed very doubtful. However, strong representations from members of Parliament, the Chinese community, and others secured a postponement. Between June 1960 and July 1970, 11,569 Chinese had their status adjusted.[75] The immigration regulation regarding equal treatment did eventually materialize, but not until 1967.

The fight for family reunification and for equality in Chinese immigration had helped to consolidate the Chinese Canadian communities, which went through a tremendous evolution from the end of the Second World War to the 1960s. The 1950s were years when the Chinese Canadians became aware of their cultural heritage, both Chinese and Canadian, and the *tusheng* activists continued to be instrumental in helping to improve the immigration law and regulations regarding ethnic Chinese.

In a 1964 letter to the *Chinatown News*, one *tusheng* observed that while the elders feared the *tusheng* were losing their heritage, they failed to realize that their heritage was North American, no matter how much they deplored it or tried to deny it.[76] By the 1970s, both the *tusheng* and the new immigrants from South China and Hong Kong were reconciled in their way of forming a Chinese Canadian identity.[77]

Chapter 4

Picture Brides, Paper Sons,
and Paper Daughters

It was a common practice in the 1950s for older overseas Chinese bachelors to send for "picture brides," women who were much younger and could look after them in their old age. Many of these young wives had never met their sponsoring husbands before the marriage. In some cases, the men also needed stepmothers to look after their growing families because their first wives had died. Through direct correspondence with relatives in China or Hong Kong, or through professional matchmakers, the elderly bachelor would arrange a "blind marriage" to a poor Chinese girl who had little hope of marrying any but the poorest Chinese boy back home. From the standpoint of the girl's family, the arrangement could be justified because she would have better economic opportunities in Canada and would eventually be able to sponsor her parents' immigration. From the standpoint of the young woman, it was far less positive, for she would be married to a man twice or three times her age, whom she not only had to care for but, in most cases, to work for as well.[1] On the other hand, for many young women from poor families it was a way out as well as an opportunity to go to *Gum San* (Gold Mountain). Fortunately, some of these cases worked out well.

The image of Gold Mountain is expressed in the song sung by Tin-Shaang in the book *The Excluded Wife*:

Old Gold Mountain guests,
Young Gold Mountain guests,
Houses full of gold, silver, and silk;

If I don't marry a Gold Mountain guest,
How could I be so carefree?[2]

In 1956 an amusing column in the *Chinatown News* raised the question: "Could *tusheng* girls be good wives?" At the time the column was written, there was an extreme imbalance in the sex ratio among the immigrant youth in the early years of renewed immigration after 1947. The male newcomers soon found that there was a dearth of suitable partners, and by the middle of the 1950s, some of them were returning to Hong Kong to seek spouses in the same way as Gina's husband, who was mentioned in the last chapter. In April 1956, this problem even aroused the sympathy of the federal government, which made a special provision to allow Chinese to send for their fiancées.[3]

The following is the story of Yee, who was a picture bride. She was interviewed in the office of the Chinese Consolidated Benevolent Association (CCBA) in Victoria in the spring of 2001. She was open and friendly, and even brought along some of her own baking for me. She spoke in Cantonese.

❖ I was born in 1930 in a village in Hoiping County. My father worked in the Philippines and sent money back to support me and my mother. During the Sino-Japanese War and the civil war in China, my father wasn't able to send money to us, and we were very poor.

My husband was born in Canada. He got married at age seventeen to a girl in China and became a father at the age of eighteen. After the repeal of the exclusion act in 1947, he applied for his wife and children to come to Canada. Unfortunately, in 1951 his wife died. He then sent money back to China for a marriage broker to find him another wife. In 1951 many Chinese were looking for a way out because of the establishment of the People's Republic of China. For the women, one way was to be a picture bride and go to *Gum San*. Marriage brokers did a good business by getting many pictures sent to them, and mine was one of them.

Until 1962, because Chinese women could immigrate to Canada only as dependants of men, picture brides were very common.

❖ My future husband was looking for a tall and strong bride. I was picked not only because I was the prettiest but I'm also tall, in fact, taller than my husband. I had never met my husband until we got married, but my mother had met him. Soon after, he picked me as his future bride. At age twenty-two I went to Hong Kong to await further news. It was easy for me to get out of China because we were poor.

In Hong Kong, I received mail frequently from Canadian Immigration, and it only took nine months before I was granted immigration status, and without a personal interview with an immigration officer! I believe that it was because the immigration officer was sympathetic to the children of my husband, especially to the youngest daughter who had to be given to another woman to care for her because he couldn't manage.

It was unusual to feel fortunate being poor, but Yee, like May, believed that poverty was what gave them the opportunity to leave China. Here again, the political climate in China played an important role in the decision to emigrate.

The fact that Yee's husband was born and raised in Canada enabled him to know how to appeal to the Immigration Department. It is not uncommon, even today, for immigration officers to have some latitude in making such decisions in a positive or negative manner.

❖ You see, in the case of a picture bride, a deposit had to be given for me before I was allowed to come to Canada, as a guarantee that when I met my husband, if either of us should decide not to marry, there would be enough money for me to return to China. I had my medical and my future husband bought me a boat ticket. The boat ticket that I received was for an eight-bedded room, but since I ended up in a thirty-bedded room with many bunks, I was very happy because I received a refund of fifty dollars. The boat went to San Francisco [no boat travelled directly to Vancouver at that time.] The trip took eighteen days, and an additional two days by train to Vancouver.

I left Hong Kong on November 7th, 1952, and the marriage took place on January 3rd in a church in Victoria. Our age difference was thirteen years. My first daughter was born the following November.

I'm used to hard work in China. I helped my husband in his shoe repair shop which he ran during the day, and he also worked as a welder in a shipyard from 4 to 11 PM. I helped until the birth of my third child. My husband had three children from his first wife and I had five of my own. I really had a handful. Life was difficult then, not like now.

Yee's frugality, practicality, and willingness to work hard helped her to fit into the role that was expected of her, one at which she excelled, and she became happy, contented with her lot. By the time Yee had her third child, her husband obviously was making enough money for her not to have to work outside the home. She had two more children subsequently. I noted that she did not discuss any intergenerational issues or how she managed her stepchildren.

❖ There were very few Chinese, mostly men, in Victoria in the early 1950s, and most of them who could send for their wives were old. Many of them were not able to bring a picture bride or picture fiancée until at least 1954–56, so the fact that I was able to enter Canada in 1952 was unusual. I'm sure it was because the immigration officer was sympathetic to my husband's children being without a mother.

Life has changed so much since the day I arrived in Victoria. In those days, if you wanted to have dim sum you had to phone someone who knew how to make them. You then took them home and cooked them yourself.

I had never experienced discrimination, but my husband had. He was born in Cumberland [on Vancouver Island], and used to tell me stories about fights between the whites and the Chinese. The minister from the church used to put a stop to them.

The discrimination that Yee's husband suffered occurred when he was growing up in Cumberland. At that time, there was institutional discrimination against all Asians. By the time Yee arrived in Canada in 1952, much had changed.

Life is so much better today because everyone has the chance to go to university. Of my five children, one son is a policeman, and of course … my youngest daughter is an MLA [member of the legislative assembly]. My life in Canada is like winning a lottery. I gambled and won. At that time, everyone wanted to come to *Gum San*, and not all turned out well. When I went back to my village in China with my husband in 1977, I felt even more fortunate because many people didn't even have enough to eat.

At the end of 2010, Yee was interviewed again and asked how she was doing.

❖ I am eighty years old now, getting forgetful and useless, and can't hear well. I stay home most of the time, just like most women in the village in China. I don't have any English friends because I can't speak English well. I have no regrets coming over to Canada as a picture bride. In the village in China we had no money, and I could have died of hunger. I have enough to eat here, and my children are doing well.

By immigrating to Canada, Yee did not live through the tumultuous time in China known as the Great Leap Forward, which was followed by a widespread famine in which up to 40 million Chinese died, and by the Cultural Revolution when society was turned upside down. When she and her husband went back to China in 1977, it was soon after the death of Mao Zedong on 9 September 1976 and before Deng Xiaoping's policy of opening up the country to the world. At that time, the majority of Chinese were very poor. Yee felt extremely lucky to be living in Canada.

Yee's is a success story. She made a risky decision and was willing to work hard for a better life. As a victim of poverty in China, she took the chance of marrying a man she had never met, and she became an agent of change in bringing into the world a second generation of Chinese Canadians, who had political power in the person of her youngest daughter. Her pride in her daughter showed not only that life was good for her but that it was even better for the next generation of Chinese Canadian women. To her, Canada is the land of opportunities.

It is interesting to read the letters written to the *Chinatown News* two months before the government announcement, in April 1956, allowing

Chinese men to send for their fiancées. The letters reveal not only the cultural differences between the *tusheng* and the newcomers but also gender issues among the ethnic Chinese. One immigrant youth vented his anger by writing: "All these [Canadian-born] girls know is how to enjoy themselves, and how to spend money and how to make up their faces as beautiful as white girls. They want a husband who must have a car, a house, or some other things representative of money. How can a young man afford these?" In his opinion, "maidens from Hong Kong" were preferable marriage partners because girls born in Canada were ignorant of "their Chinese parentage" and "prejudiced against their own kind."[4]

Given the prevalence of such beliefs among Chinese Canadian men in the 1950s and early 1960s, it was very common for them to go back to Hong Kong or China to find a marriage partner. Most of the young men who immigrated after 1947 came in under family reunification, but more and more young women came as young brides, especially in the 1950s. This was a group who was better educated than the earlier immigrant women and had urban experience either in China or Hong Kong, or both.

The following is the story of Lim, who married a Chinese Canadian man who was looking for a wife in Hong Kong. Lim was interviewed in the office of the CCBA in Victoria in the spring of 2001. She spoke in Cantonese.

❖ I was born in Macao in 1941. My father lived and worked in the
United States. I was conceived when my father was on one of his
visits back from Los Angeles. When war broke out, my mother
urged my father to return to L.A. right away, and he took my
eldest brother back to the United States with him. A certificate
had to be bought for my brother because he was born before
my father went to America. When I was born, a son's birth was
claimed for the purpose of selling the certificate in the future. So
I never had proof of birth as a daughter of an American citizen.[5]
    During the Second World War it was very difficult for my
father to send us money, so my mother and I went back to our
ancestral village in Sunwui County, where I attended primary
school. I attended secondary school in Kongmoon. In my third
year of secondary school, my father visited Hong Kong. My family applied for permission from the Chinese government to go

to Hong Kong to see him. It was there that I met him for the first time.

My mother didn't want to leave the graves of the ancestors, so she arranged to have another woman live with my father in America. From this woman were born six children. The certificate for the proof of my birth was later given to the son of the sister of this woman so that he would have a chance to go to America.

Lim's story again confirms the patriarchal tradition of the importance of sons, to the extent that when she was born, her father reported the birth of a son to the American immigration authorities. She said that a son's birth certificate could be sold for a lot of money. She told me this without anger in her voice, even though she was left with no proof that she was the daughter of an American citizen and had been deprived of the chance of going to America.

The practice of buying and selling birth certificates was common among the Chinese male immigrants in both the United States and Canada – a result of discrimination and exclusion. The practice caused a lot of confusion to the immigration departments in sorting out families and led to the raids, accusations, and recriminations described in the previous chapter.

The mothers of Gina and Lim were similar in that both were independent and did not want to follow their husbands to the Philippines or America. Similarly, both husbands also had wives and families overseas. As Lim said, she and her mother were able to get permission from the Chinese government to go to Hong Kong to meet her father in the 1950s. She did not elaborate on how they lived during the Second World War in their village in Sunwui County and after the establishment of the People's Republic of China. They were part of the Chinese exodus to Hong Kong in the 1950s.

❖ In Hong Kong I attended school part-time, and I also learned something of Chinese herbal medicine because my father was a Chinese herbal medicine doctor in the U.S. I sometimes took factory outwork home to do as my friends did, but my family was comfortable, and I really didn't need to work.

In 1966 I met my future husband when he returned from Canada to Hong Kong to look for a wife. We were introduced, and he asked my mother for permission to marry me. At the time, I didn't even know what he did for a living, I just knew that he was ten years my senior [laughs]. The marriage took place in Hong Kong. It was a gamble and I was fortunate. Even my father-in-law was nice to me. He later bought us a house to live in, because he said he wanted to be fair to both sons. He bought a house for the son who lived in China.

For the educated women from South China, Hong Kong was just a way station where they could look for opportunities to go abroad, because they were not part of Hong Kong society. Many believed they had better chances elsewhere. Some were fortunate, and some were not.

❖ I didn't work when I first arrived in Victoria. Friends arranged for me to learn English with a white teacher, who was very nice. I had lessons for four months and finished the book *John and Janet* and was ready to go to a higher level, but then I started not feeling well. I was pregnant with my daughter. I had three children in three years and was nauseous all the time. So the lessons couldn't continue.

My husband formed a partnership with friends to open two restaurants and lost a lot of money. Finally, with the financial help of other friends, we opened a small restaurant and ran it ourselves. Since I didn't know enough English, we had to hire people, and I stayed at the back to help. My in-laws helped to look after the children until 1974, when they left for Hong Kong. From then on, the whole family had to rise very early to get to the restaurant before 7 AM because we also served breakfast. After school, the children could go to the restaurant, where they did their homework and slept there until the restaurant closed, when they went home with us.

At one point my son suffered from diarrhea and vomiting, and the health department wouldn't let the children go to the restaurant anymore. Fortunately, by that time the children were independent enough to take care of themselves.

Lim did not go into details about her children except to say that they were very good children, as they would need to be in order to adjust to their parents' schedule.

❖ I worked with my husband in our restaurant for twenty-seven years, serving both Chinese and Western food. My husband has been in the restaurant business for thirty-one years. He was a good cook, and our restaurant was famous for our soups. I pitched in to do everything, from cooking to cleaning the toilets. At the beginning, we hired quite a few staff because of my lack of knowledge of English, but we were not making ends meet. I had to learn enough English so that I could take orders from our customers.[6]

I'm a very lucky person because people are always so nice to me. When my children wanted to go to Chinese school and my husband and I weren't able to take them, one of our customers, a Chinese Canadian man, offered to drive them, and he continued to do this for five and a half years. He even helped us to enlarge our house in anticipation of my sister's family coming to Canada.

I count my blessings in having so many good friends as well as kind customers. When we were short-handed in the restaurant, the customers poured their own coffee and helped clean the tables, and all I had to do was make up the bills. Working six days a week and doing housework on Sundays, I developed high blood pressure in later years and sometimes fell asleep in the restaurant. When that happened, my customers not only poured their own coffee but also left the money on the table without waking me up.

My husband and I are both retired now. Former customers are our friends. We are also fortunate that we have very nice neighbours. They always greet us when they see us in the morning. When they see me shovelling snow, they often come over to help. It's not like people in Hong Kong, who are not so nice or helpful.

This type of comment was repeated by many of my informants, particularly when they were referring to the period when Hong Kong was like a big refugee camp filled with desperate people from Mainland China.

Lim's experience with the Canadian immigration system was obviously positive. Despite the fact that she had to work very hard in helping her husband in their restaurant, she believed her immigration had given her a chance to live in a free country and a land of opportunities for her entire family.

❖ Our children are all doing well and are independent. One daughter works at UBC [University of British Columbia] and a son is a computer engineer in the U.S. Our lives were so different from this younger generation, and I'm happy that they are so independent.

   In the old days I was busy all the time, and couldn't do a lot of the housework. Now that I have the time, I still can't do it because I have aches all over. I go to a chiropractor for relief.

Both Lim and her husband had gruelling schedules running a restaurant. This was not the type of work she wanted for her children, and she is glad they are professionals. She also implied that their children had had better opportunities in the educational system in Canada. Lim's option in Hong Kong would have been to continue her studies and perhaps become a Chinese herbal doctor like her father, because she did say that she was interested in the subject. However, she chose another route, agreeing to marry someone she hardly knew, and fortunately her marriage turned out well. She could have been a victim in this kind of arranged marriage, since she hardly knew her husband-to-be. But she was lucky.

Yee and Lim had all the characteristics that Chinese Canadian men looked for in their spouses at that time – they wanted women who were frugal and hard-working. In the 1950s and 1960s, the Canadian immigration system gave such women additional options in their life-course, for it was generally believed that Chinese women from back home had different expectations from the local-born Chinese Canadian women. Their immigration to Canada gave them opportunities that they appreciated.

In response to the views expressed in the letters written by Chinese men to the *Chinatown News*, mentioned earlier in the chapter, a Chinese woman from Lethbridge, Alberta, sent in the following rebuttal upbraiding the men:

Your efforts sounded like the grumblings of a prejudiced mind when you insinuate that Chinese girls must use artificial makeup to be beautiful. Don't you realize that makeup is considered a necessity today, and not a vanity? ... How can a man afford a home and a car? Why, any young man with half an ounce of ambition can acquire these ... I have yet to meet a Canadian-born who is not proud of her heritage. And you, who harbours such thoughts, are the one who should disqualify yourself as judge and jury ... Having been born and educated in Canada we naturally are a little more fussy when we come to pick our lifetime partner. Whereas many of our distant sisters [in Hong Kong] look at Canada through rose-colored glasses – using marriage as a convenient vehicle to come to Canada, and I am sure many many must have dearly regretted their quick marriage to some of you dashing, albeit feelingless, wife hunters.[7]

These arranged marriages between picture brides and young Chinese Canadian men during the 1950s and the 1960s could indeed end up badly, as is illustrated in the following situation. An interview was arranged with Irene to learn of her experience when she immigrated to Canada as a young girl. As it turned out, she poured out her mother's story as well as describing her own experience and feelings. Thus, from the perspective of a daughter who was very close to the situation, I gained the story of three generations of women – mother and daughter, who both immigrated in 1967, and the grandmother, who immigrated in 1971.

Irene was interviewed in the office of the CCBA in Victoria in the spring of 2001. Having grown up in Canada, she is more fluent in English than Chinese, so she spoke in English, but she did add some Cantonese words during the interview.

❖ My mother was born in China, where the family owned a lot of land. After 1949, they escaped to Hong Kong. It was fortunate that my grandmother was also able to get out, but unfortunately many members of the family were not able to. My parents got married in the mid-1950s, and they had me and my sister. My father worked in a department store, and my mother did some embroidery and made plastic flowers to make extra income.

Unfortunately, my father died, and Mother was widowed at a very young age. The family lived in Macao for a year. Soon after Father died, my mother was desperate to remarry.

Irene's story of her mother's family was again one of political upheaval in China. Belonging to the landlord class, they had to escape to Hong Kong in 1949 when the Communists won the civil war. Irene mentioned that her grandmother was fortunate to get out, but that many of her family members suffered under the Communist regime. Again the political situation in China was the main reason why her mother and grandmother left China.

❖ Through the introduction of friends as well as her brother in Toronto, she [my mother] married a Chinese Canadian man who was looking for a wife in Hong Kong. It was believed that getting married in Hong Kong instead of Macao would make immigration to Canada easier, so they got married in Hong Kong. She knew little about this man, who actually had a wife in China, as well as being separated from another wife in Canada. In fact, my mother didn't know whether he was legally divorced in Canada.

My mother believed that few men would see her as a marriage partner because she was a widow with two little girls in tow. She felt she needed to remarry for security for herself and her daughters. And since it was everyone's dream to go to *Gum San*, marrying someone from there would give her family a better future. In 1967 the family left for Canada. I was five years old and my sister was three. I was scared, not because of flying but because I was leaving behind my grandmother, who had looked after my sister and me when my mother worked.

When we arrived in Victoria, we discovered that Stepfather was a market gardener who rented a farm from white Canadians. He grew Chinese vegetables, so the family lived on the farm. My family was scared because we didn't speak any English, even though the white family was very kind to us. A house was provided for the family to live in, but my sister and I were not allowed outside to play, mainly because we had to take on a lot of responsibility of housework. My mother worked on the farm alongside her new husband, but she was very disappointed by the environment we ended up in because that was not how he had presented himself to her. She used to cry a lot.

Irene's mother had looked at her prospect of a husband from *Gum San* through the "rose-colored glasses" referred to in the letter in the *Chinatown News*. She believed she would have security for herself and her daughters. But she did not know the man she was marrying. Because she was so anxious to marry anyone, especially someone from *Gum San*, who would accept her, a widow with two daughters, it is likely that she was prepared to believe whatever he told her.

❖ A little later, Stepfather rented a house on Fisgard Street with a vegetable garden in front, where they grew vegetables to sell in Chinatown. He continued to work on the farm he rented, marketing the vegetables himself, driving a green truck, going from door to door. Since he didn't contribute to the living expense for the family, my mother held three jobs, cleaning houses during the day, helping with the growing of vegetables, and washing dishes till midnight at Strathcona. I would go after school and helped her wash dishes.

When I started school, it was a difficult experience. Not only was there a language problem but also the visual difference, such as customs and clothes. There were eight Chinese children in my class, and the eight of us stuck together, having little communication with the other children. Mrs Waring, the teacher from grade school, took me under her wings because she knew how tough it was for me. I was plump as a child, and children can be mean. I was called "that Hong Kong person" because I was different. I believe that when I was invited to a birthday party, it was not because the other child regarded me as a friend but that I was just a novelty. I felt very self-conscious and so I never went to a birthday party until I was in grade 3.

Irene's mother's regret at her decision was evident in the tears she frequently shed. Irene's trouble fitting in at school was similar to that of many immigrant children who had language and culture problems.

❖ By grade 7, I felt that everything was falling into place for me at school. Besides having more confidence in myself, I also knew that I would be leaving the school after that year. In grade 8, it was easier because I was among a lot more students, many of whom I didn't know before. There was also no longer the familiarity of "my mom gave her those hand-me-down shoes." I was no longer judged by my background or that I was that girl from Hong Kong. By then, it was the 1970s and there were more immigrant children and so a lot more diversity at school.

It was the change in immigration regulations that had made life easier for Irene, because by the 1970s there were more immigrant children from Hong Kong in the schools in Victoria.

❖ My stepfather was very abusive, and the entire family learned not to say anything. My sister and I were never allowed to bring friends home. We were also not allowed in the house after school until Stepfather came home at 6 PM to unlock the door. We had to wait on the porch, even in the winter, and when we had to go to the bathroom we had to go outside, even when it snowed. My mother would prepare the food beforehand and, being the older child, I was responsible to cook the rice and reheat the food. My mother went to work at 7 AM and returned at midnight. She accepted her life, since she didn't see that she could have other options, and she justified it since others had to work as hard in the Chinese community.

In 1969 a younger half-brother was born. The situation became worse because Stepfather never wanted this child. I remember one instance when Stepfather told him not to touch the wood stove, and when he did, Stepfather put his hand on it to burn it. I still remember the blisters. I was responsible for looking after the younger children until 1971, when my grandmother came over to Canada to help out.

My stepfather took all my mother's good pieces of jewellery and sold some, while some were still in his safe-deposit box after he died. The pieces that she was left with [i.e., was allowed to keep] she sold in order to bring her mother over to Canada. After Grandmother arrived and saw the abusive situation, she told my mother to leave and return to Hong Kong, but my mother wouldn't because it would be a loss of face.

From the interview it was clear that Irene's grandmother was a strong person and her mother was not. When the grandmother immigrated to Canada, it was a relief for the grandchildren because she was there to stand up for them, since their mother could not.

❖ My grandmother had fights with my stepfather because of his abusive behaviour towards his family. Each time they had a fight, he wouldn't give us any food as punishment. My grandmother was smart; she would use the vegetables that her son-in-law had put aside, and walked to Chinatown to sell them in order to buy eggs and soya sauce, and we would have that with rice. Sometimes, an egg would have to last a week for each of us.

The money my mother made was all given to her husband, so the family never had any money. Stepfather was never a provider. It was my mother who made all the money, out of which he paid the rent and bought food for the family. He only rented and never owned anything. When he was not working, he would be out drinking, and returned home drunk every night. When my grandmother had her pension, my mother told her to keep it herself. She used this for us. I am very grateful because we never lacked anything and never starved because of our grandmother.

Since Irene's mother actually made the money to support the family, the stepfather's power was only a presumption of the mother, shown in the fact that she handed over all her earnings to him. Besides suffering a loss of face if she had left her husband and gone back to Hong Kong, she would not have found it easy in Canada either to get a divorce in the 1970s.[8] And since they lived in Chinatown, she would still have suffered loss of face if she left him and stayed in Canada.

❖ One day, my stepfather disappeared. He puffed up his pillows and put them under his blankets, and the family thought he was sleeping in because he was sick. Then we realized he had left without a trace. Later, we found out that he had discovered he had cancer, and the hospital in Victoria couldn't accommodate him, so he went to Vancouver. My mother actually felt guilty that she couldn't be in Vancouver to take care of him when he was dying of cancer.

After high school, I got into Ryerson in Toronto. For my graduation from high school, my mother gave me a trip to Trinidad to visit her cousin. By then, my stepfather was already in the hospital in Vancouver, and since he had left, my mother was able to keep all the money she made. My mother lived with Grandmother, and with her earnings and Grandmother's pension they were able to buy a house together. She was satisfied that they finally owned their own home.

When Stepfather died, my mother wanted all of us to be at the funeral to save face. My half-brother had to be forced to attend because he hated his father. I went because of my mother.

When I was at Ryerson, one day I suddenly woke up at 4 AM and said to my girlfriend that I never would see my grandmother again. That same day, at noon Victoria time, my grandmother died peacefully. It was August 16, 1980. I returned to Victoria and saw the state my mother was in. I planned to stay a year and return to school, but I never left again. I went to work at a relative's store in Colwood [B.C.].

My mother would never talk about the abusive situation at home, and would never consider leaving her husband. Up till about five years ago, she believed that, for all her suffering, her children did have better opportunities in Canada. However, in recent years, when she looked at her friends and how well some of their children are doing in Hong Kong, she was not so sure. Philosophically, she said her time had passed, and she couldn't relive her life again.

Irene's mother considered that even life with an abusive husband was better than being a refugee in Hong Kong. She lived a life of regret, believing that her children had better opportunities in Canada. Since she had moved her family to Canada, she had not kept up with the improvements made by the government in Hong Kong in response to the influx of refugees from China.

In speaking about how well some of her mother's friends were doing in Hong Kong, Irene was referring to the early 1990s, the years before the return of sovereignty over Hong Kong to China. These were prosperous years for the Hong Kong economy.[9] Since the 1970s, there had also been rapid expansion of the education system in Hong Kong.[10]

❖ To the end, my mother still felt gratitude to the man who gave her the opportunity when she believed she had no option. She remained forever grateful for the opportunity to come to Canada. My mother would not look back. She only looks forward to what she would do that day, one day at a time. She also looks forward to the grandchildren growing up, and there are four at the moment.

I have had two relationships and two children, and I never got married. But by not being married I find the situation in a separation is even worse than being married. I feel even closer to my mother since I had my own daughter. My mother is much more than a mom to me.

While Irene's mother immigrated in the 1960s, her behaviour was more like that of the Chinese wives from the old days who suffered in silence. Her belief that Canada was really *Gum San*, or Gold Mountain, was ingrained in her. It was by her own agency that she made the decision to marry a Chinese Canadian in order to bring her daughters to Canada to start a new life. In that sense, she was well served by immigration to Canada. In keeping with the traditional Chinese culture, saving face was an important factor in many immigrants' lives. If it had not been for that, perhaps more women immigrants would have returned to their communities of origin.

Irene's mother's attitude and the family's situation, as well as her perception of her husband's power over her children, had a permanent effect on Irene, who said she would never get married despite two relationships. She was also very protective towards her mother.

Irene herself had adapted to life in Canada, despite her early difficulties in school as the poor "hand-me-down" girl from Hong Kong. As she said, by the 1970s, students who were visible minorities could feel more at home. By immigrating to Canada, Irene's mother had given her children a chance in a new country, a step she did not regret, even though the children of some of her friends who remained in Hong Kong had been doing very well in recent years. Her children are the new generation of Chinese Canadians who had a chance to be well educated and independent; and the grandmother brought with her the family values of love and caring that were totally ingrained in Irene.

As well as being picture brides or marrying someone they barely knew in order to have a new life in *Gum San*, there were young women who themselves purchased papers to get into Canada. Until 1923, the Canadian Immigration Department kept a record of the number of times Chinese men travelled to China and the length of their stays.[11] For this reason, some men reported having two children if they stayed more than a year. It was anybody's guess whether any children at all were born.[12] Once a child's birth was reported, the paper became a valuable document, especially if a son was reported, as noted earlier. Because most families wanted papers for boys, these could fetch as much as five thousand dollars. Not that everybody sold their papers. Some needed them to bring their own family members to Canada, but many made a tidy profit, particularly the middlemen, who arranged for the "paper sons."[13]

A paper son was a Chinese Canadian man's son who did not qualify as a dependant to enter Canada and had assumed the identity of another man's son who did qualify. A Chinese Canadian father who did not have enough money to send for his own son might sell his son's birth certificate to a wealthier father. Some men reported the birth of a son when none actually existed, and these certificates also could be sold. The paper son had to assume the identity of the other person when he was quizzed by Immigration, and the false identity had to remain with him for the rest of his life.[14] This phenomenon could cause chaos in the case of inheritance, especially as the false identity had to be carried on by future generations.

While paper sons were common, paper daughters were unusual, though the two actually worked in exactly the same way. The following is the story of Joyce, who came to Canada as a paper daughter. She was interviewed in the office of the CCBA in Victoria in the spring of 2001. She brought me cakes from the Chinese bakery and spoke in Cantonese.

❖ I was born in 1931 in a village in Toisan County, the youngest of three children. My grandfather and father were both working in Canada. My grandfather originally went to the U.S. on a student visa and later moved to Victoria. His English was very good, and he often worked as a translator in different cities across Canada. The family also had a business in Victoria. My father was born in Canada and returned to China to marry my mother, as most overseas Chinese men did in those days.

My mother, brother, and I stayed in China. I was attending school in Guangzhou when the Japanese invaded China [1937].[15] After the Second World War, when the Communists arrived in the city [1949–50], there was a lot of political upheaval. I still remember the fighting and the bombs going off. My mother told me to return to the village. In 1949, the Nationalist troops retreated to Toisan, and the retreating troops and spies were kidnapping villagers for ransom. My older brother was kidnapped. I had to go to Guangzhou to get the money my father wired to pay the ransom for my brother. Soon after his release, my mother took him to Hong Kong. A little later, I also left for Hong Kong.

Joyce's story is similar to those of the other interviewees regarding to the tradition of Chinese men returning to the village to get married and then leaving their families behind in China. She was also of the generation who experienced the dreadful political and social disorder in China during and after the Second World War.

It is interesting that Joyce, as the younger child and a girl, was sent to Guangzhou to get the ransom money for her older brother. She was also the one left behind in China when her mother took her older brother to Hong Kong in 1949. It was fortunate that she was able to leave for Hong Kong a little later, before the Chinese government clamped down on exits by wealthy Chinese nationals. All this confirms the low regard for females in traditional Chinese culture.

❖ In 1950 my father reported to the Canadian immigration the birth of a son instead of me during his last stay in China when I was born. My father wanted my eldest brother to immigrate to Canada, but my brother was already overage, so he used my paper, reporting himself as much younger. He and my mother immigrated to Canada in 1950. [In 1950, there had been an age restriction on immigration for dependent children of Chinese families]. While in Hong Kong, I attended an English school. In 1952, when I was twenty-one, wishing me to join the family in Canada, my father bought a certificate from someone who had reported to the Canadian government the birth of a daughter in China, and the daughter's age was similar to mine. It cost my father $800. Such was the difference in value between a boy and a girl!

Paul Chan, former president of the CCBA who attended the interview, said that the cost of a paper for a boy could be as high as $8,000. He added that this was the first time he had ever heard of buying a paper for a girl.

❖ Buying a certificate to come to Canada was a very frightening experience, especially when the person who sold the paper slipped up when he was questioned about my case. During this time, that person was also bringing other members of his family to Canada. I had to assume the identity of the girl mentioned in the certificate while I was being questioned, and I had to retain the same identity for the rest of my life.

As mentioned earlier, reporting the birth of a son to the Canadian immigration authorities was an important conduit for the next generation of sons to immigrate to Canada, and it was frequently abused. If a boy's name was substituted for a girl's, it could not be checked because birth certificates did not exist in China at that time.

Joyce did not question her father about the way her immigration to Canada was handled. She believed he felt guilty using her birth for the immigration of her older brother and had later bought her a paper in recompense. By then, in response to the political turmoil in China, Canadian Immigration had loosened the age restrictions on family members, so Joyce was eligible even though she was in her twenties. One wonders whether she would have had the chance of immigrating had it not been for the sufferings of her upper-class family during the Chinese civil war.

Joyce was proud of the achievements of her father and grandfather in Canada: "My father owned greenhouses in Victoria, growing flowers and vegetables. These were located fairly close to Government House.

His flowers were so beautiful that he was a regular supplier to Government House for their floral arrangements. He was an expert in what he did and used liquid fertilizers that he made up, so he gained a name as a scientist."

❖ In 1956 I got married to a Chinese man who had immigrated to Canada in 1950. Our parents knew each other. My husband owned a grocery store for ten years. I helped out in the store, and it was very hard work because our hours were from 9 AM to 9 PM. Later, my husband got a job with the ferry service between the islands.

The Canadian government announced amnesty for illegal immigrants in the early 1960s.[16] I went to Immigration around 1962–63 to let them know of my false identity, and in July 1963 I received an official letter from the government with my real identity and got my own name back. At the same time, my older brother also got back his own age instead of being seven years younger.

Joyce told me how frightened she had been when questioned by the Canadian immigration officer. During the raids by the RCMP over immigration fraud in the 1950s her entire family must have been very worried. Their lives were much easier now.

❖ We are Christians and follow religious teachings. We first became exposed to Christianity when we brought our children to Sunday school. I do believe children who go to church are better children.

I've never had to work outside of my own environment, and that's why I never made the effort to be fluent in English. But now that I'm working as a volunteer helping seniors and new immigrants, in filling in tax forms, etc., I really have to improve my English.

We have a son and a daughter. Our son is a chiropractor and our daughter works in computers. We are very satisfied with our lives here in Canada. It's nice to live in Canada, a free society. We have good neighbours, our children are doing well, and I'm happy.

Like many of the women, Joyce was a victim of patriarchy, in that her birth was reported as the birth of a son. When her father relented and bought her a false paper, she was again a victim, this time of the Canadian immigration laws that had made illegal immigration a necessity for Chinese families wishing to reunite. At the same time, she was an agent in her manipulation of the Canadian immigration system.

After Joyce received amnesty and regained her real identity, her life changed. She gained a sense of freedom she had never had before and was able to appreciate Canada more. Illegal Chinese immigrants had the *tusheng* community to thank for fighting for their rights, not only for amnesty but also for the relaxation of Canadian immigration laws.[17]

From the 1950s on, the *tusheng* were no longer adamant in claiming the right to interpret or represent Chinese culture. This was because of the influx of the new group of Chinese immigrants who culturally had little in common with them. Both groups, however, saw the future of their ethnic group in relation to its acculturation and integration into Canadian society, and thus shifted their point of reference from China to Canada.[18] This shift was a natural process stemming from the isolation of Mainland China and strengthened by the Canadian educational system, by the sense of belonging following the government's relaxation of discrimination, and by their identification with the country in which they were born and raised.

Canadian policy around issues of human rights helped to reduce the level of overt racism in the country. However, Canadian society remained susceptible to negative stereotyping of certain ethnic groups. An article in *Maclean's* in 1962 depicted the Chinese community as unlawful and uncooperative with the government, and suggested that the immigration brokers were controlled by Triads and Communist. The same article denied that Canadian immigration laws were discriminatory. It alleged that the Chinese Benevolent Association (CBA) had told Chinese Canadians that if the military police came to the door with a search warrant, they should let them in but say nothing: "Anyone with 'irregular immigration papers,' ... should burn them." The article claimed that "Chinese feigned lack of knowledge of English with investigators," and it added: "All those people, who could have been jailed, have been granted amnesty, and still the Chinese community will not co-operate ... The CBA claims it is forced into fraud by our harsh immigration laws, by high-handed heartless immigration officials." It went on to say that instead of letting the CBA decide whom to bring in, "we could select Chinese who can assimilate ... from Hong Kong's pool of European-educated students and businessmen with money to invest."[19]

One of the best-known instances of state harassment of a visible minority group in Canada was the series of RCMP raids on Chinatowns across the country that was described in the last chapter. In their attempt to accumulate incriminating evidence, police teams barged into private homes and business offices, intimidating the occupants. The popular press fanned public hysteria with headlines such as "RCMP Squad Cracks Huge Chinese Immigration Racket." When the RCMP commissioner made the allegation that "11,000 Chinese of the 23,000 that have come to Canada since 1946 have entered the country illegally," a challenge was immediately brought by Chinese organizations, especially the CBA. Meanwhile, Liberal MP Jack Pickersgill attacked the Conservative government's effort to prove wrongdoing by a community "which has a record of obeying the law that most of us might envy."[20]

With public opinion on the side of the victims, Immigration Minister Ellen Fairclough apologized for the government's harsh measures, and offered amnesty for those who had entered Canada illegally, as described above. In the end, only twenty-eight people were prosecuted and no sentence was greater than six months. However, for Chinese Canadians, this incident remains "the 907 days of fear."[21]

One of Douglas Jung's greatest contributions during his tenure as MP was the implementation of the amnesty program, which made it possible for the Chinese who came into Canada using false names and identities to regularize their status with the Immigration Department, after which they could apply for their real families to come to Canada.[22] Jung was also instrumental in getting the immigration regulations changed so that more categories of family members could be sponsored.[23] When this change in the regulations was announced in 1962, Jung was given the credit by *Time* magazine.[24]

In his speech in the House of Commons on 9 June 1960, Jung said:

I urge that Chinese dependents regardless of age be allowed to join their relatives in Canada. Bearing in mind Chinese customs and traditions in the family, the class of dependents should be sufficiently broad to cover not only nephews and nieces but also grandchildren where the parents of the grandchildren are dead and the only relatives are in Canada.

I believe we have a moral obligation to those early Chinese immigrants who sacrificed so much and received so little to become reunited with their families ... For over half a century many of these early settlers were denied a normal family life, and it is a source of wonder to me that in spite of these handicaps they were able to build up a reputation as law-abiding and hard-working people.

Concurrent with the reunification of Chinese families there should be a quota system set up for those who have special skills and who do not have relatives in Canada ... skilled persons such as doctors, nurses and technicians.[25]

Jung's defeat in the next election revealed a disenchantment among some immigrants over his lethargy with regard to advancing the interests of Chinatown. Equally damaging to his credibility as a faithful spokesman for the ethnic group was the Conservative government's perceived hard-line approach to the issue of immigration and its crackdown on illegal Chinese immigration in 1960. However, Jung's political career was an indication of Canada's openness to its Asian minorities, and particularly to the Chinese Canadians in Vancouver.[26] He helped to reduce the remoteness of Canadian politics by giving them a voice in Ottawa.

Chapter 5

Enter Those with Education
and Language Skills

By the beginning of the 1960s, the *tusheng* community had helped to strengthen the support of the Liberal Party in Vancouver, despite the fact that Conservative MP Douglas Jung was from that community. In the election of 1963, the defeat of John Diefenbaker brought Lester B. Pearson to power. Pearson set his priority on French Canada, where he needed a powerful Quebec lieutenant, and he chose Marchand. However, Jean Marchand refused to join Pearson alone, and wanted Gérard Pelletier and Pierre Trudeau to come along too. Pelletier, the editor of *La Presse*, was welcome but not Trudeau, who was considered a wealthy intellectual dilettante. But Marchand insisted, and safe seats were found for the "three wise men."[1] Of these, Trudeau became the architect of the multiculturalism policy that had far-reaching effects on Canadian immigration for years to come.

Canada continued to face a shortage of skilled labour in the 1960s and needed to take well-educated immigrants from developing countries to cover the shortfall. Of equal importance as the need to change its immigration policy was the fact that Canada was in the process of building a positive image on the world stage. It was a Canadian, John Humphrey, who had drafted the United Nations Declaration of Human Rights in 1948, and it was Lester Pearson who had been awarded the Nobel Peace Prize for his efforts in resolving the 1956 Suez crisis, as well as for developing the concept of United Nations peacekeeping.

Mordecai Richler captured the mood of the nation during Canada's centenary year. "Vietnam and Ronald Reagan," he wrote in 1967, "have tempered my enthusiasm. Looked at another way, yes, we are nicer. And suddenly that's important."[2] Views were changing in Western society in the 1960s, not just in Canada. By this time, the horrors of racism perpetrated during the war and then the anti-imperialist and anti-colonialist struggles throughout the world, together with the American civil rights movement of Martin Luther King, had helped to discredit racism and European ethnocentrism.[3] In order to enhance Canada's economic profile among new states in Africa and Asia, as well as improving Canada's international image, the country's immigration policy had to be brought into line and made nonracist. Accordingly, Ottawa commissioned a major review of its immigration policy.[4]

Prosperity in Europe and slow economic growth in Canada, together with a policy of "selective immigration," had discouraged the entry of unskilled workers; in 1961 Canada had experienced the lowest level of immigration since 1947.[5] During 1962, a growing number of business people began to express support for higher immigration as a stimulus to economic growth. The president of the Canadian Manufacturers' Association called for "a strong, new program" in a speech in November, which drew a positive response from the new immigration minister, R.A. Bell. The *Globe and Mail* suggested that, if "we are going to get large numbers of immigrants, we are ... going to have to look to the overpopulated countries of the world ... We are going to have to look to Asia and Africa."[6]

The search for immigrant professionals was intensified by the need to replace Canadians who were accepting higher-paying jobs in the United States.[7] According to information reported in the House of Commons on 19 November 1961, of all the people who left Canada, more than half went to the United States. This pattern persisted into the first half of 1962. In February 1962, the *Labour Gazette* reported that between 1946 and 1960, almost half of the immigrants with professional and technical skills had left for the United States.[8]

During the 1960s, professionals made up nearly one-quarter of the total number of immigrants entering the Canadian labour force. The percentage from Britain declined from two-thirds to one-third, with a modest number coming from France. Meanwhile, there was a dramatic increase in the number of Asian professionals as Canada moved from "an ethnic-based immigration policy to a skill-based, universalistic one."[9] The new emphasis on labour-market skills signalled the beginning of large-scale racial and ethnic diversification in Canada. An acute shortage of professional and technical labour prompted Canada to broaden its admission standards to enable the admission of trained workers from all over the world. This policy increased the brain drain from developing countries, depriving them of their top professional workers, while at the same time bringing about a dramatic shift in the racial and ethnic origin of immigrants to Canada. This change subsequently altered the dynamics of integration.[10]

This very important policy change, which started with the Conservative government, was made partly for economic reasons. But equally important was the fact that Ellen Fairclough, minister of citizenship and immigration, and her deputy George Davidson, as well as other senior officials realized that Canada could not operate effectively within the United Nations or in the multiracial Commonwealth as long as it had a racially discriminatory immigration policy. The changes brought about by the introduction of new landing requirements in 1962 proved beneficial for Canada's international image at a time when empires were ending and many new independent states were being created.[11] However, to maintain the "historic pattern" of Canadian immigration, a preference for immigrants from certain geographic areas (Europe, Turkey, North, Central, and South America) was maintained, as mentioned earlier.[12]

The Cold War probably also affected the thinking of Canadian officials: for the first time, Canada took in refugees from Asia.[13] In 1961, Canada offered to admit 100 families from the huge refugee population of Hong Kong, a policy the *Toronto Star* called "no more than a gesture." In fact, the Immigration Department had considerable difficulty in finding 100 families qualified and willing to come to Canada, and the first did not arrive until August 1962. By 21 November, only 62 family units had arrived, totalling 139 persons. The issue then disappeared into obscurity.[14] However, by the beginning of the 1960s, with the change in Canadian immigration policies, Chinese women who were better educated or were trained in skills needed by Canada were able to immigrate as independents.[15] It was no longer necessary for them to follow the marriage route in order to enter Canada.

The change in attitude of Canadian immigration officials is illustrated through the story of Jean, who was interviewed in Victoria in the spring of 2001. She was very relaxed and spoke in fluent English.

❖ I was born in 1940 in Kingston, Jamaica, from a family of seven children, five girls and two boys. When I was five years old, my father moved the family to Hong Kong. My father had been in Jamaica a long time, but he didn't want us to grow up there and eventually intermarry with the locals. He wanted us to learn Chinese language and culture.

When we arrived in Hong Kong, my uncle [father's brother] arranged for housing for our family and they also went to fetch my grandmother from China. My first impression of Hong Kong was not good because I found it very confusing. In Hong Kong, I attended a Catholic school from grade one until high school graduation. As overseas Chinese, my siblings and I didn't know any Chinese, so we were put into a special class. The teacher didn't apply much discipline, and I regret that I didn't learn as much Chinese as I should have.

In 1956, after high school, I attended a technical college for one year to train as a secretary. After that, I worked as a secretary for various organizations. My first job was with the Hong Kong Naval Depot as the secretary of one of the officers there. When my sister went to the U.S., I took over her job in an import-export company for a few months. Then I worked for Jardine Engineering for a few years, and after that for an American import-export company until 1964.

My second oldest sister, who had left Hong Kong to study in San Diego, met her future husband there, but since neither of them could stay in the U.S. as immigrants, they immigrated to Canada in 1963 and lived in Burnaby, B.C.

By 1963, many of my siblings had left for the U.S. and Canada, and I thought it was time to make a move as well. I went to the Canadian Immigration in Hong Kong to get a tourist visa to visit my sister in Burnaby, B.C. During my interview, to my surprise, the immigration officer persuaded me to get an immigration visa instead. He said if I didn't want to stay in Canada, all I had to do was leave.

Jean's family background was totally different from that of the earlier informants, all of whom had fled from the political situation in China.

Jean was from an educated, well-travelled, affluent English-speaking family from Jamaica. She was the new type of Chinese woman immigrant to Canada. The fact that she was offered the chance to immigrate to Canada showed the discretionary powers that the immigration officials possessed in encouraging those with needed skills.

❖ After my medical and other necessary procedures, I left for Canada in February 1964. Since there was no direct boat to Vancouver, I took the *President Cleveland* to San Francisco. I had a lot of fun on the boat with the other young people. After we arrived, I visited my American boss's sister in Oakland and then took the train to Vancouver.

While staying with my sister in Burnaby, I sent letters of application to various companies to look for work. Within two weeks, I was offered a job with an engineering company. That was because of my experience at Jardine Engineering. It was easier to get a job in Canada than in Hong Kong. With my secretarial background, I was very employable, and the working conditions were very similar to Hong Kong. In comparison, the Chinese bosses in Hong Kong were generally more aggressive, and my Canadian bosses more polite. I'm very impressed with Canada.

I worked for a few months and quit my job to visit another sister in Phoenix, Arizona. On my return to Burnaby, there was a huge snowstorm. By then, my younger sister had immigrated to Victoria, and I wanted to visit her to see how she was doing. Besides, there is less snow in Victoria. In Victoria, I shared a basement apartment with my sister and a girlfriend. It was no problem at all to find work. All I had to do was to go to an employment office and there I could find out which company needed secretarial help. I found a job with a law firm within a week.

Jean's experience was again very different from those of the earlier interviewees. She was single and very independent, and jobs were readily available to her because of her work experience. While working at the law firm, she met her future husband, "who came over to Canada in 1950 with his mother and younger brother from China. His grandfather paid the head tax to come to Canada, and he and his son – my future father-in-law – ran a laundry in a tiny little fishing village up island."

❖ We got married in 1965. When I got pregnant with our first child, I was told that it was company policy that I should resign. It would be against the law for a company to do that nowadays! When I returned to work, I worked for the Department of Public Works, which later became B.C. Buildings Corporation. I wanted to work for the government because I would have more job security there. I remained with the government for twenty-nine years, and I have retired for three years now. My husband worked in a sawmill for thirty years. He was let go with a good package when the mill closed. He was only fifty-eight.

I always feel welcome in Canada and find Canadians very nice and kind, and I'm very impressed by the country. My husband has told me stories about discrimination the Chinese had endured. But then, his family had been in Canada for a few generations, and the old days were different.

Jean's comment about her pregnancy showed the importance of the Women's Movement, which started in the 1960s in Canada, in upholding the rights of women. The same topic is brought up in some of the later interviews. To her, discrimination against the Chinese was because "the old days were different."

❖ When you compare the behaviour of the ordinary people in Hong Kong to those in Canada, there is no comparison. In Canada, people would pick up magazines that have fallen from the rack in a grocery store, and the bus driver would back up the bus when they see me running for it. This would never happen in Hong Kong.

I believe it was easy for me to immigrate to Canada because I possessed skills that Canada needed at the time, and the fact that I speak English meant that I posed no problem integrating into Canadian society.

Jean's comparison of Hong Kong people and Canadians is similar to that of other informants. Jean never felt at home in Hong Kong, because it is a Chinese-speaking society and her background was that of overseas Chinese. She was the type of immigrant that Canada wanted after the passage of the 1962 Order-in-Council that changed the major criteria for the admission of independent immigrants to education, training, skills, and other qualifications.

When I interviewed Jean again at the end of 2010 and asked her to reflect on her life as an immigrant woman in Canada, she said:

❖ Every day I thank God for directing me to this country, which I love and appreciate. I do have my complaints at times about the justice system, which seems to help the perpetrators more than the victims, and I find the education system not strict enough to motivate our kids to stay in school and work hard. Having said that, I cannot complain about the freedom we enjoy in terms of speech, movement, religion, etc. As an immigrant, I couldn't have come to a better country.

From what I hear and see in the Chinese community, after living here for a number of years, I'm afraid I am disappointed. Maybe I expect more from my countrymen. I don't see the associations doing enough for each other. It is more like every person for himself or herself. It is depressing to see how a lot of them go out of their way to get their names in the paper or become name-droppers to bring glory to themselves. Unless there is an advantage, they will not go out of their way to help the community. And I mean acting to inspire and assist their neighbours without a second thought to himself/herself. Having said that, I must give credit to some of our Chinese philanthropists who have been quietly giving donations to a lot of worthy causes for years.

Nevertheless, this is a great country to live in – peaceful and free. I have been enjoying retirement life, and the grandchildren have given us so much joy and entertainment. We are truly blessed. Because of the many Canadians who have shown me generosity and kindness, I felt I had to give back to my community, and volunteering at the Cancer Clinic is my way of saying thank-you.

My garden is another sanctuary I now enjoy because it invigorates me and brings me in touch with nature. I so love that world, weeds and all, the birds, and even the apple tree that refuses to give me fruit year after year.

I never had intentions to immigrate to the United States,
despite the fact that I have two sisters there. I must admit, the
Canadian immigration officer had a far better vision than I did!

It will be noted that the majority of skilled immigrants entering Canada
in the 1960s had good language skills in one of the official languages.

In 1966 the National Employment Service of the Department of
Labour and the Immigration Service of the Department of Citizenship
and Immigration amalgamated to form the new Department of Manpower and Immigration. In the same year, the government published its
White Paper on Immigration, which was followed the next year by new
immigration regulations.[16] The white paper, intended to assist public
discussion and to analyze the number and type of immigrants that
Canada should seek, emphasized that "the answers must involve no
discrimination by reason of race, colour or religion."[17] The important
factors were that Canada was underpopulated and more people were
needed to increase the domestic market; the Canadian economy needed
highly qualified workers, and there were humanitarian considerations
as well.[18]

It is interesting to note the white paper's emphasis on international
relations: "Our basic immigration policy, which can be a means of fos-
tering friendly relationship with other countries ... [T]he country of
origin rightfully wishes to ensure that its citizens are not deceived or ex-
ploited ... [D]iscrimination, in the selection of immigrants, creates
strong resentments in international relations ... [R]emoving the last
vestiges of discrimination from immigration legislation and regulations
... [E]nsuring a high standard of protection and a ready welcome for all
acceptable immigrants of whatever origin."[19]

A completely new immigration selection system, the Canadian points
system, was drawn up by an official in the Canadian overseas immigration service, and in 1966 the deputy minister of manpower and immigration, Tom Kent, appointed a task force of four senior immigration
officials to refine and improve the new selection system. The results were
incorporated into the changes in the immigration regulations of 1
October 1967.[20] In what was a landmark decision, the Government of
Canada formally abolished all forms of discrimination with respect to
immigration.[21]

The revised regulations were popular with immigration officials as well as with immigrants.[22] A points system for selection and three categories for admission were created: independent applicants, sponsored dependants, and nominated relatives.[23] The regulations contained four important elements, though they were not all new: abolition of discrimination on the basis of race or nationality; selection for independent applicants based on the points system; creation of a nominated relatives category; and specific provisions for visitors to apply for landing status while in Canada. The system was simple and easy to understand and could be applied anywhere in the world. It did, however, require monitoring and adapting to changing circumstances from time to time. From 1947 to 1967, only 1.5 percent of all immigrants to Canada were of ethnic Chinese origin. In 1967, out of 222,876 immigrants who entered Canada that year, 6,409 were of Chinese origin.[24]

The following is the story of June, who came to Canada as an independent immigrant under the points system when it was first introduced. June was interviewed in my office in Toronto in the summer of 2001. She spoke in Cantonese.

❖ I was born in Hong Kong, date uncertain because my parents failed to keep a record of my birth, but it was probably around 1940. I am approximately sixty years old. I'm the only girl in a family of six brothers.

In Hong Kong, I attended a very good coeducational school in the English section. By the time I was in the fourth form, my brothers had already gone to Australia and wanted me to join them and go to school there. Having very strict parents, I couldn't wait to leave home. Not having a birth certificate complicated my getting a passport. My parents had to get affidavits from people stating the place and time of my birth, and my father also had to give a financial guarantee for me to go to Australia.

In Australia I studied English for one year, then took a secretarial course, and then went into nursing. I trained in one of the largest hospitals where few overseas students were accepted as trainees. I loved Australia, despite the fact that I couldn't stay in the country unless I stayed in school. At that time, in order to immigrate to Australia, overseas students had to return to their own countries to work for a few years before they could apply.[25]

It was in Australia that I met my future husband. When he graduated, he went back to Hong Kong to work for a large company while I enrolled in another course because I was not ready to get married yet. Besides, I loved Australia. While working in Hong Kong, my future husband heard from friends and relatives that Canada was a nice country to live in and that many people from Hong Kong were immigrating there. He asked me whether I would be interested in immigrating to Canada. He applied for immigration in Hong Kong and got it right away.

By that time, many of our friends had already moved there, so I thought I would like to immigrate to Canada too. I figured if I didn't like it, I could always apply to immigrate to Australia later. I applied for Canadian immigration in Australia. When I went to get the application form, I was asked to have my physical right away. My interview with the immigration officer only lasted half an hour. Within two weeks, I got my visa. The reason was that Canada had a shortage of nurses at that time, and I was trained not only in one of the Commonwealth countries but also in the largest hospital in the southern hemisphere. The process was so easy compared with immigration to Australia.

It was Canada's gain and Australia's loss when June and her husband decided to immigrate to Canada. The fact that by the 1960s, Canada had gained a reputation for being a nonracially-biased and immigrant-welcoming country helped to attract trained professionals from all over the world. June's experience at the Canadian immigration office was as easy as Jean's. She was fast-tracked because Canada needed nurses and because she had been trained in a Commonwealth country, which meant that she was given priority over nurses trained elsewhere.

❖ In 1967, when I finished my course, I returned to Hong Kong with the plan of getting married. The invitations were all ready to be sent out, but then the riots started. So we came to Canada and got married in Toronto.

When I arrived in Toronto I got a job right away at a large

hospital. But because I was not Canadian-trained, I could only work as a graduate nurse until I had my R.N. [registered nurse degree]. I waited for an opening for the course, and when I completed it, I got the balance of my back pay, which I couldn't receive before.

June mentioned the riots in Hong Kong that prevented her wedding from taking place. She was referring to the Cultural Revolution in China, which by 1967 had spilled into Hong Kong. There were riots in the streets and the population in the colony was feeling very vulnerable. Here again, political disturbance provided the incentive for immigration.

June was used to the life in Australia, and adjustment in Canada was not a problem, particularly when she was able to find work immediately in the same field for which she was trained.

❖ Our family then moved to Montreal where my husband worked in broadcasting. I worked full-time in nursing until I had my first child, and then worked part-time, partly because I didn't have help and partly because I am a baby nurse and love looking after babies anyway. After two and a half years, we moved back to Toronto, where we have remained ever since.

I consider myself a Christian even though I was never baptized, but my husband is. We have a son and a daughter. My daughter is an excellent student and graduated from an Ivy League school. We are happy that our children are doing well in Canada.

I've worked as a nurse all my life. Now that I'm retired, I still help a doctor doing his billing. My husband is also retired, and we are taking it easy and enjoying life.

June said that her parents had been "too restrictive" – another form of Chinese patriarchy – so the early hurdle in her life was to get her parents' permission to go to Australia for school. In her decision to immigrate to Canada with her husband, she was able to take advantage of the points system because of her nursing training. If she had been able to stay in Australia, she would have done so. The restrictive Australian immigration policy at that time turned out to be beneficial to Canada. This was another success story of immigration in the 1960s.

The following is the story of Karen, who also entered Canada on the new points system. Karen was interviewed in my office in Toronto in the summer of 2001. Being a conscientious teacher all her life, she came prepared with all her facts written down in case she missed some of them when we spoke. She also brought with her a copy of the page of her passport stamped by Canadian Immigration. She spoke half in English and half in Cantonese.

❖ I was born in Hong Kong in 1941, the youngest of three children. I was educated in a very good coed school in the English section. After the fifth form, I continued my education at Northcote Teachers' Training College for two years. After graduation, I taught visual arts and English for six years in secondary school and then requested to be transferred to elementary school to get primary school experience.

In 1965 I married another schoolteacher. His family was very traditional, and so we planned to look for opportunities elsewhere so that we could be independent. Life was too complicated and demanding in Hong Kong. We were contributing to my in-laws' income by renting one of their apartments, and my husband had to teach painting for free every Sunday at his father's studio as another financial contribution. Wishing for a simple life, we looked to Canada to fulfill that wish.

We applied jointly at the Canadian immigration office in Hong Kong, putting the reasons to immigrate as both husband and wife wanting to start a new life, as well as exploring teaching opportunities in a new country. At that time, two thousand teaching jobs in Canada were advertised in the newspapers in Hong Kong. Within half a year of our medicals, in 1967, we were notified that we had one year to make the decision to move to Canada.

Like June, Karen and her husband were trying to get away from traditional Chinese patriarchy. When the riots broke out in Hong Kong, they made a quick decision to leave.

❖ Political turmoil in China spilled over to Hong Kong in 1967, and my husband and I decided it was time to leave. By then, I already had one year of experience teaching primary school. My husband took a year of absence from teaching in Hong Kong, just in case he didn't like Canada, but I just resigned because I knew I would never turn back. In June 1968 we landed in Vancouver with our baby daughter.

I was shocked by what Vancouver looked like because I had a totally different and glamorous image of the city based on the James Bond movies. I visited my sister in Saskatoon with our baby daughter while my husband flew to Toronto to look for work. Within two weeks, he was offered a teaching job in Brampton. He then returned to Saskatoon to pick us up.

The education system in Ontario recognized my teaching diploma, but not my husband's university degree as a teacher. He had to make up courses in order to start teaching in September. I didn't start working right away because our daughter was too young, and we had no household help.

Qualifications for teaching change all the time and differ from province to province. In 1968, those with a university degree, and teaching experience, needed additional teaching qualifications. Teaching qualifications from a teacher's college in Hong Kong, such as those Karen had, were readily accepted because Hong Kong was part of the Commonwealth.

❖ In 1969 I looked for a teaching job, and all I had was a phone interview. It seemed that the school principal mistook my name as an Anglo-Saxon name, and since my English was very good, he thought he had hired a teacher of Anglo-Saxon background. He was in shock when he met me for the first time. I'm not sure whether I would have needed more than a phone interview if that mistake had not been made.

However, Karen never mentioned experiencing discrimination from her colleagues, the parents, or the students. In fact, teaching was a happy experience for her, and she loved her students.

❖ I remained teaching in that school for eleven years. With the constant change in the teaching system, from closed to open concept, and French immersion, I had to learn to teach English in a French immersion school. After eleven years, I remained the most junior in seniority among teachers because I didn't know French, and lost my job. However, I was offered interviews in another school board, but I would have no choice of location.

Out of ignorance, every time I had another child, I resigned instead of taking a leave of absence. Regulations changed, and by 1974 all new teachers had to have a university degree, which meant that when I returned to work, I had to have, or at least be working towards, a university degree. I worked at it in the evenings and in the summer months. At one time, my mother came to help and at another my mother-in-law also came to help so that I could complete my courses. Finally, I was able to get my degree, which secured my position as a teacher.

It seems that Karen had not looked into the education system in Ontario, and this had caused her a great deal of inconvenience and hard work. She blamed herself for being negligent. The fact that she was not advised about maternity leave and resigned each time she became pregnant could be perceived as racial discrimination, but she did not blame anyone but herself.

❖ Our first house was rented, and it cost $160 per month, in addition to $50 for heating. With a salary of $3,000 per year, there was very little money left. No matter how hard up we were, my husband, being the only son – and his sister didn't count – was expected to send $50 each month back to his parents in Hong Kong.

Karen appears to have been under a lot of stress and did not know how to deal with it. Despite having left Hong Kong, she and her husband were still living according to traditional Chinese patriarchy. They did have their options, but chose not to take them.

❖ When the children were small, I did wonder whether it was worth my while at all to work, because half of my salary went to babysitters. We also needed two cars because we didn't teach at the same school, and I also needed clothes. Now, I know it's definitely worth it because of the pension I'm getting. I'm just a little disturbed when I found out that our pension could not be passed on to our children, which means that we'll have nothing to give them when we pass away.

We came to Canada at a good time, because as time went on, it became more and more difficult to get a teaching job. There had been years that our salary was frozen, and in my last five years, the cutback in the provincial government had affected my retirement scale. So, we came at the right time, but I retired at the wrong time.

I feel very lucky to be in Canada, because at the time we applied to immigrate in the 1960s, the Canadian Immigration in Hong Kong was terribly overworked because so many people wanted to emigrate from Hong Kong. We knew some teachers who didn't get accepted, and if they were to have health problems, they would not have been accepted at all.

I have no regrets coming to Canada. I never missed Hong Kong. We have a family life here. Our life was very children-focused, but for the first ten years, we had no lifestyle at all because we just couldn't afford it.

We are practising Catholics, but we don't insist that our children go to church on Sundays. We had wanted our children to go to Chinese school, but it was always a struggle. Our children are doing well, and one daughter is a medical doctor. Both our daughters are married to white Canadians.

Karen did not mention any intergenerational issues with their children. This is probably because of her educational background in an English school in Hong Kong, which made assimilation into Canadian society much easier. Her children have grown up like other Canadian children and are pursuing their own interests.

Karen's was another successful immigrant story. As she said, her timing was good because, when she and her husband and baby daughter came to Canada, teaching jobs were plentiful. And she has been enjoying her retirement: "My husband and I are retired, and we have embarked into a new career in photography and computer imaging, as well as doing a lot of travelling."

At the writing of this book in 2010, I interviewed Karen again, and she reflected on her life in Canada:

❖ No matter how we enjoy our vacations to different parts of the world or even to the most exotic places, on returning home to Canada we never fail to let out a sigh of relief, "Home Sweet Home!" Canada has been our home since we emigrated from Hong Kong in 1969 with our little daughter. We are proud of our roots, but we feel so blessed to be living in this beautiful country with freedom of choice, old age security, free medical care, opportunity for higher education, and with great respect for different cultures.

Even as a top student in high school in Hong Kong, I was one of the few graduates who could not afford a university education. Yet in the Canadian system, I was able to complete my degree before I turned forty when I was a working mother of three. With my hard-earned degree, I could continue to teach till I retired at age fifty-five with a good pension.

Life was very challenging the first ten years, with health problems in the family. Both my baby son and I underwent major surgery. The medical bill for our son's surgery and hospitalization was thirty Canadian dollars! If we were in Hong Kong then, we would have been in deep debt to pay the medical bills. Thank you, Canada!

Just two years ago, it was the fiftieth anniversary of our high school class. We had a wonderful global reunion in Hong Kong with close to sixty classmates in attendance. Apart from my very good friends in Canada, nearly nobody recognized me. I was remembered as a tall and skinny girl who was always sick and walking with a slouch. One classmate could not help teasing, "Wow, you have changed so much! What has Canada done to you?" Ah ha! Canada has changed me into a SWAN.

Ballroom dancing has improved my poise, swimming forty laps per round has boosted my health, and doing weights with regular gym visits have enhanced my figure. In some countries, one has to be a rich member of a special club in order to swim in a twenty-five-metre indoor pool. Nowhere else in the world would one find so many inexpensive facilities and community centres for everyone. There is no place like Canada! There is no place like HOME!

Karen and her husband are grandparents now, and their parents have passed away. Despite occasional health problems, they travel a great deal and spend a few months each year in Hong Kong.

June and Karen, as well as their husbands, were beneficiaries of the points system that was introduced in 1967, as well as of Canada's recognition of the Commonwealth educational qualifications, even though their job experiences were very different. They had the skills Canada needed, and both they and Canada benefited. June and Karen brought with them the new image of immigrant Chinese women, those with education and skills, and thereby contributed to a rise in the profile of the Chinese Canadian communities.

Unlike many of the female immigrants, Jean, June, and Karen all spoke English fluently, which made assimilation to Canadian life much easier. In the 1960s, immigrant families continued to arrive from Hong Kong. The majority were part of the earlier exodus from Communist China, though the push factor for these three was the 1967 rioting in Hong Kong.

Iris's family was part of the earlier exodus. She was interviewed in my office in the summer of 2001. She spoke softly in Cantonese.

❖ I was born in Chongqing in January 1950, the youngest of four children. My father worked for the American air force. When the Communists took over in 1949, the family waited for my birth and then we moved back to our village in the Hoiping County. My father then left for Hong Kong in February 1950. The rest of the family stayed in the village for five years.

Family members left for Hong Kong bit by bit. In 1952, my older sister left, and after that it became very difficult. When I left, my mother had to make up an excuse that a daughter was getting married in Hong Kong and the family must be at the wedding; so permission was given to her to bring me and my twelve-year-old brother to Hong Kong. My eldest sister, who was sixteen years my senior, stayed with my grandmother, and she came to Hong Kong two to three years later with another relative. So in 1958 the family was finally reunited.

Like my other informants, those with wealth or with connections to the enemies of the Communist Party, such as Iris's father, had to get out of China at the end of the civil war. Many of them believed that, as an interim measure for the family, if they left the cities and went to live in their ancestral villages they could get out of the way of the advancing Communist army. But in 1949 the wealthy in the villages were targeted. In addition, travel restrictions became more and more stringent, and excuses had to be made to get permission to travel to Hong Kong, since it was British territory.

❖ My family had a very difficult time in Hong Kong because my father wasn't able to get any money out of China. We were very poor. My eldest sister had a fiancé whose father lived in Canada, but he had sold the paper of his son's birth to someone else. So when he wanted his son to join him in Canada in 1959, he in turn had to buy a paper for him. After his arrival, he applied for my eldest sister to come to Canada.

Here is another instance of buying paper to prove the birth of a son.

❖ In 1967, during the riots in Hong Kong, my older brother had just graduated from technical school with two years of drafting. Because of the new policy in Canadian immigration, he applied as an independent immigrant.[26]

At that time, there were many picture brides the same age as me. These girls took a chance marrying men they didn't know in order to have the chance of a new life in Canada. Fortunately, despite our poverty, my parents were very much against this. I was able to finish grade 12, and by that time my brother was settled in Canada and could sponsor his family.

My father was a mechanic, and my brother's employers gave a letter guaranteeing my father a job when he arrived in Canada. At the same time, my eldest sister gave the guarantee that if the need should arise, she would support us. All this made our application very easy. My other sister and I were under twenty-one, so in 1969 we had another family reunion in Canada.

I was very happy to be in Canada. Our family had to borrow a lot of money in order to make the move, and that's why my parents couldn't send me to school for much longer. My eldest sister didn't end up helping us at all. We rented one of her houses to live in.

Iris was thankful that her parents were against her becoming a picture bride, and she was able to finish her schooling. She belonged to the new group of immigrant Chinese women who opted for education rather than a "blind" marriage.

❖ I went to George Brown College to study commerce for two years and then went out to work in 1971 as a clerk at the head office of a large bank. My sister worked at OHIP [Ontario Health Insurance Plan], and together our family was able to buy our own house in 1972. I remained at the bank for nine years.

In 1973 I got married. I first met my husband in 1968 while he was working at a large bank in Hong Kong. Before that, he had studied at the Baptist College for one year, and since he couldn't get a degree he decided to go out to work. Ten months afterwards, I immigrated to Canada. He promised me that he would be in Canada within three years. He saved up for three years and then applied to a junior college in California. Within ten months, his visa was granted. He was using this to get closer to Canada so that we could see each other. He did two years' work in one, and then transferred to Boston University. Then we could be closer. He graduated three years later, and we got married.

Iris referred to herself as a housewife. She did not speak about working from the time she got married but only about volunteering in the community.

❖ I have a son and a daughter. From 1983 on, because of my son and daughter I was involved with the Chinese school of one of the Chinese organizations every Saturday morning. Since then, I got to know more people in the Chinese community. In 1987

I became a board member, and I was actively involved in fund-raising from 1990 on. I have learned a lot about people from working with the Chinese community. Over the past twenty-one years, the Chinese school has grown from sixty students to thousands of students.

I'm very thankful for all the opportunities Canada has given my family. I believe Canada gives immigrants a lot of opportunities, and as long as you are willing to work, you will succeed. Compared to United States, Australia, and New Zealand, I don't feel much discrimination in Canada.

Since Iris has had no first-hand experience of the other countries she mentioned, she was probably basing her assessment on hearsay as well as on her faith in Canada. Iris and her husband were very satisfied with their life in Canada as well as being happy about the development of their children. The children were good students and won awards, both in school and in the community as volunteers.

❖ With my community work, I have a lot of opportunities to speak to new immigrants. I always remind them that they must think of themselves as Canadians first. They are Canadians of Chinese heritage. I don't like those who take the benefits from Canada without contributing to this country, especially those who work and make money in Hong Kong, and bring their aged parents here for the old age pension. When these people get sick, they come back here for free medical care. Some even boast that it's cheaper to buy a plane ticket than to pay for medical care in Hong Kong. As a taxpayer, I feel taken advantage of.

My son is a doctor now, and my daughter is training as an accountant. My husband and I are very happy.

Iris came to Canada as a dependant of her father, who immigrated at the same time as a dependant of his son. This is a typical pattern of family chain migration. Although she was from a humble family, her immigration from Hong Kong to Canada gave her opportunities she would not have had back home. She married a man of her own choosing, and it was fortunate that he was able to come to Canada as originally planned. Iris contributed much to her community by volunteering, and she encouraged her children to do the same. She constantly reminds her children that they must give back to Canadian society.

At the end of 2010, I asked Iris to reflect on her life as an immigrant woman in Canada, and she said:

❖ I am very happy being in Canada. It is the best country in the world to live in. I think the fact that I have a good husband and successful children has contributed to the way I feel. My son, who is in public health, has had very good offers from Hong Kong as well as in the U.S., but he turned them down because he said he is a Canadian and wants to contribute to Canada. My daughter is a very successful accountant with one of the major accounting firms in Canada. Her husband is in the same profession.

My husband is still working because he is only in his early sixties. The company he works for is a distributor of heating equipment from Italy, so we get trips to Italy, which is very nice. We make about five trips a year all over the world. Our children come back for dinner once a week with their families when we are here. I don't interfere with their families, and of course I'll look after my granddaughter whenever I am asked, which is not often. We have another grandchild on the way.

I hear people talk about racial discrimination in Canada, but all through my many years here, I have never experienced any.

Iris has completely retired from her volunteering and travels a lot with her husband. Her social life remains within the Chinese community.

The points system that came into being in 1967 was a turning point in the history of immigration for Chinese women. From the vivid stories of Jean, June, Karen, and Iris we see how during the 1960s, with the changes in immigration law and introduction of the policy of multiculturalism, Canada entered a new phase in nation building.

Chapter 6

They Came for Higher Education

In the 1960s, the number of educated immigrants from Hong Kong entering Canada gradually increased. Since Hong Kong was part of the British Commonwealth, with English as the language of business and government, Hong Kongers had an edge over immigrants from many other countries, especially after the introduction of the points system. Hong Kong is a highly developed financial centre, with a high level of education, and its financial success could not have been possible without the services provided by a generation of educated professionals.[1] These were the accountants, lawyers, builders, surveyors, educators, and so on whom the Canadian Immigration Department was seeking.[2]

In order to understand the migrants from Hong Kong since the 1960s, it is important to appreciate the hardships that generations of its people went through to achieve Hong Kong's success. Its identity has a significant Chinese component in its schools and in its popular culture; it is multicultural and all-encompassing. Helen Siu quotes Elizabeth Sinn, who said, "Hong Kong cultures grew in a unique environment full of historical contradictions ... In Hong Kong, the Chinese, the foreign, the new, the old, the orthodox, and the unorthodox are mixed in a melting pot ... out of which arises a pluralistic, fluid, exuberant cultural uniqueness."[3]

Hong Kong residents, migrants, and locals, although cramped for physical space, have collectively created an unusual cultural and political space, where they could choose and act on the agendas most meaningful to them.[4] This was the background from which many of the new immigrants to Canada came. Beginning in the mid-1960s, skilled and educated Chinese women emigrated from Hong Kong, many of them were from the elite echelon of society. Others came indirectly from Shanghai. Many of these young women wanted to go to Canada for higher education.

Until 1974, it was possible for individuals already in Canada as tourists, students, or temporary workers to apply for landed immigrant status.[5] This mode of immigration was very common among Chinese who were not sponsored or nominated, and it was particularly true of university students who, after graduation, could secure employment in Canada and then seek admission as independent applicants.

The following is the story of Lucy, which shows how the immigration regulations worked for graduates of a Canadian university in the 1960s. Lucy was interviewed in my office in Toronto in the summer of 2001. She spoke in Cantonese in a soft tone.

❖ I was born in Hong Kong in 1939, the youngest in a family of two boys and three girls. I started at a very good coed school in Hong Kong, in the English section, from grade 3 until high school graduation. In 1959 I went to the U.S. to continue my studies at a college. After a year and a half, I transferred to a university, and finished my degree in 1963.

I went back to Hong Kong and taught English at a middle school, and was well liked by the other teachers as well as the students. However, my U.S. degree was considered lower in status than a degree from the University of Hong Kong. My salary was $500 instead of the $1,300 paid to the graduates of the University of Hong Kong [laughs]. I was lucky to be living at home, because my salary was only enough to buy clothes. I discovered that to be recognized, I needed a degree from a university from the British Commonwealth.

I applied to a Canadian university to do my master's degree and came to Canada on a student visa in 1965. When I finished the following year, teachers were in great demand. I opened the newspaper and saw that a school in a small town in northern Ontario was looking for a teacher in my major. I applied, not knowing it was such a remote little town, and was offered the job. Then I needed to establish my status in Canada.

According to the immigration regulations at the time, it was very easy for me. In 1966, because of my job offer, I was granted landed immigrant status that September. My teaching job was probationary because I needed to get my Ontario teacher's certificate, which meant that I had to take courses for two summers.

When I got to the town, I realized how isolated I was. Most teachers in the school, unless they lived in the surrounding areas, were single girls. There was a residence for us. We rented a car together to drive to Toronto every weekend. I had a brother who lived in Toronto, and I went to the Chinese church with him every Sunday. We are from a very religious family. It was at the church that I met my future husband. I stayed in the school for only one year because the town was just too small and remote for a person from Hong Kong.

Lucy mentioned the importance of qualifications from the British Commonwealth for anyone working within the Commonwealth. Because she was not getting pay equal to that of other teachers in Hong Kong, she came to Canada to get her qualifications without intending to stay here. The great demand for teachers at the time of her graduation became the determining factor for her application as a landed immigrant.

The isolation that she felt in a little town was not only because she was from Hong Kong, which is always crowded with people. She also felt isolated from the well-established Chinese community in Toronto. Her complaint about the smallness of the town was probably only partially the explanation. After all, she did not suffer from social isolation – she had lived abroad for a number of years and was fluent in English. I believe it was the remoteness from the Chinese community in Toronto that was the real issue.

❖ In the meantime, my brother asked me to come to Toronto to share an apartment with him. I again saw a lot of teaching positions available in Toronto, and there was going to be something like "market week" in the lobby of the Park Plaza Hotel, where all the school boards set up booths, so that teachers could do their "job shopping." I went and was offered two jobs. Not knowing where either one was [she laughed again], I picked the one that was farthest away, again teaching the same subject.

The Canadian immigration process was easy for someone with Lucy's qualification in the 1960s, but it would change in 1974, as will be explained later in this chapter.

❖ My brother and I looked for an apartment and rented one in a central area. There were two garage spaces, and the rent was $170 a month. My brother gave me his old car. Working far away meant driving thirty miles each way to get to work every day. I taught there for six years.

I was married in 1968. My husband had also come to Canada as a student to do his master's degree. In 1965 he got a job after graduation and applied for landed immigrant status. In May 1971 we both got our Canadian citizenship.

My parents were coming over for my wedding, so instead of coming as visitors, I sponsored them to come as landed immigrants. At the beginning, my parents would only stay in Canada half a year each time because my paternal grandmother was still alive in Hong Kong and my father still had his business there. After 1970, when my father closed his business in Hong Kong, my parents bought a small house in Toronto and lived here full-time. They loved puttering around the house and the garden. Since space was so limited in Hong Kong, they really appreciated having their own house and garden in Toronto.

Eventually, all of Lucy's siblings moved to Canada or the United States, and her parents were able to be close to them. This kind of chain migration made it possible for the founding of strong, socially active Chinese Canadian communities.

❖ We bought our first house, and in 1970 my son was born. I took maternity leave for a year, and even though I didn't get a full year's pay, I was guaranteed my job back after the year. I went back to teach at the same school for three years until my daughter was born.

At that time, I really wanted to quit teaching and stay home with the children, but for security's sake I thought it better not to quit altogether, so I took two years off instead. Afterwards, I went back to work full-time in order to secure a better financial future for the family. My former job was gone, but I was offered two other jobs under the same school board. One was at a high school near the airport, and the other at a junior high. Everyone warned me that I wouldn't survive teaching in a junior high because of the age group, but I thought I would try. I stayed for nineteen years until I retired.

I never regretted leaving Hong Kong. When the principal of the first school wrote me to invite me back to teach after I received my Canadian degree, I turned it down because I had already met my future husband, and we wanted to stay in Canada.

I remained a teacher until 1995, when I retired. My children have both graduated from university and are doing well. Both my husband and I go to church every Sunday, and we were church elders for many years until recently. I've remained active at my church with Sunday school and the education centre, as well as singing in the choir.

Lucy and her husband had made their choice to stay in Canada with no thought of returning to Hong Kong. Religion and the Chinese Canadian community at her church formed a very big part in their lives.

Lucy had agency all along and made a lot of choices in her life. When she made the wrong ones, she was able to carry through in good humour. Unlike Karen, she knew her rights in taking maternity leave so that she could go back to the same teaching job on her return to work. At the writing of this book, Lucy was enjoying retirement with her husband, taking cruises and travelling all over the world. Her father had passed away, and her mother is in a Chinese nursing home. She feels very fortunate at having immigrated to Canada, because Canada is a safe and peaceful country.

Immigrant women like Lucy and Karen have made their contributions to Canadian society by being the educators of the next generation of Canadians. During the 1960s and early 1970s, it was easy to immigrate to Canada, especially when the applicant had been a student in a Canadian university. The years at the university were counted as half the time of residence in Canada. Because of the time spent in the universities, these students did not have any problem adapting to life in Canada.

The following is the story of Hope, who was interviewed in my office in Toronto in the summer of 2001. She spoke very self-assuredly in English.

❖ I was born in Shanghai in 1944, near the end of the Sino-Japanese War. But then the civil war in China began, resulting in the Communist takeover of China. In 1949 my family was probably the last family to leave before the Communists took over Shanghai.

My father had wanted to attend Whampoa Military Academy with the hope of a military career, but his hopes were dashed when the Japanese invaded China. In Shanghai, he was the manager of a prestigious dance hall, and the family was well off.

When my family moved to Hong Kong, my father was not able to find work, so my mother had to go out to work for the first time in her life. She found a job as a bookkeeper-accountant and was able to support the family.

For Hope, like many of my informants, the civil war in China was the push factor – the reason why her family had to leave Shanghai and the comfortable life they had there, joining the exodus from China to Hong Kong after 1949.

❖ I was sent to a convent school because my mother had done her research and knew that the children were given a bottle of fresh milk every day at recess, which was a big deal in the postwar days in Hong Kong. There was an orphanage attached to the school, and it was then that I learnt to care for those who were less fortunate than I.

My mother had wanted to send her daughters to Canada to study one day, but in 1954 she died. In 1957 I transferred to a good coed school because of its high academic standing. When I finished Upper Six, I felt I needed a change of scene, and thinking of my mother's wish, I decided Canada would be a good place to start.

In 1963 I came to Canada on a student visa to attend McGill University, where I did my BSc and one year of my MSc. That summer, my fiancé graduated from the University of Hong Kong medical school, and we had planned to get married. I returned to Hong Kong and persuaded my fiancé that we would have a better future in Canada. We applied to immigrate to Canada, both in the independent class since we were not yet married. It was easy for me because my degree from McGill was sufficient for immigration. I came back to Canada in 1968.

While Hope spoke of the disappointments in her father's life, she did not explain how the family managed financially after the death of her mother, who seemed to be the sole supporter of the family. Hope did fulfill her mother's wish by going to Canada for university. The change in the immigration law made it easy for her as a Canadian university graduate. She was even able to convince her future husband to immigrate, despite the fact that he would have to do his internship all over again.

❖ My fiancé applied as a medical professional with two years' experience. He needed a Canadian licence to practise and was accepted into the internship program in the Ottawa Civic Hospital, even though he had already done his internship in Hong Kong. Because he was going to be in Ottawa, I finished my MSc in Ottawa under the aegis of McGill.

I became a Canadian citizen much earlier than my husband because my four years at McGill was counted as two years of residency. At that time, residency was only three years, so I received my citizenship in 1969. There was no citizenship ceremony at that time. I went into an office and was asked a few questions of which the answers were obvious, I swore allegiance to the Queen, and that was it. It was over in five minutes!

Depending on when a person received his or her citizenship, the process changed from time to time. This was mentioned in many of the interviews.

❖ I worked in research in the Ottawa Civic [Hospital] after graduation until our only son was a year old. In 1973, after my husband finished his training in the Ottawa Civic, we moved to Montreal, where he trained in neuroradiology. When his year was finished, René Lévesque came into power in Quebec, and we decided it was time to move. My husband sent out one hundred and twenty letters of application for a staff position in radiology, and out of that only four replied. One of them was a hospital in Toronto. We chose to go to Toronto because my husband had siblings there.

In 1974 I started to work for a university in Toronto as a tutor, my duty being that of looking after the students of one professor, the administration of the courses, the students' problems, as well [as] ordering materials and books, and making sure that the courses run smoothly. Should the professor get sick, I would take over the lectures.

I think I fit in well in Canada, even when I was a student at McGill. I didn't feel discrimination, only annoyance – even though others might have interpreted otherwise – especially when I was asked whether I lived on a boat [in Aberdeen] or why I didn't wear a pigtail. People were generally very kind to me, and I was always invited for long weekends. I never had to fight for marks at university. Because of the squabble between the French and the English in Quebec, I often got better service at the post office because I looked different.

Economically, we were typical of the young generation of Canadians when we first arrived [this was her interpretation]. We had $2,000 between us. My husband started with making $400 a month, and since I was working full-time I took care of most of the bills.

When I felt discrimination was during my last year at McGill when companies came to the school to offer jobs to graduating students. I was offered a research job at seventy-five cents [compared] to the dollar that was offered to a male student in my class who had lower marks than me. That was not acceptable to me, and I decided to go to graduate school. I feel, at my present level, there is no discrimination. I believe being talented is not enough. One has to be smart and know how to socialize.

It was fortunate that Hope interpreted ridiculous questions from fellow students as annoyance instead of discrimination. She brought up the topic of gender discrimination, emphasizing that it existed in the job market – in the hiring practices of companies – rather than among Canadians in general. She believed she had overcome it by having higher education and knowing how to socialize: "I think there is more discrimination in Vancouver nowadays," she said. "When I visit there, just because I look different, I'm presumed to be ignorant. Or maybe I'm just getting old and crabby." So Hope experienced both gender and racial discrimination. She had expected to be treated equally because of her high level of education. Education helps, but it does not solve the problem of the ignorance of others.

❖ I stay out of politics because of my early experience with my family's political infighting. My father had ten siblings, and they belonged to opposite parties in China. So grandparents' parties, such as birthdays, always turned out to be shouting matches.

I spend a lot of time on volunteer work. My life as a dedicated volunteer started at my church a long time ago. As a practising Catholic, I used to bring my son to church every Saturday morning while I did my volunteering, until he got older and was no longer interested to go with me. Then I brought my church together with the Catholic Women's League to raise money, and later became the bazaar chairwoman.

Religion was a big part of Hope's life as it has been in the lives of many Chinese immigrant women.

❖ After my son turned sixteen, I found I had a lot of time on my hands, so I became involved with the Federation of Chinese Canadian Professionals (FCCP) in which my husband is a member. I raised some money for the federation in the following year. In the same year, I became a docent in the Art Gallery of Ontario [AGO] and was asked to join the board of the Mon Sheong Foundation.[6]

In 1990 I left the Mon Sheong Foundation and joined the board of the Chinese Cultural Centre. In the early 1990s I joined the ballet board. How it happened was that someone noticed that I was going to the ballet three times a week. That person didn't know that besides loving the ballet, my husband was working all the time, so I actually had a lot of time on my hands. I was on that board for six years.

Since the 1990s, I've also joined the boards of the Art Gallery of Ontario, the Opera, and Roy Thomson Hall, and I remain on the advisory board of the Chinese Cultural Centre of Greater Toronto. I've found out that I'm a good outreach person, not only leading tours as a docent in the AGO but also giving pre-opera chats.

I am still in the same job at the university. Even though I valued my youthful experience in Hong Kong, Canada is, to me, still the best country in the world to live in.

Hope is an example of the new generation of Chinese immigrant women who socialize well with the members of the mainstream communities. She has made a notable contribution to Canada. She was awarded Canada's highest honour for voluntarism.

The following is another integration story of someone who came to Canada for university. Rena was interviewed in my office in Toronto in the summer of 2001. She was confident and spoke in Cantonese with some English during the interview.

❖ I was born in Shanghai in 1938 in a family of six children. My family owned thousands of acres of land, and my father also had a stock brokerage firm. Because of the civil war in China, he knew he would be targeted by the Communists, so he moved to Hong Kong in 1948 with my mother, leaving the six children behind in the care of three servants. My mother wanted to believe that the Communist regime wouldn't last and that the separation was going to be temporary, so she left behind all her valuables in the care of a neighbour.

We were very happy to be left in Shanghai. Under the Communist regime, there were a lot of meetings and activities, and students were not required to take their studies seriously. With the parents gone, we were left to do as we wished.

Here is another story about China during the civil war and families leaving for Hong Kong.

❖ In 1952 we got the exit visas to Hong Kong. I was fourteen. I believe it was because there was only enough money left in Shanghai to take care of us and no money was being remitted, so there was no reason for the government to keep us. Those who were receiving overseas remittances were having a much more difficult time leaving China. Five of us left with a servant. My eldest sister didn't want to leave because she was having so much fun and all her friends were in Shanghai. However, by December, she changed her mind and also went out to Hong Kong.

It was considered too dangerous for us to bring our mother's valuables, so they remained in our neighbour's safekeeping … [until they] were confiscated by the Red Guards in the 1960s. Strangely enough, the contents were recorded. In the 1980s we were contacted, and compensation was made in cash, with the evaluation of $50 per carat of diamonds! Even then, the money given back to us had to remain in Shanghai.

Here we have more details about life in Shanghai and how the younger generation reacted to the beginning of the Communist takeover. If Rena and her siblings had stayed in Shanghai, they would have been targeted sooner or later as the children of a wealthy family.

❖ The culture in Hong Kong was so different. I found it very difficult to adjust because I spoke only Mandarin and Shanghainese. The first day I went to school I wore shorts, because it was so hot, and was reprimanded by the head mistress. The next day I went in jeans and again was reprimanded. The following week my school uniforms, the cheongsams, were ready, and I was fine. My siblings and I stayed in this Chinese school for only three months because our mother wanted us to go to an English school.

Through a friend of my parents, my siblings and I were able to attend a Catholic school. We all became Catholics because the nuns were very good teachers and they were good to us. I had to be put back from secondary level to primary school because of my lack of knowledge of English, but I eventually caught up with the other students.

A good English education was highly valued by many parents in Hong Kong. Not only was English the language of business in Hong Kong but it was also the language for teaching at the University of Hong Kong, and, of course, a language of communication in many parts of the world.

❖ Because my father lost a lot of money in Hong Kong, my mother was very unhappy and cried a lot. As a refugee, I went to church frequently and became very devout. I went to a service every morning and every evening for ten years. Because I played the piano and the organ, I was asked to play for the parish, as well as for weddings on Saturdays and Sundays. I helped prepare the hosts for communion, washed the altar, and on Sunday evenings counted the collection money.

From the first Catholic school, I went on to another for lower six and upper six. In 1959 I enrolled at the University of Hong Kong with the intention of studying mathematics. However, the math professor was very discouraging; he believed that only men should study math. The English professor was very nice and encouraged me to take English, so I graduated with a degree in English literature in 1962. By then, I had already met my future husband, who was studying medicine at McGill. After graduation, I taught for one year at my old school.

As we see, Rena's first encounter with gender discrimination was at the University of Hong Kong.

❖ In 1963 I applied to come to Canada on a student visa to do my master's degree at McGill and to be with my fiancé. We were married in Montreal with the intention of returning to Hong Kong after my husband graduated from medical school. He graduated in 1965, and because of the political situation in Quebec, he decided to apply for internship in Ontario. I didn't finish my degree after I had my first child, and by the time my husband started his internship, I had already had my second child. My husband was making so little money as an intern that it became necessary for me to work.

I was offered a teaching job, but I not only needed to go to summer school to get a teacher's licence but also needed to be a landed immigrant. When I went to apply, I was told that, as a married woman I had no right to apply as a landed immigrant. I could only apply as a dependant of my husband. Those were the rules in 1965!

It seems ridiculous now to think that my husband applied as
a landed immigrant not because he wanted to stay in Canada
but because I needed a job. I was in the dependant category in
my husband's application, which in turn made it possible for
me to attend the Ontario College of Education to get my teaching licence.

Rena found the situation ridiculous, but as she said, those were the rules
in those days. The gender discrimination she experienced this time was
embedded in the Canadian immigration process.

❖ In 1966, after my husband's internship, we returned to Hong
Kong. By the end of the year, the riots in China had spilled over
to Hong Kong. Because of this, together with some disagree-
ments between my husband and his father, my husband applied
to a Toronto hospital for a residency in radiology and was accepted.
    At that point, I got pregnant again. My in-laws gave me the
option of leaving the two boys behind in Hong Kong and having
the baby, or of having an abortion and taking the boys back to
Canada with us. They contended that I would not be able to
serve my husband well if I had to look after all three. I couldn't
leave my children, so I was forced to have an abortion. I was in
such a terrible mental state that I was tranquilized all the time.

In her personal life, Rena never seemed to have any option after she
was married. She was constantly under the rule of patriarchy – by her in-
laws and by her husband. Not only did she not have an identity in
Canada, she also did not have it in her own family. She was being victimized by the Chinese tradition that obligated a woman to obey her
in-laws. In her case, education did not improve the situation. When I
questioned her, she said she was an obedient Chinese woman. She did
not seem to mind gender discrimination in this respect, though she did
when it was connected with Canadian Immigration:

❖ In 1967 we returned to Canada. Because of all the years my
husband studied at McGill, years that were counted as half the

time of residency, he got his Canadian citizenship very quickly. I received mine later – as an attachment to my husband, as I called it. All I received was a letter letting me know that I had become a citizen.

When we first returned to Canada, my husband went into radiology because he believed that, as a Chinese, no one would accept him as their doctor. But then, after two months into the training, he realized he was looking at films all day and not patients, so he knew that wasn't for him. In the meantime, he was making so little as a resident that he took a part-time job in a clinic. When he left the radiology program in 1968, he joined the clinic as a salaried doctor in general practice. The administrator asked him to join as a partner, which would cost $20,000. When he looked at the books, he realized the administrator was the one making all the profit while the doctors were just getting by. So he left the clinic and looked for office space. One of the drug salesmen told him that Markham was a good town to practise in.

One weekend, he and I drove to Markham and Unionville to look around and talk to the people, and we discovered that there was no doctor in the area. He rented an upstairs office in a strip mall to start his practice, and he was busy from the first day because he was the only doctor in the area. A year later, the landlord offered him exclusivity in the mall if he took a space on the street level, which would be much more expensive.

The racial discrimination the couple had expected proved to not exist. Not only did the patients not mind having a Chinese doctor, but Rena's husband ended up with a flourishing practice.

❖ We started to look around to purchase a house for his practice and found one with three bedrooms just around the corner. The Unionville by-law allowed doctors to practise in a house without living there. So that became his office until the day he died.

After we returned to Canada, I had stayed home with our sons, and I gave piano lessons to the children in the neighbourhood. We had a piano recital once a year in my home. I also took up oil painting. How that came about is that one day I was flipping through a Simpsons catalogue and saw an oil-painting set for $19.95. I bought it and did a painting of a Chinese junk and decided that it was good. So I enrolled in the Agincourt collegiate's evening course for beginners and also got myself a private teacher. My teacher encouraged me to exhibit my work with the Scarborough artists' guild. My first painting sold for $40. I was subsequently invited to exhibit my paintings at various synagogues, since most of my clients were Jewish. Later, I also held painting workshops in my home.

I got involved with the establishment of a Chinese school, to whom my sons went on Friday nights. At that school there was a Chinese painting teacher, and I learned Chinese painting techniques from him. I was also invited to show my paintings in various galleries in Toronto. Those galleries are closed now. I am starting to build up my portfolio again after a long break.

I was very happy in Canada, but my husband had always felt that he would like to be back in Hong Kong. After a while, his practice was going so well that it wouldn't have made any sense even to think of going back.

I believe that Rena's main issue was with her husband, who had to be served and was dictatorial. She would not have had a choice to stay in Canada if he had insisted on returning to Hong Kong. Meanwhile, as an intelligent woman, Rena filled her time with work that was meaningful to her.

❖ I did a lot of volunteer work as well as fundraising for different charities, and I got to know many people in the Chinese as well as mainstream communities. That was in the 1970s, when there was a lot of talk about multiculturalism, and I was very vocal about the topic. When I gave my exhibitions, I talked about the multicultural aspects of my paintings.

Here is a departure from the assimilation pattern of the earlier immigrants. Rena was vocal about the rights of minorities in Canada, especially immigrants like herself, because of the federal government's policy of multiculturalism.

❖ My profile was raised when I was asked to speak at the Scarborough Education Department. That was when Bill Davis was premier, and his executive assistant asked if I would be interested in running in the next election. The riding under Tom Wells was going to be split into two, and at that time the Chinese population in Scarborough was already 10 to 15 percent. And presuming that they all came out to vote for me, I could win. If I did, I would likely get a portfolio because I am Chinese and a woman. I considered it and decided against it because my husband wasn't keen.

The lack of support from her husband was to be expected. Despite her education and ability, she was still under the control of patriarchy.

❖ In 1978 the Council of Chinese Canadians in Ontario (CCCO), held a conference in Toronto with the guest speakers talking on the topic of multiculturalism. The following year, another conference was going to be held, and they needed a coordinator. I applied and got the job. The conference was called "Living and Growing in Canada: The Chinese Canadian Perspective." It was planned for November. Then, "Campus Giveaway" was aired on CTV in September.[7]

At first I didn't know anything about it [the CTV broadcast], but the Chinese students downtown were very upset. They went around asking for help from Chinese and non-Chinese, as well as different lawyers, and were told they had no case. They then came to me when they heard about the upcoming conference. They came to show me the film and asked me to have the floor at the conference so that they could air this issue. When I saw the film, I said, "Of course."[8]

By the time of the conference, the students had solicited help from seventeen cities across the country. Many people came to the conference and donated money.

After the conference, there had to be a follow-up. An ad hoc committee was formed called the CCCO against W5. I was going to chair the committee, but my husband was very much against it. He said I wasn't spending enough time looking after him and the family, and I was slipping behind in my housework. He also didn't want me to be so involved with the community. So instead of me, he took over and chaired it. However, I still did all the background work, did a lot of the writing, contacted people, and spoke to them, but he was the one on the films and getting all the headlines!

In both instances, whether it was running as a member of the provincial parliament or chairing the CCCO against W5, it is surprising that her husband's decisions were acceptable to Rena. The housework part was a poor excuse.

By the following April, CTV wanted to negotiate. The Chinese Canadian Council for Equality had by then been founded, which later became the Chinese Canadian National Council. Rena told me that she had subsequently been appointed an immigration judge, and later an appeals judge in immigration, by the Mulroney government. Her appointment was in recognition of her contributions to the community. It was also recognition of the importance of immigrants to Canada from the Asia Pacific region. She must have seen the irony of being an immigration judge when she had suffered gender discrimination by Canadian Immigration in the days before the points system was introduced.[9] "I am now widowed," she told me, "but I keep busy by sitting on a number of boards."

Rena had chosen not to fight for equality for herself in her own home, but she was consistent in redirecting her energy to fight for equality for people of Chinese origin in Canadian society. Her life was an ironic mix of agency and victimhood. In 2010, in an update to her interview in 2001, she said:

❖ In 2002 I began to prepare a Shanghai cookbook, as the city was about to come into the limelight on the world stage once more. Shanghai is where my roots are, and my attachment to Shanghai culture and cuisine never waned despite the years I have been in Canada.

Things moved along relatively smoothly. Just as I was about to line up the restaurants for interviews and inspections, SARS broke out in 2003. That instantly put a stop to my project, as travelling to China at the time was unwise and undesirable. My intention was to resume my work once the SARS episode was over, but other things kicked in and the cookbook project remains on the back burner to this date.

During the course of preparing the cookbook, I also resumed oil painting, which I had put aside for almost fifteen years because of a skin allergy to turpentine. By the beginning of 2004, I had completed five 24″ x 13″ canvasses. Fairly happy with the progress, I decided to work towards an art exhibition – do another fifteen paintings and mount a show by early 2005.

However, in the same year I was offered a business proposal to produce a Canada China television co-production series. It was to be the first of its kind between the two countries. As it turned out, after working on a co-production for eighteen months, Telefilm, the Canadian authority on international co-productions, discovered in 2006 that the co-production treaty signed in 1985 by Canada and China did not include television production. It was for films only. We had to redirect the project into a Canadian production with participation from China. At the end of almost four years of unrelenting efforts, we completed a twenty-episode television drama series. It was the first of its kind, in that cast and crew are selected from both Canada and China, and the two teams worked closely in association with each other. The series began to air nationwide in Canada in October 2009. It was aired a second time in early 2010.

Completing the television series was a highlight in my life. Now, in addition to my being a musician, an artist, a writer, a judge, a realtor, a teacher … I can proudly call myself an independent television producer. As always, I am known as a Jack of a hundred trades and master of none.

Looking back, for four generations our family has had to abandon everything and relocate to a new city or a new country on account of political instability. In the nineteenth century, my great-grandfather left his native city of Kaifeng, Henan Province, and migrated to Nan-Chang, Jiangxi Province. My grandfather established himself in Nan-Chang as the sole distributor for Standard Oil of New York [predecessor of Exxon Mobile] only to leave his business empire and seek refuge in Shanghai when his house was taken over by Generalissimo Chiang in his campaigns against the Communist guerrillas. My father prospered in Shanghai but had to forsake his assets when he went in exile to Hong Kong when the People's Liberation Army approached to take over Shanghai. For my generation, all my siblings and I made our way to Canada.

By choice I came to Canada, and by destiny I arrived to witness this nation in the wake of its multicultural reality. Inspired and encouraged to envision the eventual culmination of Canadian cultural richness, I found myself extremely fortunate to have the opportunity to express myself culturally and artistically within the framework of a multifaceted, diverse country.

Be it music, painting, television production, or writing, it has been my motto to let the past serve the present, and progress to the future. I draw sustenance from the heritage and tradition I inherited in my childhood and youth; the imprint of my past will always remain the foundation and backbone of my work. I gather knowledge and experience in my present surroundings, and I look forward to a fully culturally diverse Canada.

I would like to think that Canada has offered me a channel to make a minuscule contribution towards its complex and intricate social fabric, however insignificant it may be. In the process of my growth and development in this country, I have attained fulfillment and gratification for my existence. I am much indebted to this country.

Despite all the setbacks she has had in her life, Rena is a very accomplished woman, one whom all Canadians can be proud to call their own. She is now a grandmother and has found peace in her life. She is a very good example of the new Canadian woman of Chinese heritage.

Hope and Rena were immigrant women who became part of the Canadian social as well as political scene. They represent a significant development in the Chinese communities since the time of Jean Lumb. This new group of Chinese women took up the fight for equality in the public domain for the Chinese community as Jean had done in the 1950s. The difference is that many of the former group ran small family businesses, including Jean, who did not have a postsecondary education and was a restaurateur. The later group consisted of university graduates and professionals from Hong Kong who had been exposed to activism before they came to Canada.[10] Hong Kong immigrants emerged as leaders of the Chinese Canadian community on account of their numbers, education, occupations, age, and civic culture.[11]

At this point, some explanation should be given about the educational system in Hong Kong. The Chinese immigrant women who had attended the Protestant and Catholic schools were from the minority of the population in Hong Kong. It was an elite system that was available only to those who were from more affluent homes and of high academic standing; there were public exams at the equivalent of grades 6, 11, and 13. Because of the limited number of students that could be admitted to the University of Hong Kong, only the best were accepted. Even after the establishment of the Chinese University of Hong Kong in the 1960s, only approximately 2 percent of the high school graduates could enter university. The Chinese women who graduated from either university were thus the elite of Hong Kong.

The standard of English in the English-language schools, as well as in the schools that had both Chinese and English sections, was very high, as seen in the case of Karen (see chapter 5), who was mistaken for an anglophone by the school principal who interviewed her on the telephone. In most Hong Kong schools the educational standards were far higher. For example, a mark of C in a Hong Kong grade 11 exam was equivalent to a pass in the London General Certificate of Education (GCE) exam.[12]

The above is illustrated in the life of Susan, as is the cost of education in Hong Kong compared with that in Canada. Susan is someone I have known for a long time. She was interviewed by phone in Toronto in the summer of 2002 and spoke in Cantonese. Susan is a shy person who keeps her personal life very much to herself. Few have ever heard her life story and her immigration experience.

❖ I was born in 1929 in Tangshan in Hebei Province from a family of farmers. I had four or five siblings, I really don't remember, because I was adopted at age six by my aunt. My aunt, who was my father's older sister, had no children. She had wanted to adopt one of my brothers, but grandparents decided that I was the one to be adopted.

I went with my adoptive parents to Qingdao in 1935 and have since lost contact with my own family. When I was ten years old, a boy was also adopted. During the Sino-Japanese War the family went to Tianjin, where I went to school and later went into nursing. Tianjin was liberated by the Communists the year I graduated. It was the first city to be liberated, and it happened in three days. On my graduation, there was fighting in the streets. I remember the many injured soldiers and civilians who were brought into the hospital where I worked, and for two days and three nights we worked continuously and had nothing to eat. My adoptive parents left before the Communists arrived, and went back to Qingdao. I was left behind in Tianjin.

The Communist troops wanted nurses to go with them as they went south to liberate cities such as Wuhan, Hankou, and Guangzhou. I would certainly be picked because they preferred to take nurses who didn't have families in Tianjin. I didn't like the way the Communists worked, with constant political meetings and self-criticisms. My adoptive father died of a heart attack when he saw in the newspapers that Tianjin had fallen to the Communists, for he thought I had died in the fighting. I went to see my adoptive mother in Qingdao. Two months later, I left with a friend for Guangzhou, and never saw her again because she and her adopted son went back to Tangshan and became victims of the terrible earthquake in the 1970s, together with all my own birth family members.

From Guangzhou, I planned to get to Hong Kong. In 1950 it was easy to get into Hong Kong. No papers were needed. To enter, particularly from Guangzhou, one only had to answer a few questions verbally. It was a little more of a problem for people from north China. I crossed the border with a Cantonese woman whose son had gone to school with me in Tianjin. I married him a few years later. This woman's family had gone to Hong Kong earlier, and she came from Hong Kong to bring me through the border. She had family members who worked at the border crossing at Lo Wu [Luo Hu], so they had many friends there. She told the customs officials that I was her daughter. We did look a bit alike, and they knew she had a few daughters, but they didn't know how many. She told them that I was raised in northern China since I was a child, and that's why I couldn't speak Cantonese. So it was easy to get through.

Because of her adoption, Susan was fortunate to have received a good education, unlike her siblings. Her interview gives us a vivid picture of what life was like for young people in northern China during the civil war, of the fighting in the streets, and her predicament as an unmarried nurse during the war. Since she did not want to live under Communism, her only option was to get to Hong Kong, like other refugees. This was her first migration out of China and her adjustment to living in a society with an English influence.

❖ In Hong Kong, my nursing licence was not recognized, so I worked as a private nurse. After a while, I found a job working in an ear, nose, and throat doctor's office. Later, I found work in Hong Kong Central Hospital, but without a licence. I did the same work as the other nurses, even in the operating room, but I was paid less. I was not happy. In 1953 I got married, and in [the] following year, my eldest daughter was born. My husband worked as a clerk in an office.

In 1964 I arranged to work for free at the Kwong Wah Hospital for six months in exchange for a letter that would allow me to take the nursing exams for the Hong Kong licence, which I got. And when Hong Kong Central wanted to hire me back, I turned them down to work in private nursing care. In the same year, I was pregnant with my second daughter. In Hong Kong, I was able to have live-in help with the children, and at that time, I was working on twelve-hour shifts.

The lack of recognition in Hong Kong of her Chinese nursing training was similar to Lucy's experience as a teacher in Hong Kong with a United States university degree. They both did the same work as the others but with lower pay. This was a prelude to what Susan was going to face in the next stage of her migration.

❖ Sometime between 1967 and 1968, my in-laws immigrated to Canada, and they wanted us to join them. At first, I was worried about my English-language skill and that it would be difficult for me to find work in Canada. Besides the fact that the grandparents wanted to be near the grandchildren, the main reason for my decision to immigrate was for educational opportunities for my children.

When my eldest daughter reached fourth year of high school, I became very worried that I would not be able to afford to send her to university. Besides, she was not a top student, and her chance of getting into a university in Hong Kong was not good. Private school fees were high. We were already spending hundreds of dollars for my younger daughter in primary school. University fees were much higher. If we were to stay in Hong Kong, the chances of my daughters going to university were slim. Canada was an option for them to have the best possible education. I decided that if I had to struggle financially, it would have been worth it.

Susan did not explain under what category her in-laws had immigrated to Canada. The decision for her immediate family to immigrate was clearly hers and for educational opportunities for her daughters, since access to university was much easier in Canada than in Hong Kong.[13] Like Karen in the previous chapter, the cost and difficulty of obtaining a university education in Hong Kong was the push factor that caused Susan to immigrate to Canada.

❖ My husband and I applied to Canadian Immigration. We were co-applicants because we needed to put both our points together to have enough. Being an office clerk, my husband didn't have enough points, and I had more points for being a nurse. We arrived in Canada in August 1970.

For the first two months I didn't work. I applied to George Brown College to study ESL. It was a six-months course, five days a week, six to eight hours each day. We were living with my in-laws at the time, so the children had someone to look after them while I was at school. The government paid me $40 as a subsidy, and each day that school was missed, an amount was deducted. At the end, I got a certificate to say that I had graduated. However, I still didn't feel confident to look for work where English is used.

Around this time, I moved out with my daughters. My husband stayed with his parents. My younger daughter was only five years old. Not wanting to leave my younger daughter to go out to work, I took in sewing to do at home. In the following year, a friend from California asked me to look after their baby and they would pay me the same as doing the sewing, so I was given a little boy to care for who was only two months old. A year or so later, I spoke to the parents that they should really look after their own son, otherwise he wouldn't know them. Besides, with my family problems, it wasn't convenient to have another child there. They took their son back.

Susan had a very hard time settling and integrating in Canadian society, partly because of her family problems and the separation from her husband. Added to this was her difficulty with the English language, despite having lived in Hong Kong for many years. English was not a language she had needed for her work in Hong Kong, and by the time she immigrated she was already forty-one years old. She did understand the language, but in her case it was a lack of confidence rather than a lack of knowledge that made her reluctant to use English for work.

❖ I didn't know people to introduce me to do private nursing work, and my English was not good enough to write the nursing exams, so I applied for the nursing aide exams. Part of the form that had to be filled had to be done by the nursing school, which meant the one in Tianjin, since my licence from Hong Kong was not accepted because I didn't go to school there. I sent it to Tianjin and never heard back from them. So I couldn't take the exams.

Susan's problems were compounded by moving out of her in-laws' home and having to support herself and her daughters by whatever means. She never mentioned whether her separated husband contributed to the support of their children. Her lack of confidence in the English language held her back from working towards qualification in her profession. But even in trying to be a nursing aide, she came up against the same problem as other immigrants who had obtained their training during times of war and political instability. Certification is often a major issue in the settlement process.

❖ What should I do? I knew I had to work. A friend suggested I take a course to do keypunch. I did, but the noise the punching made was nerve-wracking to me. I had to take medication to calm my nerves, so that wouldn't do. By 1975, I found work with the Mon Sheong Foundation giving nursing care in the old people's home.[14] The night duty that I had was good for my family, since I liked to be able to spend time with my children during the day, and I also had two days off every weekend. I had a very nice neighbour who offered to keep an eye on my daughters. She asked them to knock on her wall whenever they had any problems. She had the key to go in to check on them.

In 1982 the workers at the Mon Sheong were getting unionized. I was no longer able to have the same schedule. They wanted me to rotate with others, which meant that I would end up with different times for duty every week, which would not work for me because my younger daughter was still young and needed me to spend time with her. I think some of them were jealous that I was getting more pay because evening work paid twenty-five cents more per hour. So I quit, and for a short time I didn't work.

It had taken five years for Susan to find her professional niche within the Chinese community where she could make use of her nursing training. Although she said that her younger daughter was still young and needed her to spend time with her, this daughter was then in her late teens. Susan may have felt extra protective because of her separation from her husband.

❖ I was able to get a part-time job at the Sheppard Lodge, which is a seniors' home.[15] I worked the 3–9 PM shift. I was in great demand because of my nursing training, so my hours were increased to the equivalent of a six-day week. I didn't need a certificate of qualification because the lodge hired a lot of health-care workers, many of whom were only trained for a short time in community colleges.

At that time, a fashion designer was looking for home knitters, so I went to pick up knitting to do. I'm happiest when I'm knitting and sewing. A year later I found the work at the Sheppard

Lodge was affecting the nerves in my lower back because of degeneration, exacerbated by having to lift the old people from time to time. Around that time, the same fashion design office was looking for someone full-time. I was hired and I quit the job at the Sheppard Lodge. I stayed at the same designer office until I retired at age sixty-five.

In respect to my family situation, there is regret in coming to Canada, but family problems might have happened even if we had stayed in Hong Kong anyway. In respect to my daughters, I did absolutely the right thing for them. They were my purpose for immigration. My career in nursing was not important. If we had stayed in Hong Kong, I doubt my daughters would have had the opportunities to graduate from universities. They would probably have to come out to work after high school. They may not be brilliant, but now one is a researcher in a lab and the other is a dentist, and I'm satisfied.

Like some of the earlier women I had interviewed, Susan had come to Canada for educational purposes, but in her case it was for her daughters. Immigration to Canada, she believed, was the only chance that her daughters had of going to university. Because of her decisions and sacrifices, her daughters have had a better future.

When I interviewed Susan in 2010, her husband was in the same seniors' nursing home as the one she worked for, but at a different location. Susan was a grandmother who helped to look after her grandson. Her daughters remained in the same professions for which they were trained. I asked her to reflect on her decision to immigrate to Canada and whether she had any regrets. She said:

❖ That was the best decision I have ever made. My daughters were able to become professionals. What happened with my profession was not important. I am happily retired. I go to the St Paul l'Amoraux Centre four mornings each week to exercise with other seniors. Afterwards, I walk around in the mall and maybe do some shopping. In the afternoons, I often watch TV or get CDs of Chinese movies. I still like to do crafts whenever I have the time.

My eldest daughter, who never married, still lives with me, and my younger daughter is in the process of moving back from the U.S. with her husband. Their son is here now, living with us for the time being and going to school.

Life in Canada is so much better than in Hong Kong. As a retiree, I have CPP [Canada Pension Plan] and my RRSP [Registered Retirement Savings Plan] and free medical care. Every time we travel, especially to the U.S., we have to buy health insurance; otherwise, any medical emergency would be absolutely unaffordable. Even for drugs, we only pay a few dollars for dispensing fee.

Canada is home to Susan and her descendants, the only surviving members in her entire biological family. Educational opportunities were the major draw in immigration in the 1960s and 1970s, whether for the immigrants or their children.

By the beginning of the 1970s, because of the huge backlog of immigration cases, it had become obvious that changes had to be made in section 34 of the Immigration Regulations, which had come into effect in 1967, permitting visitors to apply for landed immigrant status from within Canada. The Immigration Appeal Board Act of 1967 had given everyone who had been ordered deported the right to appeal to the board, no matter what his or her status was under the immigration act.[16] The Canadian government had been granting immigrant status to all who applied, with little or no review of their cases, a practice that helped account for the great increase in Chinese immigration in the early 1970s. Floods of visitors had been arriving in Canada with the obvious intention of applying for landed immigrant status; if refused, they could submit an appeal to the Immigration Appeal Board, which then had the power to permit them to stay on compassionate or humanitarian grounds.

As the number of visitors from various parts of the world increased, so did the number of cases before the Immigration Appeal Board. Approximately 45,000 visitors in Canada applied for landed immigrant status in 1970 – one-sixth of all applications that year. By 1972, the situation had become critical, with the numbers increasing by the month. During one weekend in October, as many as 4,500 arrived at Toronto's international airport. The Liberal government decided that action must be taken to bring the situation under control.[17]

On 3 November 1972, section 34 of the 1967 Immigration Regulations was revoked, and on 1 January 1973 regulations were introduced requiring all visitors staying in Canada for more than three months to register, and for all those seeking employment to obtain working visas. By the end of May, there were 17,472 people awaiting hearings before the Immigration Appeal Board. In July 1973, Immigration Minister Robert Andras announced a sixty-day Adjustment of Status Program, with the intention of accommodating most of the people caught by the revocation of section 34, as well as those who had been living in Canada for years without legal status.[18] The result of the program, together with the earlier attempt to reduce the backlog at the appeal board, brought the final number to around 52,000 people. This was widely thought in Canada to be a great success.[19]

In 1974 an order-in-council was passed prohibiting non-immigrant residents in Canada from applying for immigration status from within the country. However, even with these restrictions, Chinese immigration did not appreciably decrease until 1977, when further government restrictions were instituted, leading to an almost 50 percent decrease from previous levels.[20]

On 3 February 1975 the government tabled the *Green Paper on Immigration*, a four-volume document that reviewed Canada's immigration policies and suggested alternatives for future policy. The green paper was accompanied by a statement by the immigration minister that said, "What finally is at stake is no less than the future of Canada's population – its size, rate of growth, distribution and composition – and the basic principles that should govern our decisions to augment the nation's human resources through the admission of migrants from abroad." This would require close collaboration between Ottawa, the provinces, and the municipalities.[21]

Given the importance and complexity of the issues, the government established the Special Joint Committee on Immigration Policy to study the green paper and canvass the opinions of various groups across the country. This culminated in the introduction of the Immigration Bill in the House of Commons on 24 November 1976.[22] For the first time, the act stated clearly the fundamental objectives of Canadian immigration law.[23] It emphasized family reunification and the settlement of refugees, unlike the earlier regulations, which had attached considerable importance to skill and education.[24] The preamble of the act reflected concern not just for Canada's immediate immigration needs but also for the welfare of the immigrants. It committed Canada to easing the distress of refugees, the displaced, and the persecuted, and affirmed the government's continuing commitment to family reunification.[25] Section 3 (f) was later amended to preclude discrimination in a manner inconsistent with the Canadian Charter of Rights and Freedoms.[26] In sum, the act symbolized the virtual end of the white Canada policy.

In discussing the government's policy on refugees, reference must be made to the undocumented migrants from Southeast Asia who were admitted during this period. Many were ethnic Chinese from Vietnam, Laos, and Cambodia.[27] From the fall of the Thieu regime in 1975 to the end of the 1980s, Canada admitted a great flood of refugees.[28] Many of them moved into the traditional Chinese communities in the major cities.[29] To what extent they have integrated into the Chinese communities will need further scholarly studies. In 1985 the Supreme Court of Canada ruled that refugee claimants were under the protection of the Canadian Charter of Rights and Freedoms.[30] By the end of the 1980s, the government had agreed to admit more than 60,000 "boat people" from Southeast Asia. Per capita, Canada absorbed for resettlement a higher number of these desperate refugees than any other nation.[31]

Despite taking in refugees, Canada continued to need immigrants with skills. The points system established in 1967 was revised in 1978 to place more emphasis on practical training and experience than on formal education.[32] It became a barometer for measuring the intention of the government in immigration and planning. In 1985 further changes in the points system for independent immigrants made it easier for the government to raise levels and achieve announced targets.[33] With this revision, entrepreneurs were given priority processing as a subcategory of the independent class of applicant.[34] The revision ensured the selection of highly qualified workers by not awarding any points for having a relative in Canada who could assist with establishing the applicant. Furthermore, the minimum required points for independent applicants were increased from fifty to seventy, making it more difficult for some potential applicants to qualify.

From the time when racial preferences were removed from Canadian immigration policy in 1967, there had been an upsurge of educated

Chinese immigrant women coming into the country, both as students seeking higher education and as immigrants with skills needed by Canadian society. These women brought with them a new sense of social and political activism, which helped to change the face of Chinese Canadian communities.

Chapter 7

Multiculturalism and
Chinese Canadian Identity

In the 1970s the formation of a multicultural policy and the establishment of diplomatic relations with the People's Republic of China were important milestones of Canadian internal as well as foreign policies. In the following years, the negotiations between Britain and China over the return of sovereignty of Hong Kong to China in 1997 became an important turning point in Canadian immigration. In the Chinese communities across Canada, the emergence of a new identity was closely linked with other developments in the country.[1] During the 1960s, there had been increasing awareness of the unequal treatment accorded to Canada's two major language groups. Yet the Québécois were not the only force for change; the postwar immigrants also wanted a Canada without allegiance to the old British ways. Even the armed forces became a controversial symbol of change as their uniforms were "Canadianized." The new maple leaf flag was adopted. The question for the federal government, then, was what to do about the situation of the two major language groups and also the ethnic minorities, which, as a group, were growing in importance.

The origin of official multiculturalism in Canada had little to do with the ethnic Chinese. It grew out of the federal government's attempt to deal with the separatist movement in Quebec. Until the 1960s, Canadian society in general had assumed the supremacy of the British over the French as well as all other ethnic groups, and assimilation of the latter into the Anglo-Canadian identity was expected. As we know, this was one of the reasons for the disaffection in Quebec. The Royal Commission on Bilingualism and Biculturalism was appointed in 1963 to examine the issue of Canadian identity and related national policy. Public discussion of the issue gained momentum after the various ethnic minorities joined in the popular demand for cultural rights. The participation of the Chinese in this debate was modest compared with that of other immigrant groups.

In the 18 February 1964 issue of the *Chinatown News*, the Reverend Andrew Lam wrote: "To be proud of our origin and to appreciate it fully is an attitude of mind that is not inconsistent with good citizenship or loyalty to Canada."[2] This was much what Prime Minister Diefenbaker had said in the House of Commons in 1960 – that Canadians of all racial origins should be assured that their heritage would be maintained undiminished and handed down to generations yet to come.[3] In June 1965 the *Chinatown News* applauded its editor, who had appealed to the royal commission in Vancouver for due recognition of the cultural and linguistic rights of the Chinese. This emphasis on cultural retention was a notable departure from the earlier position of the *tusheng* on conformity to Canadian culture. The Canadian pluralistic society encouraged the *tusheng* to invest positive meaning in their ethnic background.[4]

The multicultural aspect of Canadian society was brought sharply into focus when on 14 July 1967, French President Charles de Gaulle made his infamous pronouncement in Montreal: "Vive Montréal! Vive le Québec! Vive le Québec libre!" That same year, Canada's centennial, the forces of disintegration found a leader in René Lévesque, who issued *Option Québec* in September, making a clear demand for Quebec independence. In 1968, Canadians gave a national mandate to a new leader in a new era, and Pierre Trudeau became prime minister.

The Royal Commission on Bilingualism and Biculturalism heard the aspirations of ethnocultural communities aside from the English and French. The commission's reports, particularly the fourth and final report, *The Cultural Contribution of the Other Ethnic Groups*, along with the Liberal government's awareness of the increasing numerical strength of Canada's population of neither French nor English origin, led to Canada's multiculturalism policy.[5] Another landmark result of the royal commission was the Official Languages Act of 1969.

The multiculturalism policy was announced in the House of Commons on 8 October 1971 by Prime Minister Trudeau, who said: "A policy of multiculturalism within a bilingual framework commends itself to the government as the most suitable means of assuring the cultural freedom of Canadians ... National unity ... must be founded on confidence in one's own individual identity; out of this can grow respect for that of others and a willingness to share ideas, attitudes and assumptions ... [O]ther cultural communities ... are essential elements in Canada and deserve government assistance in order to contribute to regional and national life in ways that derive from their heritage yet are distinctively Canadian."[6] Robert Stanfield, the leader of the opposition, said, "I am sure this declaration by the government of the principle of preserving and enhancing the many cultural traditions which exist within our country will be most welcome ... the cultural identity of Canada is a pretty complex thing."[7]

One of the main reasons the Liberal Party adopted multiculturalism was to win ethnic votes in anticipation of losing much of its traditional support from Quebec as the province sought independence. The federal government's adoption of official bilingualism in 1969 and then multiculturalism in 1971 was a compromise for the demands of French Canadians and the aspirations of those not of British or French origin. Bilingualism constituted linguistic rights and institutional obligations, while multiculturalism represented personal cultural choices. Federal policy provided only moderate financial assistance to ethnic groups for their pursuit of cultural expression. However, the most significant achievement was the shift in attitude and policy assumptions away from assimilation. The policy of multiculturalism has made a great difference in Canadian society.[8]

In the 1970s, particularly in Vancouver with its large and well-established *tusheng* community, the multiculturalism policy helped give a specific meaning to Chinese Canadian identity, which could best be expressed by radio programs such as *Pender Guy* in Vancouver. The policy and its progressive implementation meant that in major cities in particular, the pressure on immigrants to assimilate were greatly reduced throughout the 1970s and 1980s.[9] "Chinese Canadian" did not equal "Chinese" or "Canadian" because it had its own identity and culture. A

Chinese Canadian is anyone of Chinese descent who has been in Canada long enough for Canada to affect her or his identity.[10] In 1976, in recognition of the contribution of the ethnic Chinese to Canadian society, Jean Lumb became the first Canadian woman of Chinese heritage to be awarded the Order of Canada.

Another important development in the late 1960s was Canada's relationship with China. By the end of 1969, United States President Richard Nixon and Secretary of State Henry Kissinger had launched their secret diplomatic efforts to normalize relations with the People's Republic of China; thus, Canadian fears of American economic retaliation subsided.[11] Normalization of relations was supported not only by the Canadian public and by Trudeau's strong convictions but also by Canadian diplomats and government officials, who believed that it would be a notable foreign policy achievement.[12] Negotiations began in Stockholm at the beginning of 1969, and diplomatic relations between Canada and China were established on 13 October 1970.

The leadership in the Chinese Canadian communities, particularly in British Columbia, had been dominated by supporters of the Republic of China (Taiwan) since the 1930s, but this situation changed after the establishment of diplomatic relations between Canada and the People's Republic of China. In the early 1970s the Chinese Cultural Centre (CCC) was founded in Vancouver, with the clearly expressed idea of emphasizing the contribution of Chinese Canadians as a distinct cultural group.[13] This was resisted by the pro-Taiwan Chinese Benevolent Association (CBA).[14] The conflict was ultimately challenged in the courts, and the traditional leadership of the CCC was finally replaced by young professionals.[15] The CCC of Vancouver was established with a democratic constitution and open memberships, and thus their election is a major event in the Chinese communities there.

In 1973 Trudeau visited China, a move that marked the real institutionalization of the Canadian Chinese relationship. Trudeau met with Premier Zhou Enlai of the People's Republic of China, and they signed agreements on a range of issues. The most important one that pertains to this book was the agreement to reunite families, meaning that China would permit the emigration of its citizens to join their families in Canada.[16] From the early 1950s, it had become increasingly difficult for Chinese nationals to leave the country, as mentioned earlier. This humanitarian agreement had a significant impact on Chinese immigration, for people could now come directly from Mainland China, rather than by escaping to Hong Kong as a first stop. On 24 October 1973, an agreement was signed by Maurice D. Copithorne, chargé d'affaires ad interim, and Ma Wen-po, vice-minister of foreign affairs of the People's Republic of China. In order to facilitate family reunions, it was agreed that the Canadian official based in Hong Kong be accredited to Beijing (Peking) and Guangzhou (Canton) and that a Canadian embassy be established in Beijing.[17]

Applications for Mainland Chinese who wished to emigrate had to be initiated by family members in Canada. Once an application was submitted, the relative in China applied for an exit permit. The emigrants were given no special consideration by Canadian immigration authorities, nor were they classed as political refugees. In 1971 some 2,000 emigrants had left Mainland China for Canada, and in the following year 21,000 had come. In 1973 the number increased to 55,000.[18]

Thus, in addition to the new definition of Canada as a multicultural society, the changing popular perceptions and diplomatic standing of China, as well as an outburst of community consciousness and social activism centring on Chinatown, brought new life to the Chinese Canadian communities across Canada.[19] This was achieved through the reunification of members of Chinese Canadian families from China, the immigration of many educated ethnic Chinese, mainly from Hong Kong, and the renewal of cultural pride among the *tusheng* communities.

In order to understand why the agreement between Canada and China was necessary for the reunification of families of Chinese Canadians, we need to look at the situation in China under the rule of the Communist Party. The overseas (*huaqiao*) Chinese legacy was about the most complex and intractable issue the Communists inherited in China in 1949, and it became an ongoing problem for more than thirty years. The Chinese government vacillated in its classification of this group inhabiting rural southern Guangdong Province within the Communist regime. The dependent households of the overseas Chinese were composed mainly of women and children, since all able-bodied men had emigrated. Therefore these families suffered from a shortage of labour power, and their livelihood depended primarily on remittances from overseas.[20]

Overseas Chinese investments in southern Guangdong had increased substantially after the 1911 revolution, many members being supporters of the revolution. By the 1920s, the returned overseas Chinese (*guiqiao*) and the family members of the overseas Chinese (*qiaojuan*) came to constitute a class of nouveaux riches in some areas, distinguished by their foreign dress, their foreign-style houses, their self-segregation in exclusive villages, and their reputation for lavish outlays on weddings, funerals, and other forms of conspicuous consumption. This same geographical area of southern Guangdong was also a major base of Nationalist support during the civil war.[21]

Land reform in southern Guangdong Province followed a tortuous course until 1953. It was the last province to complete the process, which was achieved only after the dismissal of up to 80 percent of the local cadres and a massive infusion of "northerners" to complete the task. The new cadres failed to distinguish properly between real landlords – those who deliberately profited from feudal exploitation – and overseas Chinese households, whose main source of income came from labour overseas and who had no choice but to rent out their land because of their lack of able-bodied men. These households were unfairly branded as landlords and subjected to expropriation of land and houses. Land expropriation was judged irreversible, but in order to ease the injustices and resentments, the Guangdong People's Government felt compelled to establish a special Commission for Handling Outstanding Problems of Overseas Chinese Houses.[22]

A perfect example of the situation in China after 1949 is the following story of Nui, who was interviewed in the office of the CCBA in Victoria in the spring of 2001. It is a poignant story of how Chinese family members of Canadians who had not managed to leave fared in China during the years following 1949. In this story, we also learn of the difficulties that these family members had in immigrating to Canada after the signing of the 1973 agreement.

Nui's interview was done with her husband's help as translator into Cantonese, since she only speaks the Szeyup dialect.

❖ I was born in a village in Sunwui County in 1928, the eldest of six children. Since I was the eldest, it was my job to look after my younger siblings and to help my mother work in the fields because my family owned a bit of land. I had a few years of schooling.

I was married in 1946 to the son of our neighbour in the same village. The marriage was arranged by our parents. My husband's family was on the verge of starvation during the Second World War because they didn't have any land to farm because his father, who had a restaurant in Saskatoon, was not able to send money to them. So right after the war, his father sold the restaurant to return to China in order to buy land and to see to his son's marriage.

In 1949 the land my father-in-law bought was confiscated by the Communist government, and we suffered greatly for belonging to the landlord class. Life for us under Communist rule was like being prisoners, except we were not locked up. Now that the government owned everything, everyone worked for them. The landless peasants were doing well, and they became the bosses. We never had enough to eat. All the children had to be put into government nurseries while the parents worked.

My husband and I, as well as other family members, had no freedom. Every morning we had to report to work, on our knees, to the village cadres, and they would assign work to us for that day, such as cutting a hundred catty[23] of firewood or repairing a dam. At the end of the day, we had to return to report, again on our knees, not only what we'd done that day but also what we'd had to eat. That was only until the communes were established in the late 1950s and everyone ate at public dining halls. When we got sick, we still had to report in the morning, and if the cadres believed us, we would be excused from work that day. Pregnant women had to work until labour started, and for those with small children, the mother had to carry the baby on her back while she worked. Women attached fans on their backs to shield their babies from the sun.

This story was told to me with great emotion because of the memory of their suffering. Nui painted a clear picture of what life was like under the Communist regime in the countryside. As mentioned above, the Communist cadres did not care how land had been acquired in Guangdong by the overseas Chinese, who had to work very hard in order to save enough money to purchase land in their ancestral villages. When Nui spoke about the pregnant women, even though she spoke in the third person, she may have been talking about herself, since she had two children within six years of her marriage.

❖ In 1955, my husband was able to get to Hong Kong, where he had to stay for ten years before being able to immigrate to Canada. During his stay in Hong Kong, my mother-in-law was able to get out of China to see her younger son [under the age of twenty-one and unmarried] off to Canada. At the same time, she also took my second son to Hong Kong. He immigrated to Canada in 1968.

Nui did not mention how her husband or her mother-in-law got out of China. During that time, many Chinese nationals took their chances and escaped by land or water, joining the exodus to Hong Kong. Nui's husband had not immigrated to Canada when he was in his teens, as so many young Chinese adolescents from South China did. Her father-in-law may have thought that this son should stay in China to look after the land that he had purchased right after the war, which had been confiscated by the Communist government. Later, he could not immigrate because he was over the age limit and was married, and therefore not a dependant of his father, a Canadian citizen. "The circumstances of his immigration, in 1965, were unusual, because by then he was thirty-one," Nui said.

Nui's husband broke in to explain how he had eventually been able to come. During the federal election of 1963, a large donation was given to the Conservative Party by a Chinese Canadian who wanted to bring his son (who was the same age as Nui's husband) to Canada. The immigration rules were bent, not only to allow older children but also those who were already married to come to Canada as dependants. He benefited from this bending of the rules. I have not been able to substantiate from Citizenship and Immigration Canada the softening of the age limits or the status of a married person as a dependant in immigration around that time. However, we do know that he entered Canada in 1965. Nui continued:

❖ In 1973, when Prime Minister Trudeau visited China and agreements were made for family members of Chinese Canadians to reunite with their relatives who lived in China, my husband applied to Canadian Immigration and filled in the form with the information of our family in China. But the local Chinese officials [at the commune level] wouldn't let me and the rest of our family out. My husband went to his MP, and found out that the procedures were correctly done by Canadian Immigration but it was not complied with on the Chinese side. I believe that it was because of jealousy on the part of the Chinese officials because they themselves could not leave the country.

On one of the visits of the Chinese ambassador to Victoria, my husband asked him to inquire about our case in China. Whether he did or not, we are not certain, but soon after, in 1978, I was allowed out of China, and by then I was already fifty years old.

My husband then applied for the rest of our family members to come to Canada, one by one. It was a painful process. We believe that the problem was not the Canadian government, nor the central Chinese government, but the government at the commune level, because, as long as there are family members of overseas Chinese in the village, money will be sent back for their living expenses, which would be good for the local economy.

The People's Republic of China had long regarded remittances as a principal source of its foreign exchange earnings, and in February 1955 a decree had been passed protecting remittances.[24]

❖ I believe it was Deng Xiaoping's policy that had made China freer. If it had not been for him, many people like us would not have been allowed out of China. But, you know, public security in China is bad now because of the freer market economy.

My husband worked in a variety store in Victoria, and later as a cook at the Chinatown Care Centre when it was established. When I arrived in Canada, I worked in a greenhouse growing vegetables for a few years. Then I worked in a Chinese restaurant washing dishes. My biggest problem was learning English. When I was preparing for questions to become a citizen, I used a tape recorder and remembered a few answers by heart. I was allowed to use a translator for more complicated questions.

Coming directly from a village in South China, and living under Communist rule, Nui did not have the education or Western exposure that other immigrant Chinese women had who entered Canada at that time. So it was understandable that her settlement in Canada remained within the ethnic community in Victoria. Because of language and cultural problems, she was more comfortable working in Chinatown.

❖ When the Chinatown Care Centre was built, my husband also applied for me to work there. He did the cooking and I did the laundry. The centre accepts residents from all ethnic backgrounds, but the majority are ethnic Chinese. There are many care centres like it, but this is the only one that serves Chinese food. My working experience in Canada is pleasant, and everyone had been very kind to me. The Caucasian boss at the care centre kept trying to teach me English. Every time he passed me, he would ask me something in English. He was very kind. But I just couldn't catch on.

The Westerners are very nice to me, and I wish I could talk to them in their language. My life in Canada is so much better than in China. In China, no matter how hard I worked, I still had nothing, and I lived in fear all the time. In Canada, we can enjoy the fruits of our labour, and we have freedom.

Both Nui and her husband were fortunate to have found their way out of China. The only mention she made of her children was of her second son leaving for Hong Kong with her mother-in-law and of his immigration to Canada in 1968. Even though Nui worked mainly in Chinatown in Victoria, by the time of her immigration, many Chinese Canadians had become integrated into the host society, having gradually moved out of Chinatowns across the country into other residential areas. Chinatowns then became centres for business and tourism.

Vancouver's Chinatown underwent a commercial revival. The Chinatown core was designated as a heritage area, and in 1974 it was subjected to detailed planning controls by the city government in an effort to preserve its distinctiveness.[25] When developers eyed Toronto's Chinatown in the 1960s, Jean Lumb had set up the Save Chinatown Committee and convinced City Council to move Chinatown to its present location in the Dundas and Spadina area. Laura Larson has described the mediator role that Jean Lumb played as being the interpreter of the past, present, and future of Chinese Canadian women.[26]

By the 1970s, Chinese men and women were immigrating in equal numbers, and women leaders such as Jean Lumb were gradually being replaced by the well-educated, urbanized and Westernized women from Hong Kong, as mentioned in the last chapter. Because of the policy of multiculturalism, Chinese Canadians were able to celebrate their heritage and culture as part of the Canadian mosaic.[27]

The following is the story of Lily, who immigrated in 1977 with her husband and daughter. Both Lily and her husband have skills that were needed in Canada. She was interviewed in the summer of 2001 in my office in Toronto. She spoke in a low voice in Cantonese.

❖ I was born in Hong Kong in 1949, the sixth of seven children. My family escaped from China just before the Communist takeover in 1949. My father was a scholar and a teacher in China, and my mother was a doctor trained in Tokuang Hospital in Guangzhou. Life was very difficult for our family in Hong Kong. We opened a small factory doing embroidery for a living because we are from Swatow [famous for embroidery]. My mother didn't have a licence to practise, but she helped a lot of poor people who were their neighbours in the refugee area where we lived. After a time, my father gave up the embroidery factory and worked for a canning company. He was later converted to Christianity, and worked at Chek Lap Kok [an area in Hong Kong] spreading the gospel. In 1964 the whole family was baptized in the Baptist Church. My mother continued to work in health care as an assistant because she didn't have a licence.

Lily's story about her family escaping from China in 1949 is similar to that of many of my informants. Despite her parents' education and former occupations in China, refugee life was a struggle for the entire family. Her father's conversion to Christianity and becoming a pastor had been a revelation to the family.

❖ I was a sickly child and was often hospitalized in public wards in government hospitals, and because of that, I didn't start school until age seven. By then, I often didn't want to go to school. In grade 2, I was put in a Chinese school and stayed there until high school graduation. From there, I went to Chung Chi College to study music because I have always loved music.[28] In fact, I had been making my own money teaching piano since I was fourteen.

By the time I was in Chung Chi College, some of my older siblings were already overseas. I have a brother in Canada who was in the hairpiece business.[29] He sponsored me as a landed immigrant in 1969 after I finished my first year at Chung Chi College. It was very easy to immigrate to Canada at that time. I studied at the Royal Conservatory for a short time but returned to Hong Kong because of a young man I met just before I left Hong Kong. That was my future husband, a musician, who came out of China by himself and is eight years my senior. My parents were against this relationship because they wanted me to be engaged to another young man, who I didn't like. That was the main reason I left Hong Kong in the first place.

I returned to Hong Kong without my parents' permission, and married the man I was in love with. We worked very hard to save up enough money to go to Vienna. By the time we left Hong Kong, we already had a daughter. In 1971, my parents immigrated to Canada.

Music was the common bond between Lily and her husband. She did not say what she and her husband planned to do in Vienna. The city attracted them because it is one of the music capitals of the world. They were probably aware that they would not be able to settle there, so this may just have been an adventure for them.

❖ We remained in Vienna until 1977. We decided to immigrate to Canada because of my parents, and my husband wanted to immigrate so that he could sponsor his family from China. When we applied to Canadian Immigration in Vienna, I discovered that I still had landed immigrant status, but by then there were three of us. We were sad to leave Vienna because we really loved living in the music capital of Europe, where we were both working and making a decent living, and where we'd made a lot of friends.

There were very few Chinese in Vienna, and the Viennese were very interested in Chinese culture. Of the forty overseas Chinese students, I got a job with a large department store, managing their import business from China. I realized then that I had talent for business. I had a lot of press coverage, and trips with my whole family were paid for by the company. We had a wonderful time!

Lily and her husband had adjusted well in their first migration experience. They were confident that the second, and permanent, migration would work out just as well, if not better.

❖ When my husband and I were interviewed by the Canadian immigration officer in Vienna, we talked mainly of music. The immigration officer told us that we should apply as music teachers instead of musicians because at that time Canada needed more music teachers. At the same time, another brother, a psychologist, also sponsored us. Within two months, we were granted immigrant status.

After we arrived, I looked for a job with Manpower but couldn't find any. I was willing to wash dishes or serve in a restaurant. I believed it would be difficult to get work as a piano teacher because I'm a Chinese woman. Since I wasn't working, I went to my church and offered to teach the three children of my minister for free. Soon, the word got around, and more and more students came. And before I knew it, I was sending them to competitions and exams. I also got work playing the piano for ballet classes. These classes were very long, and I was getting backache from them. Within a year, I had so many students that I could no longer play for ballet classes.

We often hear of similar experiences from immigrants who were accepted into Canada because of their skills but, when they arrived, found that no jobs were available. However, when Lily and her family arrived in 1977, there were already well-established Chinese communities in Toronto, and getting jobs in the ethnic communities had become much easier.

Lily had a perception about discrimination similar to that of Rena's husband, and in both cases it turned out to be erroneous. Her misapprehension is surprising, considering that she had lived for a number of years in Vienna and did not mention experiencing any discrimination there. When she said that she had been willing to wash dishes, she was inadvertently stereotyping Chinese immigrant women in that role. In fact, she did well: "I gradually established my piano schools and music houses, selling pianos as well, in three locations in Toronto. I feel God's hand in guiding me in my life. My husband is a conductor, and our daughter is studying music in the U.S." Being resourceful, Lily has been able to create work for herself and became successful in business within the ethnic network. Immigration to Canada had been good for her and her family. As of 2010, Lily's daughter had graduated from a music academy and was an accomplished musician. She herself had become a grandmother. When asked to update her life as an immigrant woman in Canada, she said:

❖ I am very happy with my life. Canada is a good country for my entire family. I am consolidating my business in the sale of pianos, and, in the last few years, musicians from Vienna have come to watch me teach piano and even videotaped me, because they like the way I teach. I have been invited to Vienna to teach as well.

Chinese immigration had become a family affair by the 1970s. This had affected family work patterns and domestic organizations, and led to the development of institutions catering to the very young and the very old.[30] These included the Mon Sheong Foundation, Yee Hong Foundation, and the Chinese Cultural Centres of Vancouver and Toronto, as well as many Chinese churches and Buddhist temples.[31]

By the end of the 1960s, the increase in Chinese immigration had broad implications in major metropolitan centres in Canada, where immigrants most often choose to live. Those coming from Hong Kong brought with them distinctive Hong Kong consumption values that raised the standard of living in the communities, particularly in connection with high-quality food items. They also brought with them a proclivity for social action on civil rights, human rights, and freedom to protest. It is noteworthy that the protests against the airing of "Campus Giveaway" on CTV (mentioned in the interview with Rena), the formation of the Chinese Canadian National Council, and the 4 June protests were all organized by Hong Kong immigrants.[32] These, along with other activities helped to increase the assertiveness of the entire Chinese Canadian community.

Unlike the early Chinese who migrated to Canada, the latter immigrants intended to make Canada their home. For those who came from Hong Kong, emigration did not mean a change of loyalty, because they had not felt any nationalistic sentiment towards the colony while it was under British rule. Many of them considered Hong Kong an unhealthy place to live and raise a family.[33] Despite the higher income levels since the 1980s and low taxes, it is very expensive to live there at the same standard that the majority of middle-class Canadians can enjoy. In the 1970s and 1980s, a sense of Hong Kong identity did emerge, however, and it became a matter of pride to call oneself a Hong Konger.

As the Chinese community grew in terms of educational achievement, occupation, and wealth, the assertion of Chinese ethnic identity took on particular significance. Since the end of the 1960s, immigrants of Chinese ancestry had been coming to Canada from all over the world – from areas as diverse as South Africa, the West Indies, India, and South America – as well as from China, Hong Kong, Taiwan, Vietnam, Singapore, and other countries in Southeast Asia. The most dominant group, however, was the Hong Kong Chinese.[34] It was the Canadian government's belief in the potential contribution of this group to Canadian society that prompted its shift of immigration resources to Hong Kong to attract well-qualified immigrants and to establish a major Canadian presence in Hong Kong.[35]

On the tenth anniversary of the proclamation of Canada's multiculturalism policy, Trudeau stated, "Our multiculturalism policy had helped to reduce cultural discrimination and has helped to promote a better understanding of the federal government's dedication to creating a keener awareness of ethnic groups as full partners in the growth of our country. The government ... guarantees the right of all Canadians to preserve, enjoy and develop their cultural and linguistic heritage."[36]

By the 1980s, because of the passage of the Canadian Charter of Rights and Freedoms (1982) and the gradual changes in the racial composition of the Canadian population, the federal government was more sensitive to issues of racial equality, and this in turn created new expectations among minorities. During this period, immigration from developing countries was expanded, and the concentration of immigrants in such cities as Toronto, Vancouver, and Montreal heightened public awareness of racial discrimination and inequity.[37] This awareness was partly the result of public debates preceding the enactment of the Charter of Rights and Freedoms and the Employment Equity Act of 1986. By the mid-1980s, it had become clear that there were two different orientations towards the official multiculturalism policy – one for cultural retention and the other for equality. The former was enunciated by the established European ethnocultural groups; the latter was stressed by visible minority groups.[38] However, there was crossover to a certain extent.

Even though the multicultural policy had been proclaimed in 1971, the Multiculturalism Act was not passed until 1988. The act acknowledges freedom of cultural choice, promotes multiculturalism with full and equitable participation of individuals and communities of all origins, enhances the development of communities sharing a common origin, provides for equal treatment and protection for all individuals while respecting their diversities, promotes intergroup interaction, gives recognition and appreciation of the diverse Canadian cultures, and preserves and enhances unofficial languages while strengthening the official languages of Canada.[39]

During the first ministers' constitutional debates that took place in 1987 and 1990 following the Meech Lake Accord, it became clear that to recognize Quebec as a "distinct society" required the federal government to strengthen its commitment to multiculturalism in order to show the acceptance of Quebec's special status was not at the expense of cultural protection for other minority groups. In 1990 the Department of Multiculturalism and Citizenship was formed. However, judging from the expenditures allocated to the new department, it would appear that the renewed commitment was more symbolic than substantive. After the failure of the Meech Lake Accord and the federal election of 1993, the new Liberal government split the Department of Multiculturalism and Citizenship into the Department of Canadian Heritage and the Department of Citizenship and Immigration. A secretary of state for multiculturalism within the portfolio of the Department of Canadian Heritage was appointed.[40]

Despite the official policy of multiculturalism, with the influx of the Chinese from Hong Kong in the 1980s, particularly after the signing of the Sino-British Joint Declaration in 1984, racism was again on the rise, mainly in Vancouver and Toronto, where the new immigrants tended to concentrate. Expressions of racism against wealthy Chinese immigrants often manifested themselves in statements related to struggles over control of land and boundary protection, statements such as "goddamn Chinese, it's the Chinese moving into our neighbourhood."[41] This will be further discussed in the interview with Belinda in the next chapter.

In Vancouver, where there is a long heritage of anti-Asian prejudice, the price increase in real estate was frequently blamed on the influx of immigrants from Hong Kong. Net migration to Vancouver from the mid-1970s was high, and the supply of housing could not meet the demand. However, internal migration, mainly from Ontario, as well as natural increase in the population by 25 percent, outweighed international migration by a ratio of three to one.[42] The Hong Kong Chinese just happened to be made scapegoats in a situation that was not within their control.

The derogatory language that was used – terms such as "monster homes" and "unneighbourly houses" – referred only to large homes bought or built by Hong Kong immigrants and never to large homes in West Vancouver or the British Properties, where there were also wealthy Asian immigrants, but they were not conspicuous.[43] The stories reported in the media was frequently reminiscent of earlier anti-Chinese rhetoric.

Vancouver was the city where the most virulent racial language was hurled at the Chinese immigrants. The intense dismay expressed over the city's aesthetic and economic changes betrayed the fear of erosion of the symbols of the established domination of Anglo-Canadians. White residents also feared their exclusion from the business practices of Hong Kong entrepreneurs, whom they perceived as directing their capital and opportunities along racial, regional, or family lines. This was evident in the anger and resentment over the 1988 marketing in Hong Kong of the Vancouver Regatta condominiums. The media fanned the fear by using threats of engulfment by Hong Kong Chinese.[44] It is therefore not surprising that Prime Minister Brian Mulroney appointed David Lam as the lieutenant governor of British Columbia in 1988.[45]

Despite the stature and respect the new lieutenant governor commanded, the Hong Kong Chinese in Vancouver continued to face antagonism caused by "latent racism" and the "fear of economic displacement." At a public forum on immigration and housing organized in 1989 by the Vancouver mayor, some speakers raised their concern about the racial origin of immigrants. The *Vancouver Sun*, on 14 April, reported one speaker saying, "I'm frightened for the Anglo-Saxons in Canada in the next twenty years. If the doors are wide open to immigration, what's going to happen to Caucasians?"[46]

Vancouver also saw the greatest number of hate incidents. A potential real-estate buyer was spat at by the person living next door, and "Hongcouver" T-shirts were sold everywhere. Stones were thrown at elderly Chinese women exercising in a park. Swastikas and anti-immigrant slogans appeared on school walls and in public places. The British European Immigrant Aid Foundation and the Immigrant Association of Canada lobbied for more European immigrants. Members of the Aryan Nation disseminated hate literature at integrated schools.

There were similar stories in the Toronto media. In the November 1990 issue of *Toronto Life*, a Caucasian Canadian talked about the spending power of the Hong Kong Chinese: "We'll take the other sixteen (houses). It's obvious they were buying for all their friends back in Hong Kong ... [Many] regard the injection of Oriental capital into the city as a threat ... that money will translate into power. And since power is a zero-sum game, the rise of Chinese power will leave her crowd with less."[47]

In the same article, the writer noted:

Many of us who are inclined to regard the Chinese as commercial marauders [should recognize that] ... the recent influx of Hong Kong immigrants ... makes up less than ten per cent of the total Chinese population ... Wealth and the pursuit of influence do not characterize the Chinese in Toronto. Diversity and disunity do ... The lack of geographic cohesion is compounded by an increasing multitude of dialects ...

Perhaps the most misleading aspect of the current media depiction of the Chinese in Toronto is the over-stated impact of the city's emergence as a conduit of flight capital from the Pacific Rim … This obscures the fact that North American and European interests continue to dominate foreign investment in the city. The largest pools of Oriental capital, moreover, are controlled by a small group of globe-trotting industrialists, many of them "astronauts" who divide their time among homes in the Far East, Europe, the States and Canada.[48]

In Vancouver the city officials, in the interest of development and of attracting international investments – realizing the Pacific orientation of the British Columbia economy – attempted to block neighbourhood movements that were against change by increasing bureaucratic entanglements and fees, and by proposing stricter city-wide zoning laws. All in all, it was the reduction of physical and social barriers, along with Vancouver's spatial integration into the global economy, that had increased the overall value of the city.[49] Despite the virulent discrimination expressed in certain media and some neighbourhoods, the majority of Canadians surveyed believed that Canada should admit more people from Hong Kong.[50]

What was happening in contemporary Canadian society was a form of backlash racism, reflecting resentment of the success and economic power of non-European immigrants and cultural communities. In terms of Hong Kong immigrants since the 1980s, one cannot stray far from the concept of the globalization of capital, since Hong Kong people were the largest group targeted by the Canadian government in its policy of business immigration, and the same was true of the policies of many other governments of developed countries. This topic will be discussed in more detail in the following chapter.

Looking at the Canadian population as a whole, the Asian component was an important one, even though there was no homogeneity in this segment. Given the immigration trends, this component will increase as a proportion of the Canadian population. According to Statistics Canada, 42 percent of immigrants were from Asia and Pacific areas in 1991, and the majority of them were ethnic Chinese from Hong Kong.[51] One of the most prominent organizations dealing with the issues arising from government policies and private concerns has been the Laurier Institute, with its headquarters in Vancouver. The goal is to "contribute to the effective integration of the many diverse cultural groups within Canadian society into our political, social and economic life by educating Canadians of the positive features of diversity."[52]

In looking back, Canada's rejection of its racist immigration legacy after 1966 greatly affected the character of Canadian society, as did the country's commitment to multiculturalism in 1971 and the policy of inclusion of a continuous and substantial obligation to refugees in the immigration act of 1976. Jeffrey Reitz concluded in 1988 that Canadians' "positive institutionally-sanctioned perceptions of immigrants as an economic asset helped to dilute social conflict." In Canada, non-white immigration occurred within the context of a long-term program of national development.[53]

Chapter 8

Racism and Business Immigration

When in the 1980s Canada began to introduce a business immigration program to attract wealthy immigrants, many who met the criteria came from Hong Kong. In order to understand the situation better, we need to look at the development of Hong Kong society since the end of the Second World War. A new generation of Hong Kongers grew up during the time when China turned inward and Hong Kong projected itself to the world. Many parents of this generation of baby boomers were refugees from Mainland China after 1949, and their children had been educated and gained professional achievements that were particular to Hong Kong. Consequently, a distinct Hong Kong ethos began to emerge among the young in the 1960s.[1]

When the shock of the pro-communist riots of 1967 subsided, the Hong Kong government realized that social issues had long been neglected, and it began to invest heavily in housing, education, health care, social services, and transport, as well as infrastructure in the colony. This brought about Hong Kong's eventual role as an Asian financial centre, which triggered a surge of upward mobility.[2] Hong Kong became brashly prosperous from the late 1970s on. While few would deny their Chinese ancestry, Hong Kongers made it clear that this did not automatically mean political commitment to China, and this presumption was zoomed into focus with the approach of 1997.[3] Fear of the change of sovereignty triggered a flood of emigration from Hong Kong to different parts of the world, with Canada as the country of first choice.

In the discussion of business immigrants from Hong Kong and the influx of their capital into Canada, it is important to understand the background to the business immigration policy. As far back as the 1950s, even though there was then no business immigration program, it was clear that Canadian officials were paying increasing attention to the financial worth of immigrants. Canadian policy explicitly recognized sponsorship in cases of "exceptional merit," including "immigrants bringing in capital to start businesses of their own." Under the government of John Diefenbaker, the immigration focus shifted from "a broad range of low-skill occupations to an emphasis on a narrow range of high-skill professionals and entrepreneurs with capital."[4]

It will be recalled that in the white paper of 1966, the last hints of an immigration policy based on racial and ethnic criteria were removed, and the new policy accentuated educational and occupational criteria by introducing the points system. For an independent immigrant, points were assessed based on the applicant's training and education, occupational skills, knowledge of English and French, employment opportunities, arranged employment, and personal qualities such as adaptability, resourcefulness, motivation, and initiative. In the beginning, independent immigrants had to meet at least fifty points out of one hundred. A prospective immigrant might be automatically awarded twenty-five points if he or she intended to set up a business in Canada and was judged to have the "financial resources to do so with reasonable chance of success."[5]

In the immigration act of 1976, business immigrants became a separate category. They were still qualified under the points system, but their business skills were now the primary entry criteria. Two subcategories of business immigrants were specifically recognized: entrepreneurs and self-employed persons.[6] Canada's Business Immigration Program (1978–92) began at the same time as the country was entering a recession. In 1978, there were 449 entrepreneurs entering Canada, but the following year, as the recession took hold, the figure declined to 285. In 1980 the numbers declined again to 266 before they rose to 449 in 1982. The program showed promise as a potential source for securing foreign capital. In 1982 the amount brought into Canada by business-class immigrants was estimated at $718 million; in 1983 it was $821 million and in 1984 it decreased to $723 million.[7]

When the Conservatives under Brian Mulroney came to power in 1984, the economic importance of business-class immigrants was not lost on them. Minister of Employment and Immigration Flora Mac-Donald reviewed the immigration policy and suggested in her annual report for 1985 that a third category in the Business Immigration Program be added – the investor category.[8] The introduction of the investor category was timely because of the emergence of a privileged and mobile international capitalist class in the era of globalization. As mentioned earlier, those in this group were the type of immigrant most sought after by developed countries, a situation that, in effect, endorsed the purchase of immigration and citizenship status.[9]

For an entrepreneur immigrant, the special requirements include the intention and ability to invest, active participation in the management of the business or commercial enterprise in Canada, with one's own traceable financial sources, and a solid, verifiable business track record of owning one's own business as well as financial resources to carry out a range of activities. The investment must make a significant contribution to the economy of Canada and create one or more jobs for Canadians, excluding family members. In addition, the admitted entrepreneur must establish or purchase a business within two years after landing and must report to the business immigration office, which monitors the "entrepreneurial and family business immigrants to confirm compliance with the law."[10] Failure to do so will probably result in the rescinding of permanent resident status and the order of removal from Canada.

The following story of Daisy will illustrates how business immigration worked. Daisy was interviewed on the telephone in the summer of 2002. She spoke in Cantonese.

❖ I was born in Hong Kong in 1953. My father started working in garments on a very small scale right after the Second World War. By the time I was born, he had a growing business in garment manufacturing in Hong Kong and would like to expand to Macao. When I was a month old, my mother, who was a concubine, moved her own family to Macao. His wife's family stayed in Hong Kong, while his family by the concubine gave him a base in Macao. The two families had lived together in the same house in Hong Kong before then, but with an expanding family, I believe it was a better idea that they moved to separate quarters anyway.

In Macao, my mother, who's very capable, helped my father in getting his business established. My mother had five children, and the wife had six. Altogether there were eleven of us.

The old Chinese tradition of concubinage has so far not been discussed. Even though bigamy is illegal under British common law, it was always accepted in the colony of Hong Kong. There could be only one wife, but a man, usually a wealthy one, could take as many concubines as he could afford. Concubines are usually accepted by the wives as part of their families. Their children are legal, having equal rights with the children of the wives.

❖ My father's business prospered. We had factories weaving yard goods [cloths]. We dyed them, then designed, and made them into garments. We exported our products to Europe and the United States, and we also made private labels for large companies. I grew up in that environment, helping in the factories and in the business.

I went to school in Macao right through till high school graduation. My father wanted me to stay in Macao to help in the business. He was of the old school, and didn't think it was necessary for girls to have too much formal education. However, I wanted to go to a university in Taiwan. At that time, my father was doing business with China, and because of the political situation between China and Taiwan, he preferred that I go somewhere else.

In 1974 I went to Centenary College in New Jersey to study accounting. In that same year, my younger sister went to study in Canada. In 1976 I was going to transfer to Northeastern in Boston. I went back to Hong Kong for the summer, and my father was not well. He needed extra help in the business because we were expanding very fast. He persuaded me to stay to help. I worked between Hong Kong and Macao, and travelled back and forth a few times a week.

I got married in 1978 to a social worker. My son was born in 1979. I continued to work until 1982, when my daughter was born. It was then that I wanted to stay home with the children.

In the 1980s there was talk of transfer of sovereignty over Hong Kong to China, and I was worried about my children growing up under Communism. At that time, I considered immigrating to Canada, not only because I've always had a good impression of Canada, but it was also an easier country to immigrate to. By that time, my younger sister had already moved to the U.S. with her husband.

The fear of Hong Kong's forthcoming return to China in 1997 was a major push for emigration from Hong Kong, and many developed countries were trying to lure affluent Hong Kongers. As Daisy noted, Canada was the favoured destination for Hong Kong emigrants.

❖ In 1985 I applied to Canadian Immigration as an entrepreneur and head of household in the garment business, and I applied to immigrate to Montreal, advised by the immigration lawyer, because Montreal was the centre of garment manufacturing. The application went in at the beginning of the year, and I was called for interviews within six months – once in Hong Kong and once in Montreal. I had to present a proposal of my business plan. Because of my youth – in my thirties – the immigration officer in Hong Kong went to see our operations and factories to confirm my capabilities.

Thus, by helping her father in the business, Daisy had been able to gain experience in the garment industry, which proved to be useful in enabling her family to immigrate to Canada.

❖ As an entrepreneur, my requirement was to employ between two and ten people. I was going to start by setting up a wholesale business of garments produced from our factories in Hong Kong and Macao. The intention was to open a factory in Canada if business went well. My business had to be established within two years. My immigration lawyer advised me to go to Montreal because it would be easier to get landed status for someone in the garment business, but he didn't take language into consideration.

My family immigrated to Montreal in mid-1986. I was under the impression that I could use English in Quebec and that I could learn French gradually. After we arrived, I found that Quebecers wouldn't speak to me in English. Even in the schools, not only did my children, aged six and eight, have problems, since they only knew Chinese, but as a parent, I had difficulty communicating with the teachers. Despite that, I established my sales office and hired a French Canadian sales manager.

As a Hong Konger, Daisy had not realized the sensitive language issues in Quebec. Unfortunatel,y she was not forewarned by her immigration lawyer.

❖ We shipped both fabrics and garments from Hong Kong for wholesale here. Sales volume was very small compared to Hong Kong, and it was difficult to collect payments, even with extended credits of six to nine months. I found my sales manager ineffective. In my experience in Montreal, we only had orders in the thousands. In Hong Kong, orders were in the tens of thousands. When we made thousands in Hong Kong, it would only be for samples. I also found that Canadians at that time were not fashionable like people in Europe or in Hong Kong. Business just didn't go well.

As long as we lived in Montreal, it was not possible for my husband to find employment in social work. He stayed home to look after the children, and he was not happy. Besides, I really wanted my children to go to an English school. So we decided to move to Toronto. When we moved to Toronto, I looked into the garment business there. That summer, many garment workers were on strike, and businesses were closing. So I decided that I had to give up the idea.

After we moved to Toronto, I stayed home with the children. My husband tried to find employment in social work and found that it's very different from Hong Kong, since most of the projects were on a contract basis with the government. He went to George Brown [College] to study heating and air-conditioning, and he found work in maintenance. One night, he was called in the middle of the winter to fix the heating that was on the roof of a shopping mall. While he was doing the servicing, the ladder blew off. He would not have been able to get down if a kind person, who happened to walk by had not put the ladder back for him. Since that experience, he didn't want to do that kind of work anymore.

My husband then went to George Brown again and took a Chinese cooking course. By 1988, Chinatown was very busy and crowded, and business was booming.[11] Since my husband was interested in Chinese food, a friend told us that one of the businesses in the food court in the Dragon Centre, at Dundas and Spadina, was for sale. We went to look and decided that he could manage because it wasn't too big, since neither of us had any experience with the food business. He ran it for four years.

Settlement in Canada had not been easy for Daisy. Like many immigrants to a new country, she had found it difficult to re-establish her business. The boom in Chinatown in Toronto was because of the influx of Hong Kong immigrants at the end of the 1980s. There was an impetus for the growth of Chinese businesses, which also brought about the expansion of ethnic Chinese communities.

❖ By 1991, Scarborough began to boom, and Chinatown was gradually being taken over by Chinese immigrants from [Mainland] China and the Vietnamese.[12] The Chinese from Hong Kong were going less and less down to Chinatown. I suggested to my husband that we should sell the business and move uptown, especially because we lived in Unionville. We found a restaurant uptown, but now it would be absolutely necessary for me to get back to work full-time, particularly when I'm the business person who knows how to deal with people. By then, the children were getting older and we could get a part-time person to help with the housework.

Even though I worked every day, I still spent a lot of time with the children. I would go home during lunchtime and the dinner hour when the children were back from school. By 1994, I found out that my husband had a mistress who was a masseur from China. She phoned me at the restaurant to tell me, but my husband continued to deny it for more than two years.

In 1997 I was diagnosed with cancer. I had surgery but not chemotherapy because I would be too weakened to be able to work. My son was just entering university that year, and my daughter was still in high school, and they both needed me. They are both good students, and since their father had lost interest in them because of his girlfriend, I wanted to be there for them. So I took care of my health by eating right, exercising, and taking Chinese herbal medicine.

After surgery in 1998, I took three months off to recover. I knew I had to be psychologically strong to survive and decided to separate from my husband because I just couldn't take it anymore. But my husband didn't want to move out. I found out from my lawyer that we could have a legal separation if we have separate bedrooms, even if he were to live in the same house. I still hoped that we could get back together again. But it didn't happen because he kept his girlfriend.

In 1999 I returned to Hong Kong to be able to think clearly about my life. When I returned, I asked my husband for a divorce. In 2000, even though he was reluctant, the divorce came through, and I changed the name of the restaurant slightly to signify the change in my life, but not to the extent that patrons wouldn't recognize it.

Daisy's personal life fell apart when she learned of her husband's affair. Besides running her business, she had to deal with both her health and her relationship with her husband. Fortunately, her family was well settled in Canada by then. It is amazing that she was able to overcome her health problem and remain strong for her children.

❖ My husband has left for Hong Kong, but without the girlfriend. She continued to bother me by phoning the restaurant demanding money and threatening to have her underworld friends beat me up, and even threatened the waiters. The police had to be called and she has been warned, but she still sends her people to try to get money from the restaurant.

I am happy that my children are good students and we are very close. My son has just graduated from university. Their father has completely lost touch with them. My health has been fine, and I'm carrying on with my business of running the restaurant.

Daisy has been the head of her household all along, and it was by her own agency and initiative that the family immigrated to Canada. Daisy's experience in settling in Montreal as an entrepreneur illustrates one of the inherent problems with the business immigration program. As of 2010, Daisy remained in good health. Both her children have graduated from university, and her restaurant business is thriving. When I asked her to reflect on her life as an immigrant in Canada, she said:

❖ I am really enjoying my life. We are going to celebrate my restaurant's twentieth anniversary next year. I have never regretted coming to Canada. No matter how my original home, Macao, has changed and prospered, I am very grateful to Canada for giving me the great opportunity to raise my children with a good education and bright future. I am proud of my son and daughter. They are doing well in their own fields, and I have a fourteen-month-old grandson.

The great thing I learned in this country is love. And I am going to give and share this love with people for the rest of my life.

With the signing of the Joint Declaration between Britain and China in 1984 and the impending return of sovereignty of Hong Kong to China in 1997, business people in Hong Kong, like Daisy, became favoured immigrants to more than twenty-four countries. At the same time, these developed countries, including Canada, which had had an open immigration policy since 1967, began to erect legislative and administrative barriers to the entry of non-bourgeois refugees and immigrants. The problem created in developed countries by globalization was the increase in unemployment rates as a result of the free flow of capital, which placed a downward pressure on wages and benefits while at the same time reducing the capacity of the governments to tax corporate profits. In order to deal with this crisis, countries resorted to a host of means of "capturing" capital, one of which is the sale of immigration status to wealthy individuals.[13]

In Canada, at a 1986 conference called "Multiculturalism Means Business," Prime Minister Mulroney was unequivocal about the pragmatic reasons for promoting a new multiculturalism. He made the link between Canada's need for export markets and the increased trading opportunities offered by Canada's ethnic members, who might have ties to other parts of the globe. This was in reference to Asians from the Pacific Rim countries. He said, "Canadians who have cultural links to other parts of the globe, who have business contacts elsewhere are of the utmost importance to our trade and investment strategy."[14]

The government began to focus more and more on better race relations and on attracting wealthy investors, particularly from Asia. The connection between these was made in several government publications, albeit indirectly. In 1984 the Mulroney government had established the Asia Pacific Foundation as a non-profit think-tank on Canada's relations with Asia. With its head office in Vancouver and an office in Montreal, it focused on information and analysis for business policy making.[15] Geoeconomist Katharyne Mitchell believes that it was not entirely coincidental that the national public education campaign to mark the International Day for the Elimination of Racial Discrimination was organized less than a month after a couple of racist articles appeared in the *Globe and Mail*.[16]

The following story of Belinda, an investor immigrant, may help the reader understand the relationship between racism and the Business Immigration Program. Belinda is someone I had known for a long time. She was paying a short visit to Toronto from Hong Kong in the summer of 2001, and I was fortunate to be able to arrange for an interview with her by telephone. She spoke in fluent English.

❖ I was born in Hong Kong in 1963, the youngest of four children. I have three older brothers. My family is very wealthy. I left Hong Kong for school in England at a very young age and subsequently went on to study in the U.S.

In 1987 I was living in the U.S. and applied to immigrate to Canada in the investor category. The application was done through an immigration consultant in Vancouver. From the time the application went in till the time I heard from the Immigration Department was about nine months.

Belinda never mentioned why she wanted to immigrate to Canada. At that time, it may have been easier for her to immigrate to Canada than to the United States, even though she was living there. Also, because of the United States' worldwide taxation rule, she may not have wanted a

U.S. passport. However, the push factor that impelled her to emigrate was that of so many other Hong Kongers: the return of sovereignty of Hong Kong to China and the fear of living under Communist rule. Belinda probably wanted to have a Canadian passport as insurance because of the uncertainty of Hong Kong's future after 1997.

❖ In 1988 I went from California to Montreal for an interview with Canadian Immigration. There was a panel of four or five interviewers; I couldn't quite remember the exact number. I was asked various questions similar to the ones asked in my application form, such as family background and educational background. They were not difficult questions. I think the immigration officials just wanted to see the applicant. They particularly wanted to know why my father and my brothers weren't applying with me.

I was probably a very unusual investor applicant because I was a twenty-five-years-old single woman. I was asked a lot about my investment experience. I actually started investing in the equities market since I was eighteen. I brought a copy of my portfolio to show them just in case they asked. It was a U.S.-dollar portfolio and there was an approximate amount of three hundred thousand Canadian dollars in it. The application was approved, and within a year my visa arrived in the U.S., where I was living. Within two months I moved to Canada. I would have liked to live in Montreal but chose Toronto because it is an English city.

As an investor, the entire amount of three hundred thousand Canadian dollars was held for a period of three years. Maybe the Canadian government took the money, put it in bonds or term deposits, and then released it after three years. But whoever managed the money for investors, that person or persons would be making pure profits! You know, investors were not required to work. I could have chosen to just sit for three years and get my citizenship.

I didn't get my citizenship after three years because I needed to apply and then go for an interview. I took my time and got my citizenship four years later. I believe the amount required for investor was increased soon after my application.

I had been living in the West since age twelve, so I had no

problem adjusting to living in Canada. I first found a job with an insurance company, working as a sales agent for three years. I was the company's top sales person. After that, I went into real estate development with a few partners, and that's where I first encountered racism.

The real estate development that we were involved in was mainly geared to the ethnic Chinese population. There were a lot of public hearings and encounters with the neighbours. In the neighbourhood question-and-answer sessions, in which councillors attended, I confronted a lot of anti-Chinese sentiment. I believe that, in any business, there is a target market, which is based on profit margin and not on ethnic origin. Changes are bound to occur in a society when people of different ethnic backgrounds come together. There was a real fear that the local neighbourhoods were being controlled by Asians.

The neighbours around our developments, both in Richmond Hill and in Mississauga, failed to understand that no one wanted to destroy the neighbourhoods. Most of the neighbourhood meetings took place in the evenings, and after each session, while I was driving home, I wondered why I stayed in Canada. My partners and I realized that these were not just development projects, but arm-wrestling matches with the cities and the neighbours, and they were very tiring.

Here we see that conflicts of culture and economic interests, and racial discrimination may not have been the whole picture. Such conflicts became very prevalent in Toronto and Vancouver, where there were large concentrations of affluent Chinese immigrants from Hong Kong. Belinda's settlement in Canada was fine for the first few years. It was only when she had to deal with overt racism that it became unpleasant to the point that she wanted to leave. She did not persevere, as did many other immigrants who encountered racism in their work. This was probably because she did not have to.

❖ By 1995, I had already decided that I would return to Hong Kong, but since our last development project was not finished, I delayed my departure. By then, Hong Kong was booming despite the impending change of sovereignty to China. In February 1998

I left. When I returned to Hong Kong, I was able to compare the racism I mentioned before to what I see there. Hong Kongers also fear that the Chinese from the mainland are invading the city.

Many of my friends who are immigrants have difficulties with their foreign degrees in Canada. Even degrees from the U.S. are discounted, and many of them have found it difficult to find the same level of work as they did in their home countries. A Canadian passport to me means that it's easier for travelling abroad and not much more. Being born in Hong Kong, I have a Hong Kong ID card. When I travel in China, I use something that looks like a credit card.

I'm happy to be back in Hong Kong, but then I wasn't unhappy living in Canada. I loved the experience of working in Canada, despite the aggravation. I feel that I had gained from these unique experiences in my life. It took some decision for me to move back to Hong Kong because I had not lived there since I was a child. I was surprised how easy it was to adjust to life in Hong Kong.

Belinda's return to Hong Kong was actually more of a culture shock than her move to Canada from the United States. She found it easy to adjust to life in Hong Kong because she is wealthy.

❖ You know, the tax system in Hong Kong is a real attraction and is the main reason why I returned there to live. I have one brother living there as well as some relatives. There is only one tax in Hong Kong, and that of earned income. There is no capital gains or dividend taxes, and the tax on earned income is only 16 percent, so it is a real advantage for people [like me] to build up their investments.

As a transnational, Belinda could choose to live virtually anywhere. Although her immigration interview had presented no problems, there were in fact significant problems with the investor program. These became evident when improprieties in the administration of immigrant investor funds were revealed. The revelations led to lawsuits and in some cases to criminal charges. Other defects in the program included a lack of federal enforcement and monitoring, its complexity, and allegations of unfair competition.[17]

As the program evolved and expanded, business immigration as a percentage of total immigration increased. In 1980 business immigrants made up only 3.6 percent of all immigrants; in 1991 they constituted 8.5 percent, rising to an all-time high of over 11 percent in 1992. Statistics Canada estimated that the total amount of money held by investors entering Canada between 1989 and 1992 was $11.5 billion.[18] Since the early 1980s, Hong Kong had been a focal point of this search for investment capital by many governments around the world. Between 1983 and 1992, 36 percent of all business immigrants, 40 percent of all entrepreneurs, and 48 percent of investors to Canada came from Hong Kong.[19]

Hong Kong's direct investment in Canada grew from $8 million in 1961 to $19 million in 1971, $87 million in 1981, and $2.306 billion in 1991 (Canadian dollars). One official estimate from the Canadian Commission in Hong Kong indicated that as much as Cdn$5 billion in Hong Kong capital from all sources flowed into Canada in 1991 alone. From the inception of the Immigrant Investor Program in 1986 until 1992, about 40 percent of the capital inflow was contributed by Hong Kong immigrants. The program is often referred to as a "cash-for-visa" program.[20] As seen in the story of Belinda, transnationals who came into Canada under the program tend not to have the same sense of loyalty to Canada as immigrants who entered under other circumstances.

In 1981 the three leading countries of business migration to Canada were the United Kingdom (11.9 percent), the United States (11.8 percent), and West Germany (10.9 percent). By 1985, Hong Kong was responsible for 40 percent of all business immigration into Canada.[21] By 1988, it accounted for 14.4 percent of total immigration to Canada, and by 1994, 19.7 percent.[22]

It is interesting to note that in 1989, 514 immigrants in the investor category invested more than $100 million in Canada in meeting their immigration requirements; in addition, they brought $65 million upon landing in Canada. According to Employment and Immigration Canada, in 1990 the rapidly growing investor category alone was responsible for approximately $1 billion a year, which amounted to 10 to 12.5 percent of direct foreign investment in Canada annually.[23]

Since the majority of entrepreneur and investor immigrants were Chinese, and most of them came from Hong Kong, authors L.L. Wong and N.S. Netting have referred to this phenomenon as the "Asianization of business immigration." This was especially important for the economy of Vancouver, since its location is more convenient for "astronauts" – immigrants who fly in and out of Canada for business purposes.[24] Their large numbers are the result of the rapid economic expansion of Asia Pacific Rim countries in the 1980s, which led to significant capital formation, and the political uncertainty of these regions. The capital flight from Hong Kong accounted for its dominance in business immigration.[25]

Was Canadian society ready to welcome the influx of Chinese migrants from Hong Kong? The census of 1981 shows that, irrespective of the educational and occupational mobility of the Chinese in Canada, they had not attained income equality relative to those of other ethnic origins. It suggested that the ethnic Chinese had adapted to the unfavourable market conditions by moving into certain occupational niches where their ethnicity is less problematic than elsewhere.[26]

When the Canadian Charter of Rights and Freedoms was passed in 1982, it became prominent in any discussion of citizenship and citizenship education in Canada.[27] The study of the extent and limits of rights became vitally important.[28] In 1986 the Employment Equity Act was passed, with the purpose of achieving equality in the workplace.[29] While the Charter prohibits racial discrimination in law, it does not require governments or legislatures to promote racial harmony.[30] It is important to note that the Charter also guaranteed gender equality, a point that some Chinese immigrant women took very seriously.[31] Educated women from Hong Kong who immigrated after 1967 defined their lives on the basis of multiculturalism and the status of women; consequently, race and gender have become important issues. With women's lives increasingly defined by education and work, these women would settle for no less than equality, from pension to pay scales. And when they encountered difficulties, many found a way of overcoming them.

In reference to racism in the context of business, we shall now look at the experiences of Chinese businesswomen who came to Canada originally as students and subsequently became landed immigrants. The following is the story of Amber, who was interviewed by telephone from Toronto in the summer of 2002. Since she is an extremely busy person, that was the only possible way of interviewing her. She spoke in English with a heavy accent.

❖ I was born in Guangzhou in 1953, the fifth child in a family of seven children. My family was wealthy, and my grandfather and uncles suffered greatly from the Communists. Fortunately, my father was frequently in Hong Kong after 1949, so did not have the same bad experiences. My own family moved to Hong Kong when I was a few months old.

We are Cantonese. My family had owned branches of a well-known Chinese medicine shop in Guangzhou for three generations, with my father's generation being the last. When my family moved to Hong Kong, the head office also moved there. Since the name of the company was very recognizable, it was easy for us to get established in Hong Kong, where we opened three branches.

I went to Chinese primary and secondary schools, and that's why I wasn't able to enter the University of Hong Kong when I graduated. I taught for a year in math and science for grades 6, 7, and 8. In Hong Kong at that time, I could do that without teachers' training.

Like my other informants, Amber spoke about the political disturbances in China. She did not elaborate on how such a wealthy family managed to leave China in 1953. Amber mentioned that she could not enter the University of Hong Kong because the language of instruction is English. Students from the Chinese middle schools in Hong Kong usually do not have enough English-language knowledge to be accepted. It was also very difficult to get into university in Hong Kong because of the limited number of seats available compared with the huge number of graduates from high school each year.

❖ In 1974, when I was twenty, I came to Canada on a student visa to study at McMaster University to do a commerce degree. It was there that I met my future husband, who was doing his MBA at the time. I graduated in 1978 and returned to Hong Kong to work as a credit analyst in a bank.

In 1979 I decided to go to University of Toronto to do an MBA, with emphasis on finance. I graduated the following year, at which time I got married and started working for a bank in the investment and pension funds areas as an analyst. Since my husband was already a Canadian citizen, it was easy for me to become landed even though I was born in China. I didn't have a passport, only a Certificate of Identity from Hong Kong. It took three years and an examination before I received my citizenship in 1983.

I stayed at that first bank for four years. I was the only person with an MBA in my department at the head office, managing pension funds in the billions of dollars. I was paid $40,000, which was considered very high pay in 1980. My department managed the stock portfolio of pension funds, and there were very few members on the team. In the last half of the four years, a Caucasian woman joined the team, and even though she was new in the department, she was made my immediate supervisor. All the reports I wrote had to be passed to her first. She would correct the English, and with the excuse that I didn't communicate well in English, she would also take the reports to present to the board. So when things went well, this woman got all the credit, and when things didn't go well, I got all the blame. I was infuriated because I was made to feel inferior to a person who knew much less than I did. That's just because I am an immigrant woman that I'm treated that way. It was then that I decided to make the move to another bank as a broker.

I was way overqualified as a broker, but the advantage would be that I would no longer have to report to a board, and there would also not be a hierarchy to deal with. I would rather move into an environment where I'm dealing with the general public on the same level. I became an investment adviser, and my pay was reduced to one-third of what it was before, but with commission. I was confident, however, that within a couple of years I would make back all the money I lost. I did it within a year. I believe that if a person is determined, he or she can do anything.

It is fairly common for members of ethnic minorities to act as Amber did. She used individual effort rather than collective effort to overcome discrimination. The entire corporate system was probably too daunting for her to fight, and she chose to get on with her life and show how successful she could be if left alone.

❖ As an ethnic minority and a woman, I always have to fight for what I want. In the early 1990s, after I had been at the present bank for six years, I became, and still am, the top performing investment adviser. Since there has been so much talk about equality in Canadian society, equity in hiring, as well as equal pay for equal work, I wanted the bank to assign me in an officer role as I should have been. Again, I had to fight for it. I went to the different departments and put the pressure on. After one year, I got it. There were no females and no Chinese in that position. Now there are more females, but I'm still the only ethnic Chinese in that position. I could have been a director, but I don't want it, because I would have to give up the role of investment adviser and just become a manager.

I never wanted to return to Hong Kong to live since my four years of university here, because I don't like the lifestyle back home. You know, those immigrants who returned to Hong Kong use high Canadian taxes as an excuse for the fact that they were not happy in Canada. Tax is an issue, but not a determining factor.

Amber may be referring to the so-called transnationals, who were afraid that Canada might introduce worldwide tax reporting. Probably, many of these wealthy immigrants were her clients.

Amber had a son and a daughter, and a good relationship with her mother-in-law, who helped her raise her children. "She has lived with us now for eleven years," Amber said. "I do believe in this old Chinese tradition, and it had worked very well for me. I have also been very lucky in my career path. I have no religion, but I do believe in a God." In many ways, Amber's luck was the result of making the right choices in her life.

I believe that Amber spoke in English to make the point that she could communicate in English even though her immediate superior in the first bank said she could not. Because of her achievements, she has become highly successful and a very well-respected member of the Chinese Canadian community.

Amber mentioned that immigrants who leave Canada often use high Canadian taxes as an excuse, but in fact they leave Canada because they are not happy here. Looking back at Belinda's interview, we see that she left Canada because of the discrimination she experienced in her work. Subsequently, she mentioned the tax advantage in Hong Kong, but that was not her prime reason for leaving.

Illustrating the same issue of the lack of equity for an ethnic minority immigrant woman is the story of Carol, who was interviewed by telephone in the summer of 2002. Carol is highly spirited and spoke very fast in fluent Cantonese.

❖ I was born in Hong Kong in 1954. My father was from Guangdong Province and my mother from the New Territories. My family was of humble means, involved in small business.

I went to a government primary school, and for secondary school I attended Hotung Technical School for Girls. After the fifth form school certificate examinations, my sister, who was already a landed immigrant in Canada, applied for me to come to continue my education. That was 1972, and I remember that that was the year when the Canadian government gave general amnesty to illegal immigrants.

My sister told me that if I worked for a year, I would be eligible to get a student grant and student loan for university, so I studied at Jarvis Collegiate in the evenings to finish grade 13, while working during the day as a bank teller. My sister advised me to take science courses despite the fact that only arts courses were given at the Hotung Technical School for Girls, because she was afraid that I would not be able to compete with local Canadians in English.

Because both my sister and I had to send money home to help the family, I decided not to go to university but to the Toronto Institute of Medical Technology, so that I could get my diploma in two years and would be able to work in laboratories. I articled at the Toronto General Hospital, and from 1975 to 1980 I worked in the biochemistry laboratory at a Toronto hospital.

My sister and I applied for the entire family to immigrate to Canada. The only exception was my older brother, who was over the age limit to be sponsored under the family class. He immigrated to the U.S.

In 1977 I married a young man I met who was working in the

Immunopathology Department at the same hospital. In 1980, when my father was discovered to have cancer, I decided the work I was doing in the hospital with close contact with patients was getting me down, so I decided to take up French at Berlitz [language school] as a diversion.

While at Berlitz, I was asked if I wanted to be trained as a teacher in Chinese, which would mean that I would have to pay very little for my French lessons. I went through the training, and my students in Chinese were mainly air hostesses, which gave me the idea to apply for a job at Canadian Pacific [Airlines]. I was wondering whether I would be hired, because at that time, most air hostesses were pretty single girls, and I was already married, and perhaps I wasn't pretty enough. I remember buying a new dress for the interview. I was offered a permanent job working the route between Toronto and Vancouver, and I quit my job at the hospital. Unfortunately, because of recession, there was a cutback at CP Air, and my permanent job became a summer job instead.

At the end of the summer, I didn't want to go back to work at the hospital and to try working in travel instead. By so doing, I was making a lot less than in the hospital. I found a job working for a Malaysian tour operator, which brought mostly Malaysian tourists to Canada. I took inbound tours from Malaysia and the Far East.

In 1984 Margaret Thatcher signed the agreement to return sovereignty of Hong Kong to China. Many people in Hong Kong were nervous and wanted to immigrate. That year, I led a group – two busloads – of wealthy tourists from Hong Kong who wanted to see Canada with the prospect of investing in real estate. I made friends with them, and they asked me to introduce them to real estate agents. I ended up going to see the properties with them. They then asked me why I didn't take out a real estate licence. I did, and never looked back.

As mentioned earlier, the signing of the joint declaration between China and Britain gave a strong impetus for emigration from Hong Kong. It was unsettling for the inhabitants, who had gained their own Hong Kong identity in the 1970s, and it was especially worrying for those who were refugees from China in the years following the Second World War.[32]

❖ In 1985 the same group asked me to go back to Hong Kong to set up an agency for them, with the purpose of bringing tourists from Hong Kong to buy real estate. I did that for one year but returned to Canada because my father became very ill. In the same year, he passed away. A year later, because of too much competition, the agency closed.

From 1987 on, I've been working in real estate full-time. In 1990 I became a partner and the principal broker of a firm, being responsible for the operation of the company, as well as dealing with the government. In 1994 a large mainstream real estate company recruited me to be a branch manager in one of their Toronto offices. The only other ethnic Chinese was a man who was transferred to Vancouver, and he didn't stay very long with the company. Out of one hundred and ten branch managers in this company, I was the only person from an ethnic minority. I felt that this was my chance to see how a large, mainstream real estate company worked, even though I had to give up selling.

Work was very difficult in a mainstream company, especially as an ethnic minority woman, but I did gain good experience. The remuneration of this company was not competitive with other smaller companies, so they had few Chinese agents. However, since I became the manager of this particular branch, within three months I was able to hire twenty-four agents, twenty-three of them Chinese. I was later transferred to another branch where there were more Chinese residents in the area.

The growth in sales in real estate was similar to the growth in Chinese restaurants that we saw in Daisy's case. Both were responses to the influx of Hong Kong immigrants to Toronto.[33]

❖ You know, as an ethnic minority woman, I had to fight for everything I wanted, as well as having to work twice as hard. I needed to overcome difficulties with perseverance and determination. My position as a branch manager was particularly difficult, because the Chinese agents believed I was helping the non-Chinese agents more in order to advance myself, and at the same time the non-Chinese agents thought I would help the Chinese agents more. I had to be very careful and fair, and kept a record of all sale assignments.

In 1999 the company downsized, and my branch merged with another, under an Anglo-Saxon man as manager. Not wanting to let me go, I was given the title of Asian market manager, with a pay cut, but I was able to sell again. However, a year later, my position was gone.

The company, being very large, had a relocation contract with the Department of Defence, with a position of relocation consultant. I applied and got the job, which was supposed to be for two years. I found the discrimination in the Department of Defence very bad, particularly towards an Asian woman. They wouldn't even take any notice of me when we met for consultation. Another team was asked to take over, and my team was let go. I was asked to pursue this with the Human Rights Commission, but I chose to get on with my life.

Carol did not go into details of her experiences with the Department of Defence, nor did she try to get her job back. Instead, like Amber, she resolved the problem by her own efforts: "I joined another real estate company, which is Chinese owned, and was hired as selling manager, and I'm still with the same firm. I am on the real estate board as one of the six directors, and I'm going to run for the position as president. My husband has retired now, and we have two sons."

Carol has been successful by making use of the opportunities provided by the demographic trends of immigrants from Hong Kong. Like Amber, she felt the burden of being an ethnic minority woman, but despite discrimination, they both ended up achieving what they wanted by "fighting" and "working twice as hard." Both Carol and Amber are good examples of the new Chinese immigrant women from Hong Kong who have refused to accept the unacceptable.[34] In cases like these, intelligence counts. Since the interview, Carol has been elected president of the real estate board. In December 2010, when she was asked to reflect on her life as an immigrant woman, she said:

❖ In terms of life in this fast lane, I have no regrets about immigrating to Canada, a land full of golden opportunities, except that, as a female and a visible minority, I need to work four times as hard – twice as a female and twice as a visible minority – to convince people to give me the opportunity as an equal. In hindsight, it had taken a lot of blood, sweat, and tears to take me to where I am today. I have no complaints, and I have to thank God for this amazing training ground for cultivating perseverance and persistence.

A recent incident around an article in *Maclean's* is a great example of the importance of educating Canadians in the reality of accepting the multicultural mosaic of our country so that our next generation may overcome this identity issue.[35] I quote the "ABC" theory from the late Honourable David Lam, lieutenant governor of British Columbia, who recently passed away. He said that we must first "accept" each other so that we can have a sense of "belonging" to be able to "contribute" our best to this great country, Canada.

The above stories reflect the reality faced by visible minority women despite the employment equity legislation of 1986, which provided a framework to support a diverse workforce and also required all federally regulated employers to file an annual report with the Canadian Employment and Immigration Commission. Equality in employment means that no one is denied opportunities for reasons that have nothing to do with inherent ability. While the language of the federal act was not itself racialized, systemic discrimination continued, as shown in the interviews with Amber and Carol. Efforts to make the Canadian public service more representative of the Canadian public also failed, as evidenced in the 1996 annual report of the Canadian Human Rights Commission, which documented in stark numbers the huge gap between the government's commitment to a public service that mirrors the diversity of the Canadian population and its dismal record in promoting minorities.[36]

The same report revealed that the pay of women over a multiyear period was only 75 percent of the salary of men when full-time work was measured. In the federal public service, the total number of positions held by women continued to decline. In the executive group of the public service, women's share was only 21.3 percent, even though it had increased from 19 percent. Representation of ethnic minorities in the public service remained extremely low. In the executive category, it was at only 2.3 percent in 1996.[37] The expectations of new, educated, Chinese immigrant women certainly did not meet the reality of Canadian society.

In the case of the transnational elite, what is the implication of their lifestyle and their way of doing business internationally on the business immigration program? Is the federal government overestimating the contribution to Canada of these immigrants or underrecognizing their potential?[38] Does it mean the rise in power of Asians in this country?

With regard to the change of source countries of immigrants to Canada since the 1960s, from 1964 to 1966 Europeans and Americans constituted 85 percent of total immigration, and Asians counted for less than 7 percent. By 1991, European and North American immigration accounted for 29 percent, while Asian immigration accounted for 52 percent. In 1991 and a few years before that, Hong Kong was the top source country, representing 9.7 percent of total immigration. Immigrants from China constituted 6 percent, and those from Britain were down to 3.3 percent.[39]

In the past, increasing numbers of immigrants of an ethnic minority caused fear and racial tensions. Since the 1980s, the wealthy influx of Hong Kong immigrants whom the Canadian government worked so hard to entice has aroused similar reactions from some Canadians. The fear and resentment were fanned by certain mainstream media, including the *Vancouver Sun*, in their coverage of "monster homes," huge Chinese shopping malls, and even the cutting down of trees.

The fact that many Hong Kong immigrants have returned to Hong Kong has also garnered criticism – that they have no loyalty to Canada – but it is important to note that many of them were professionals who were not able to find employment commensurate with their education and training during the economic recession. Some of these immigrants, who came into Canada in the 1980s under the business category, are members of the transnational capitalist elite and are therefore global citizens. While their capital has no borders, they did help and will continue to help Canada's integration into the global economy within the transnational context.

Chapter 9

Women in the New Chinese
Canadian Communities

In the era of globalization, the Chinese immigrant women are no different from the men. The women have not only immigrated as dependent wives and daughters; they have also immigrated as independents or as heads of households. Some came to Canada as students and then applied as landed immigrants upon graduation, as mentioned previously. By the end of the 1980s, applications to immigrate to Canada from Hong Kong were still increasing. The average processing time had risen from 288 days in 1988 to 461 days by 1990. By far the largest numbers of applicants were in the entrepreneur and independent categories.[1]

Women from Hong Kong had high expectations from Canada with respect to human rights and democracy because of their achievements in Hong Kong since the 1960s.[2] A law firm was first established by a woman in Hong Kong in 1961, and in 1963 a Joint Committee on Equal Pay for Equal Work was formed by various women's and social organizations.[3] In 1966, the first female legislative councillor, Dr Ellen Li, was appointed.[4] These milestones were followed by many other achievements by women, not the least of which was the appointment of the first female executive councillor, Mrs Joyce Symons, in 1976.[5]

As noted in earlier chapters, many improvements were made to the Hong Kong education system after the end of the 1960s, and for the children of the middle class, not only was superior education available, but many were fluent in English.[6] Many of these students went abroad to study and were completely comfortable in Western cultures. Daughters were now brought into family businesses, as is evident in the interview with Daisy. As for families with international financial interests, their children, both sons and daughters, were sent to schools in different parts of the world, and most now have multiple passports. Many of these were the women in the new Chinese Canadian communities in the 1980s.

After the signing of the joint declaration between Britain and China, there was great anxiety in Hong Kong at the prospect of living under Communist rule, even though Hong Kong was to be a Special Administrative Region within China. In an interview conducted by the Hong Kong Women Christian Council, Angela Kwong Siu-kuen said, "Human rights in Hong Kong are not supported by its present government [British colonial] … In addition, the Chinese government claims that Hong Kong's Bill of Rights, such as it is, will be abolished altogether after 1997."[7] Because of such fears, there was a mass exodus of people to different parts of the world. Many of these emigrants came to Canada. The topic of emigration was so popular that there were magazines published, such as *Emigrant*, to give information to those who were planning to emigrate.[8] But not all wanted to leave. A thirteen-year-old Hong Kong girl said, "I don't like 1997 because my parents want to migrate to Canada. I want to stay in Hong Kong. I don't want to leave my friends."[9]

The following is an interview with a professional woman who came to Canada with her family at the end of the 1980s because of the political situation in Hong Kong. Faith was interviewed in my office in Toronto in the summer of 2001. She spoke in Cantonese with a few English words added.

❖ I was born in Hong Kong in a family of four. I attended two prestigious English middle schools, and when I graduated in 1969, I entered one of the universities in Hong Kong to study social science. In 1973, after graduation, I went to a university in Europe to pursue a master's degree. This university had many international programs, with English as the language of instruction. That was how I was able to study for my master's degree there.

In 1977 I returned to Hong Kong to teach. A year and a half later, in 1978, I went to work in administration in one of the universities in Hong Kong. That was where I met my future husband. We were married in 1979, and in 1980 our first son was born. In 1983 my husband and I were in the U.S. to further our education. On our return to Hong Kong, after having received a master's degree in higher education administration from an Ivy League university, I went back to the same university to work at a more senior level, looking after one of the sections of the administration.

Around the time we went to the U.S., my husband and I began monitoring the political situation in Hong Kong, particularly after the signing of the Sino-British Joint Declaration and the establishment of the Basic Law. In 1988 the Hong Kong government changed the rules and went against what was promised to be a more democratic election, so we decided that it was time to leave.

Faith was referring to the white paper published by the Hong Kong government in 1988 on the future of Hong Kong saying that the government felt it was not prudent to make constitutional changes at that time. Many Hong Kongers felt betrayed by this action.[10]

❖ During the years we lived in the U.S., Canada had become our conscious choice of a country to live in, over the U.S. We believed Canada to be an enlightened country because of its policy of multiculturalism. My husband also has an aunt who lives in Canada, so he was very aware of what was happening in the country.

In 1988 my husband and I applied to immigrate to Canada. It was decided that I should be the principal applicant because of the occupational demands of Canada at the time. The need was for administrators and counsellors, and I was in that category, which meant that I would get more points in the points system, whereas my husband would receive no points for his occupation. In 1989 we landed in Canada and then went back to Hong Kong to tie up loose ends.

At the beginning of 1990, our family came to Canada to stay. I started looking for work in the areas of my training and experience. By that time, the economic cycle was already on its way down. Despite the fact that my training was supposed to be more in need in Canada than my husband's, he was the one who got a job, soon after our arrival, that was related to his qualifications.

The way jobs were advertised in Canada was very different from Hong Kong, particularly the type of jobs I was interested in. I approached churches to do administration, but none was hiring. What I was able to get in the universities were positions I was overqualified for. Part of the problem in my job search was a misunderstanding of job titles between the British system in Hong Kong and Canada. For instance, an administrative assistant to the president of a university in Hong Kong has a great deal more responsibility than someone with a similar title in Canada. Another problem could be that, in Hong Kong, as an administrator, my Chinese had to be very good as well as my English, whereas in Canada, my English would be considered too bookish for socializing among office colleagues and Chinese is not needed.

This is often a problem for immigrants. Applicants in the independent class were given up to ten points if there was a demand for their occupation in Canada. However, by the time the successful applicants arrived in Canada, the occupational demand pattern might have changed. The immigration experience would be even more disappointing when the immigrant suffered status dislocation in the process, as Faith did.[11]

❖ After a few years working in a university, I decided to apply to do a PhD. On reflection, my work experience at a university in Canada was not all bad because there was far less politics than working at a university in Hong Kong. But in terms of career, it's been disappointing for me even though it has worked out much better for my husband. Those I worked with in Hong Kong have moved to much higher positions, and besides, salary scales are also much higher in Hong Kong. I believe my husband's involvement in society or in shaping social policy is minimal in Canada compared with what it could have been in Hong Kong. However, as time goes on, things will change.

There is an element of regret in Faith's settlement experience as well as in the comparisons made with how well her friends are doing in Hong Kong. Experiences such as hers was the reason why many Hong Kong immigrants returned to Hong Kong in the 1990s.

At the end of 2010, when Faith was asked to reflect on her life as an immigrant woman in Canada, she said:

❖ I finished my dissertation in 2005 and received my PhD in 2006. From 2005 to 2007, I taught a course at one of our Canadian universities. I fully enjoyed sharing my knowledge and expertise with the younger generation. By sheer coincidence, when I began teaching in 2005, another opportunity arose. I was able to be involved with work that I had aspired to for decades. In 2007, between an academic/research career and the other that I also loved and felt called to, I opted for the latter and have been serving in that capacity since. I find my present work most rewarding and challenging.

While still sentimental about Hong Kong, I found that most of what I missed is the Hong Kong that I grew up in – the space and the people of my formative years. Now my identity, as well as my family's, is very much Canadian. The family is very involved in political and social issues facing Canada.

My family and I chose to come to Canada because of its commitment to a just society, as well as its inclusiveness and multicultural character. We have not been disappointed, although there are signs that the gap between rich and poor is growing, and that is a cause for concern.

In this interview, as in the interviews of Hope, Amber, Carol, and Rena, it is evident that there is a great difference in expectations between the earlier immigrant Chinese women and the ones who entered Canada after the end of the 1960s. Instead of being happy just to have the opportunity to live in a democratic society, these highly educated women have higher expectations. These are also the women who were the agents of their own migration and career choices.

In the era of globalization, people and capital, as well as goods, move freely across political jurisdictions. With respect to immigrants from Hong Kong, Canada and Hong Kong share many social and cultural connections and family networks, and there is a large number of Hong Kong students in the Canadian education system, all of which has contributed to setting up family business networks between Canada and Hong Kong.[12] This is evident in the case of Carol, who sold properties to

Hong Kong immigrants, as well as helping to set up a travel and real estate company in Hong Kong.[13] Some students from Hong Kong who graduated from Canadian universities have not only used their connections with Hong Kong in their business ventures but have extended their reach to China and other parts of Asia.

The following interview with Rose helps to illustrate the importance of the networks established by immigrants from Hong Kong who have formed links with China and other parts of Asia that have become part of the business culture in Canada. The recognition of this was the reason for the establishment of the Asia Pacific Foundation by the Mulroney government.

Rose was interviewed by telephone in the spring of 2002. She spoke in Cantonese.

❖ I was born in Hong Kong in 1953. My father was an officer in the Nationalist army. My parents met when my father was posted to Yunnan. My mother was the eldest daughter of a land-owning family, and Grandmother wanted her to have a good education. Grandmother died when my mother was fourteen, and she became my grandfather's right hand in supervising the family's property-owning business. After graduation from high school, she became a teacher.

In 1949, after the Communists took China, my father had the choice of moving to Taiwan, but he chose to move to Hong Kong. Life was very difficult in Hong Kong because my parents didn't know anyone. They first started a cottage industry, hiring people to do piecework for garment manufacturers. My parents later opened their own factory in To Kwa Wan and later moved to Kwun Tong. They also changed to the manufacturing of toys. By the time I was ten years old, life was comfortable for us. My mother was the one who gave my father courage in business, and she always worked alongside him. She was very capable and was the driving force in the family.

In Rose's story, we hear again of the exodus from China in 1949 and how her family joined the refugee population in Hong Kong. Hong Kong became a manufacturing hub in Asia after 1949 through the knowhow of the refugees from China.

❖ I attended a Catholic English girls' school from grade one to upper six, and in 1974 I came to Canada for university on a student visa. My older sister came at the same time, studying at a college.

I met my future husband while I was at university, where he also was a student. After he graduated, he worked with a travel agency for two years, and in 1976 he opened his own agency. My sister and I helped him. I was still a student then. In 1977 we were married. My husband was a Canadian citizen when we got married, and with me having a British passport with the right of abode in Britain, it was very easy for me to be landed. Right after I became landed, I applied for my parents to come to Canada. My sister and my parents lived with us, and my parents helped to raise our children.

To get my citizenship, I still had to be interviewed and tested by the Department of Citizenship. I became a Canadian citizen in a ceremony three years later.

Rose did not mention whether she had ever contemplated doing any other kind of work aside from running a travel agency. It would seem that she had options, but she chose to follow her husband and build a business with him, the way her mother had done with her father.

❖ As far as adaptation to life in Canada, I didn't have any problem since I was already fluent in English before I came to Canada to university. Because I helped in my husband's travel agency while I was still a student, I just continued when we were married. Our agency did well with the business from many of the students at the university, which gave us a good start. We expanded to arranging group fares for students, and we were so busy we had to employ extra help.

As you know, in 1970 diplomatic relations [were] established between Canada and China. And in 1973 Canada and China signed an agreement for the reunification of Chinese Canadians with their family members in China. By the end of the 1970s, China was beginning to open up to foreign tourism. Our travel agency was able to benefit from this situation, particularly because my husband had very good relationships with the

Chinese embassy in Ottawa, as well as with the China International Travel Service in China. We were able to get quotas for tourist visas for our customers, as well as arranging tours for them. This became the main concentration for the growth of our company. At the same time, we also arranged tours for our Canadian clients to different parts of Asia.

The credit must all go to my husband, who understood politics and the political situation in China, and who also understood the Canadian psyche in the 1970s in opening up tourism for Canadians to different parts of Asia. He not only travelled back and forth to Asia making tour arrangements, he sometimes guided large groups as well. I was the one staying in Toronto, looking after the business, with the help of my older sister.

In 1982 on one of his business trips to China, my husband's plane crashed and he was killed. In the same year, my younger sister graduated from university, and she joined our company, so the company was run by three sisters. In 1994, unfortunately, cancer claimed my older sister's life. I have a brother who's a doctor, so he's the only one in the family who's not involved with our company. Since 1980, we have opened offices in New York, Beijing, and many branches across Canada. I think my eldest daughter, who is studying business in university, will join the company when she graduates.

Our company is well established, despite a lot of competition from smaller agencies on price points. We are able to get special deals from airlines that smaller companies can't get because we work in both wholesale and retail. Having our own specialty, which is Asia, and the fact that we have our own distribution channels, airlines still need to rely on us, despite the fact that they are cutting commissions to travel agencies; as well, many customers are now booking online. The most important thing is that we are able to provide special value to our customers. My client base is mainly Westerners, even though my social base remains in the Chinese community.

The company Rose owns continues to be successful despite difficult economic times in the travel industry, for it satisfies the needs of Canadian society, particularly because of the growth of the Asian population in Canada and the country's interest in Asia.[14] The link between Canada and Hong Kong cannot be overestimated. Besides cultural and family ties between Hong Kong and Canada, there is the fact that until July 1997, both Canada and Hong Kong were part of the British Commonwealth, making it easier for Hong Kongers to adapt to Canadian society. Another important factor was the relative political stability of Canada compared with the situation that Hong Kong people envisioned with the impending return of sovereignty to China. In addition was the encouragement for business immigration, and the disparity between Hong Kong's high capitalist economic development and Canada's relatively lower development.[15]

Globalization of capital, as discussed earlier, involves the intensification and acceleration of global linkages. Many of the transnational elites were Hong Kongers who were courted by the Canadian government as immigrants.[16] These professionals and business people live and work in several global locations, controlling the capital and information flows, and they negotiated these to their supreme advantage. An example can be seen in Mitchell's article, in which a highly successful real estate agent spoke of her efficacious use of the fifteen hours' (or sixteen, depending on whether it was standard time or daylight saving time) difference between Hong Kong and Vancouver and how she is able to maintain nearly continuous buyer-seller information and connections.[17]

It has been a common practice of these elites from Hong Kong to locate their children strategically in universities in different parts of the world in order to acculturate them to different areas where there may be the potential to live or do business. This has partly been to safeguard the family's wealth and well-being in case of negative ramifications following the return of sovereignty over Hong Kong, but also because of the desire to extend the family network. In this regard, sons and daughters have been equally involved. This power to control travel, transcultural communication, habitation, education, and business leads to new and different forms of cultural identity and gives new meaning to race and national identity.[18]

In the mid-1990s, a number of wealthy Hong Kong immigrants left Canada because the Canadian government was considering requiring every citizen to report worldwide assets. As businesswoman Anna Lo explained, throwing a going-away party for friends departing for a new life in Canada or the United States had become a waste of money because so many of them ended up returning to Hong Kong.[19] "The real reason is that it's easier to make money in Hong Kong," she said.

At the beginning of the 1990s, 75 percent of the immigrants to British Columbia (mostly to Vancouver) were from Asia, and the majority of them were from Hong Kong, with almost one-quarter having entered in the business immigrant category. This is partly because of the economic links with the Asia Pacific region and partly because some economic activities serving those who have moved to Vancouver originated in Hong Kong.

Canada's anticipated benefit from Hong Kong immigrants was their investment in Canada. Large numbers have been quoted, but no absolute figures can be attributed to immigration because of the different kinds and terms of investments made by immigrants (the exception being what they brought in when immigrating as investors).[20] Sometimes it is difficult to determine whether the investments are in the form of purchasing homes, and it is even difficult to know whether the investments were made by Canadian citizens, immigrants, or non-residents. It is also difficult to attribute the amount brought in by immigrants for their own use.

However, the economic impact of the activities by immigrants was significant. During the 1980s and on into the 1990s, Vancouver's manufacturing sector was expanding, producing commodities that often were for the high-end market, and the entrepreneurs involved in these activities were typically Chinese from Hong Kong, who had honed their skills in the dynamic economic conditions in Hong Kong and southern China in the late 1970s and the 1980s. Vancouver became a region for diversification of economic activities in the global economy.[21] In the areas of professional services, such as banking, insurance, transportation, and legal matters, the practitioners in Vancouver also were often Hong Kong Chinese immigrants who had learned their professional skills in Hong Kong and in the global marketplace, in which Hong Kong had come to play such an important role. At the same time, the increased role played by China, and China-based activities in the North American economy, especially since the 1980s, had put a premium on those who were culturally familiar with the business practices of Hong Kong and South

China. The changing structure of the global economy has given the Chinese entrepreneurs and professionals in Vancouver important advantages that were even more marked by the beginning of the 1990s.[22]

One element of the immigration process that discriminated against all working women who entered Canada as dependants, even those who had careers in their home country, was the fact that job and language training were often available only to the independent heads of households, who are usually men. If these women wanted to take advantage of the program, they had to pay for it.[23] However, in the 1970s, language classes were available to immigrants, not necessarily to help them in the job market but to help them to integrate into Canadian society, as expressed in the following interviews with Wing and Han. As mentioned earlier, informant Susan noted that she received language training in 1970 when she immigrated to Canada, though she did not specify whether it was language training for her nursing profession.[24]

The following is the immigration story of Wing who, together with her friends, Han and Lee, described the existing Chinese communities in Toronto. Wing was interviewed in my office in Toronto in the summer of 2001. She and her two women friends lived in the same seniors' apartment, and they had just been out for a dim sum lunch when they came to see me. They were laughing as they walked in, obviously having a good time in each other's company. Wing spoke in Cantonese.

❖ I was born in Shanghai in 1926, the ninth child out of fourteen children. When I was seven, the Japanese invaded China, and our family decided to move back to Hong Kong, where we originally came from. My family was very prosperous. My grandfather had one wife and four concubines.

I attended a Protestant school. My education was interrupted by the Japanese occupation of Hong Kong [December 1941], but it was resumed after the Second World War until I graduated from high school. Just because my family was wealthy didn't prevent me from working, because I didn't like sitting at home. I worked as a clerk for a foreign-owned company and later I worked in a bank. I got married in 1949 and had three daughters, all of whom were educated in English. Because we had servants, I continued to work outside of my home.

When my eldest daughter graduated from a Catholic school, she worked for Canadian Immigration in Hong Kong for a few years. She decided she liked Canada and applied to study here. In 1970 she came as a student. The other two daughters also wanted to come to Canada, and since the eldest daughter had her friends at Canadian Immigration, it was very easy for us, even though the younger daughters were already over twenty-one. I was widowed by then, and since my daughters all wanted to come to Canada, I thought I should too, even though I was happy working in an office in Prince's Building. Canadian Immigration allowed us to come as a family in 1974.

Here again we have proof that there was always a lot of room for Canadian immigration officers to make exceptions to the rule.

❖ My daughters had no trouble finding work because of their knowledge of English. By the time I came to Canada, I had already worked for the company in Hong Kong for ten years and really missed my work. After I arrived in Canada, because of a lack of knowledge of English and the fact that I was getting on in age, I stopped working. I took English courses for immigrants at George Brown College for six months. I have little trouble understanding English, having come from Hong Kong, but it's the spoken language that I had difficulty with.

As a new immigrant, I received $200 a month from the federal government and $60 subsidy per week for transportation and living allowances. The English courses were very strict in the training for spoken English, and I really appreciated it. I had enough knowledge for everyday use, but I would have difficulty explaining an ailment to an English-speaking doctor. At the beginning, I regretted coming to Canada because I missed my work and my friends in Hong Kong, but as time went on, I came to like Canada, particularly in the last ten years, because the Chinese here have gained the respect of Canadians, and I'm very proud.

Now that I have reached retirement age and I'm receiving a retirement income, life is peaceful. Comparing the life of seniors in Hong Kong with that of their counterparts in Canada, life for seniors in Hong Kong is much better now; but, to me, it's still better in Canada. For one thing, the air is better here.

I live in a seniors' apartment and have lots of friends in the building. I spend my days playing mahjong, going out for dim sum with friends, reading Chinese newspapers, and watching Chinese TV programs. My life is carefree. My only concern is that the provincial government may cut back on certain prescription medication, because medical care is so important for the elderly.

Wing was only forty-eight when she immigrated to Canada. In the integration process, she had done well despite the fact that she missed her work and her friends in Hong Kong. Like many other seniors across Canada, she has chosen to live in a seniors' apartment. The idea that different generations of Chinese families live together in the same household in harmony is often a myth. Many Chinese women who have worked all their lives do not want to be tied down with the responsibilities of caring for their grandchildren on a daily basis, and no matter how much they love their families, they opt for their own social worlds when they reach retirement age.[25]

In an oral history containing interviews by Chan Kwok Bun, one informant explained: "We call the government 'the good old man.' The Canadian government is very nice to us and we feel very, very grateful. Every woman I know looks forward to turning 65 when she will get the old age pension. I have more than enough to live by."[26] In another interview by Chan, a social worker said, "This client of mine is quite bitter about the way she was treated by her family when she was living with them. She moved into Chinatown three years ago. Now she is happy with her neighbours and housemates. Twice a week she calls her son and grandchildren ... They call her a lot too ... Sometimes they talk for more than an hour on the phone ... She always spends Christmas and New Year with her family ... Her son comes ... every Monday ... to see her."[27]

The enjoyment of being independent at retirement age is enhanced by the proliferation of Chinese media. Even though Chinese newspapers and magazines can be read only by those who have a certain level of Chinese education, Chinese-language television can be enjoyed by all. The availability of a variety of Chinese print materials and of Chinese radio and television programming has made life enjoyable for many immigrants. Other developments, such as shopping malls where a huge variety of Chinese goods are available and where Chinese is the spoken language, have made Chinese immigrants feel very much at home.

Furthermore, the existence of a large number of Chinese restaurants that serve different types of Chinese food from different areas of China has improved the quality of life for Chinese immigrants. Going out for dim sum has become one of the favourite pastimes for Canadians, including those of Chinese heritage. This environment allows Wing to feel very much at home in Canada.[28] Wing mentioned that she takes great pride in the progress of the ethnic Chinese in Canadian society in recent years. This is an important aspect of the Chinese Canadian community, which is increasingly more connected with the mainstream community. This is not only because of the large number of Chinese immigrants to Canada, but it is also the result of the multicultural policy of the federal government. By the end of the 1980s, many of the social agencies that started as Chinese organizations, such as Carefirst and CICS in Toronto, became more inclusive of other groups and offered services to everyone in the community.[29]

Other voluntary groups, including the Heart and Stroke Foundation and St John Ambulance, have their Chinese chapters. In many fundraising events, especially the Cancer Foundation and the telethon for the Hospital for Sick Children in Toronto, the Chinese Canadian communities have been very much involved. On the other hand, fundraising for the Mon Sheong Foundation and Yee Hong Foundation is supported and attended by many from the mainstream community. To the Chinese Canadian communities in Toronto, the positive exposure of their members in mainstream media has given them a feeling of inclusiveness that did not exist before the 1980s.

The importance of the Chinese media to the members of the Chinese Canadian and mainstream communities cannot be overestimated. In the 1980s, because of the influx of wealthy immigrants from Hong Kong, Canadian business communities began to pay a great deal of attention to these newcomers. Advertising and public relations companies that helped the mainstream communities to reach their prospective ethnic Chinese clientele appeared on the Canadian scene. These companies had a symbiotic relationship with the magazines, newspapers, radio, and TV stations, and supported them by buying advertising for their clients.[30]

The advertisements were often translations of English messages into Chinese.

The following is an interview with Heather, who came to Canada at the end of the 1980s. She was able to benefit from the expansion of the use of Chinese media. Her interview was done by telephone in the summer of 2002. I had never met her before, but she felt quite comfortable speaking to me because her training was in communications. She spoke entirely in Cantonese.

❖ I was born in Hong Kong in December 1950. My family left China around 1948. I am one of two children in the family. My father was in business, selling clocks and watches. I went to a Chinese school for both primary and secondary education. After graduation, I went to Baptist College to study advertising and public relations.[31] It was a four-year course, and I graduated in 1973 with a diploma in communication.

I worked as editor for a Chinese women's magazine in Hong Kong for four years, and then I worked for a TV station as the editor for their weekly magazine. Unfortunately, this station went bankrupt. In the meantime, I got married in 1976. My husband is also in advertising. When the TV station went bankrupt, I was already pregnant, so I decided I wasn't going to work full-time anymore. Soon after my first son was born. I continued to work as a freelance writer for magazines and newspapers.

My husband worked as creative director in a large American-owned PR firm, making close to four hundred thousand Hong Kong dollars annually. As a freelance writer, I was making approximately two hundred thousand Hong Kong dollars, so we were in a very secure financial position, and by 1988 we had already paid off our mortgage.

I believe it was God's will that we moved to Canada. A few months before we decided to immigrate to Canada, my husband had a new boss who discriminated against the Chinese. Many of the Chinese personnel were not only suddenly not trusted with work responsibilities, despite their experience in the company, but their salaries were frozen. My husband and a few others were very unhappy. Normally, it was very easy for him to find a new job, but not during those few months.

At an advertising reception, my husband met a friend who told him he was immigrating to Canada the following month. He also said that for applicants with advertising experience, they would be awarded ten points in the points system. When he came home, he discussed the possibility with me and asked me to pick up an application form from Canadian Immigration when I was in Central [central part of Hong Kong] the next day.

Heather's story of her husband's encounter with racism in Hong Kong proved that it can, and does, happen anywhere in the world. Their reason for immigrating to Canada was partly because their friends were going to immigrate and partly because of the points system that would award ten points to anyone who had advertising experience. This was in the late 1980s when there was a great need in Canada for mainstream corporations to reach the Chinese Canadian communities, so those with advertising experience from Hong Kong were very welcome because they would be bilingual in English and Chinese. Heather's migration story was one of chain migration – but of friends, not family:

❖ We had little reason to leave Hong Kong because both our parents were in Hong Kong, and we were both making good money. However, many of our friends were immigrating to Canada, and we were often asked when we were going to emigrate. We didn't look into job opportunities in Canada and had no idea how we would be able to maintain our standard of living.

In April 1987 my husband applied to immigrate as an independent immigrant. He was given ten points as his friend said, because Canada needed people with advertising experience. We put in our application, and within ten days we were asked to fill out the detailed application. Three months later, we were given landed immigrant status and were informed that we had to come to Canada within a year. In fact, August 8 would have been the last day for us to leave for Canada. When the new South African boss heard that my husband was leaving, he turned around and told him that he was doing a good job and even offered him a raise with back pay.

We came to Toronto with our son that summer. Even though I didn't have any family here, my husband's younger brother and his family were here. We do have a lot of friends through our church, so we were well taken care of. In our first two months here, we stayed with a friend from our church.

In Heather's life, the social group at their church played an important role. As more Chinese Christians immigrated to Canada, Chinese churches of different denominations were established across the country. In the stories of Lucy, Hope, and Lily, the social circles at their respective churches were a very important part of their lives. It was the same for Heather.

❖ We sold our residence in Hong Kong when the price wasn't at its highest. Because we were leaving Hong Kong, we had to leave some money for our parents, so we came to Canada with little more than two hundred and forty thousand Canadian dollars' cash. After buying a house, a car, and household appliances, there was only a thousand dollars left in the bank. We were advised by our friends at church to pay cash for the house because the interest rate was very high at the time. Times were so tough then. I still remember writing down every day what I spent that day, and I had never done that before. I also remember, for half a year, I only spent three hundred dollars.

After we arrived, my husband was offered a job at a Chinese newspaper. We didn't have a car at that time. He was commuting to downtown every day, two hours each way. After two weeks, it became too much for him and he stopped. He was then asked by friends to help sell products because Christmas was approaching. He did it, but he was only paid six dollars an hour, and for someone who was used to high pay, it was a great disappointment.

You see, our difficulty was that we could only work in Chinese, and the market for that is limited. My husband had high recommendations from his former PR company in Hong Kong to the branch in Canada, but it wasn't much use because he could only work in Chinese. We kept praying for God's guidance. In January 1989 my husband was introduced to work for a Chinese cable company. He did a variety of jobs for them, such as broadcasting and PR. He remained there for eleven years. In 1990 he was asked to work for a company that had its head office in Hong Kong.

He was with them seventeen months, and the company went bankrupt.

Since we came to Canada, because I didn't have a car myself, and no household help, I thought it best that I should work freelance at home. I worked for different magazines and newspapers, but the pay was very little for a lot of work. In the summer of 1989, my mother died and I went back to Hong Kong for the funeral. On my return to Canada, I found out I was pregnant again. I was really desperate because we were financially strapped and hesitated having another child that we didn't think we could support. However, we believe in God, and since God gave him to us, we should have him.

The financial dilemma that Heather and her family were in was not uncommon to many immigrants even though they had good well-paying jobs before they immigrated. Her husband was given ten points in the points system because of his profession, but he was not able to find similar work when he arrived in Canada because of language difficulties. Her husband's situation was similar to that of Faith, whose profession was highly prized in Canada. After arrival, they were not able to find jobs commensurate with those they had before emigration.[32]

❖ By the end of the 1980s, the Chinese market was beginning to boom because of the influx of immigrants from Hong Kong. That was around the time my second son was born. There was more work for both my husband and me, such as making Chinese brochures, various advertisements to the Chinese communities, as well as other media work. My husband was also working freelance to supplement his income from the Chinese cable company.

I also started getting busy with freelance work from 1989 on. I worked with different magazines for the Chinese market, such as publications that feature homes, women, as well as business. At the same time, I was writing articles for Hong Kong newspapers about the life of Chinese Canadians for the Hong Kong readers, such as the beauty of the autumn leaves and the phenomenon of the popularity of garage sales, etcetera. I was sometimes asked to translate press releases from English to Chinese. I also worked on the monthly magazine published by the Chinese cable TV, wrote some of the programming as well as advertising scripts.

In 1992 I started writing as a volunteer for a Christian monthly, mainly targeting non-Christian readers. By 1998 I became a paid staff member and since 1999 I have been its chief editor and writer.

The wealth of the Hong Kong immigrants as a group that the mainstream companies wanted to target was beneficial to Heather and her husband professionally. The proliferation of Chinese media by the end of the 1980s not only provided employment for people like them but also gave a great deal of enjoyment to Chinese seniors such as Wing.[33]

❖ By 1990 we felt more settled. We are really glad we came when we did because my eldest son was about nine years old, so he was young enough to integrate into Canadian society. He has just finished university, studying computer science. We never want to go back to Hong Kong because we like the family life here. Canada is a wonderful country for children to grow up in, and there are so many opportunities available to them.

My husband doesn't like social life much, but in Hong Kong he had to go out all the time because of his work. Here in Canada, we have a lot more time together. My husband is a handyman. He likes building things and making things for our home. I have learned to cook since I came to Canada, and we like putting potluck dinners together with friends. Even though we both work very hard, our life is very relaxed. We sometimes go to places like Niagara-on-the-Lake on the weekend and stay overnight. We always go to church on Sunday.

Heather's comments about family life in Canada were similar to Karen's. They both gave very distinct examples of the differences between family life in Canada and the lack of it in Hong Kong.

❖ Our parents never immigrated to Canada. Mine have both passed away now, and my husband's mother was not eligible because of illness, so his parents live in Hong Kong. Whenever we visit Hong Kong, my husband doesn't look up his former colleagues because he doesn't want them to persuade him to go back there to work. In fact, he had an attractive offer in 1989 from the company he worked for before, but he turned it down because he really liked the life in Canada.

The settlement story of Heather reflects how much the Chinese Canadian communities have changed since the end of the Second World War. By the end of the 1980s, it had become necessary for mainstream Canada to reach out to these communities in all the major cities across Canada, and especially in Toronto and Vancouver.

In order to have a better understanding of the Chinese Canadian communities by the end of the 1980s, aside from the story of Wing, more will be said about informants who were sponsored by their children. The phenomenon of children sponsoring their parents in immigration began at the end of the 1960s. Because of the immigration regulation that was introduced in 1967 which allowed applications for landed immigrant status from within Canada, many Chinese students came to Canada on student visas and, upon graduation, having been offered employment in Canada, sponsored their parents and other family members (see, for instance, the interviews with Carol and Rose).[34]

The following is an interview of Han, who was sponsored by her son in 1980. Han was interviewed in my office in Toronto in the summer of 2001. She was one of the two women who came with informant Wing. Han spoke in Cantonese but did not give me her age. Judging by what she said, she would have been born in the 1920s.

❖ I was born in Macao and went to school there. Because I believe the Portuguese were oppressive to the Chinese, I refused to learn their language. I spent my youth helping my parents in their restaurant business. I got married in 1945 in Macao and have five children. My husband worked on shipping lines and later in restaurants. When my children were older, I went to work for relatives, first in a theatre, which lasted for quite a while, and later for an import-export company, owned by relatives, exporting goods from China.

In 1966 there were riots in Macao which had spilled over from the terrible political conditions in China [these preceded the ones that took place in Hong Kong]. I felt it was unsafe in Macao, so I sent my children to school in Hong Kong. When my eldest daughter graduated from high school, she went into nursing and worked at one of the government hospitals. In 1968 I wanted to immigrate to Canada. By then, the riots had already spilled into Hong Kong, and I thought it was time to plan for the family to go abroad.

Here is another story of a family wanting to leave Hong Kong because of the influence of the Cultural Revolution in China, which had led to riots in Macao and then in Hong Kong.

❖ In 1969 my second son applied to come to Canada to study electrical engineering. That was during the time when Trudeau was prime minister, and immigration regulations were changed so that students studying in Canada could apply to become landed immigrants. My second son applied immediately. When my third and fourth sons graduated from high school, they also came to Canada as students. By then, I was left in Hong Kong with my youngest daughter because my husband had passed away.

In 1979 my second son applied for the rest of the family to immigrate to Canada. It was very easy because, in less than a year, my daughter and I were granted landed immigrant status. In 1980 I was very happy to be with all my children again and to live in Canada, which is a more peaceful society than Hong Kong.

Even though I had a good job in Hong Kong and was making a good income, I didn't have unrealistic expectations when I came to Canada. I didn't expect to be working in a similar job as in Hong Kong and was willing to do anything. I worked in a factory in an import-export company and also did some home knitting. I retired in 1992.

People were so nice to me when I first arrived in Canada. The bus drivers were polite, and people always greeted me by saying good morning. People didn't use to lock their doors at home, but now public safety is no longer the way it was.

Since my retirement, I had been volunteering at church – the whole family is Catholic. I have also helped seniors by driving them to go out, like today, and I have made many friends over the years. I have been living in a seniors' apartment for ten years now.

Han, like some of my other interviewees, migrated twice. The pattern of double migration is very common among Chinese immigrants, as of course is family chain migration, which also was part of Han's experience. Her friend Lee is another who was sponsored by her son. Lee was interviewed in my office in Toronto in the summer of 2001 after Wing and Han. She spoke in Cantonese.

❖ I was born in 1913 in Macao. My family moved to Hong Kong when I was two years old. I was educated in Chinese schools until the third year of middle school. In 1935 I got married and subsequently had six children. I've been a housewife all my life.

When the Japanese invaded Hong Kong, my family went to China. My husband was in the import-export business before the war. At the end of the war, we went back to Hong Kong, and my husband went into the real estate business and remained in it until he retired, when we moved to Canada in 1968.

In 1957 my eldest son went to McGill to study. In 1960 my second son went to McGill. Subsequently, my third son also went to McGill. In 1967 riots started in Hong Kong. In 1968 my eldest son sponsored my husband and me and our youngest son to Canada. Our two daughters were educated in Hong Kong and worked there, but they also moved to Canada, one in 1968 and the other in 1975.

After we moved to Canada, I was bored at home because the children had all grown up, so I worked at Inn on the Park, doing mending. I like doing needlework. I retired in my sixties. I also did some home knitting subsequently.

When I first came to Canada I regretted it. The most difficult thing for me was the language. I have never had any interest in learning English, even in Hong Kong, so I found it difficult in Canada. But then it was my own fault because I never bothered to take lessons. Somehow, I am able to understand what is asked of me in English.

I volunteered for a few months at the Gar Lan Centre.[35] I was asked to visit old people to see how they were doing, and to chat with them. I didn't particularly like doing that because it's not very helpful unless I could clean their homes for them. In 1980, when my husband and I moved into a seniors' apartment, I stopped volunteering because the commuting was too inconvenient, since I didn't drive. I used to drive in Hong Kong, but because of the language problem here, I would never be able to explain myself if I ever got into a car accident.

Public security now is so different from when I first came to Canada in 1968. People were much more honest then. Lost wallets would be returned, and parcels could be left at the front door for days and people wouldn't take them. Now, the world has changed.

I get a pension of $900 a month, with one-third going to pay for the seniors' apartment. I appreciate the social security in Canada despite the high taxes my children are paying. Besides old age benefits, young people get subsidized education and free health care, plus a lot of other benefits.

My husband passed away at the age of ninety-two. He was eleven years older than me. In the seniors' apartment, I still have the company of my friends and neighbours.

It is interesting that Lee should mention the relationship between the high taxes paid by her children and her own social security benefits. This had been a major concern of policy makers in the Immigration Department. There had been various schemes to reduce the dependency ratio of immigration to population in order to support pensions for the elderly.

By the 1990s, the ethnic Chinese communities in Canada had become linguistically and culturally very diverse. One now meets Spanish-speaking Chinese from Peru, French-speaking Chinese from Mauritius, and Hindi-speaking Chinese from India. However, by far the majority of the Chinese immigrants until 1998 were from Hong Kong.[36] Since then, the majority have been Mandarin speakers from Mainland China.[37] From 1998, there was a gradual decrease from Hong Kong to just 1,324 in 2008. This decrease was partly the result of the booming economy in Hong Kong and the lack of job opportunities in Canada, as well as greater confidence in the political future of Hong Kong.

When the Tiananmen Square incident happened on 4 June 1989, the Canadian government allowed visa students from China studying in Canadian universities to become permanent residents. It was at this point that immigration from the People's Republic of China started to rise, and within two years the number reached 14,203 before dropping down to 9,485 in 1993. Subsequently, it continued to rise to 42,292 in 2005, the highest number in recent years.[38]

Today, the ethnic Chinese remain one of the largest groups of immigrants entering Canada. The groups from Hong Kong, Mainland China, and Taiwan, being culturally different, have their respective organizations in major Canadian cities. As of 2010, Chinese Canadian identity entered a new phase.

Chapter 10

Conclusion

Since the 1960s, the immigration of Chinese women with skills and education has been an important milestone. The fact that some of these women immigrated to Canada as heads of household would have been unheard of previously. In recapping the immigration of Chinese women, we note that before the 1960s, Canada's immigration policy was explicitly racist, favouring the entry of white immigrants, particularly those of British ancestry. The policy was based not only on race but also on class. Between 1884 and 1922, a head tax was imposed on Chinese labourers to discourage their entry, but this did not apply to Chinese merchants and those of the educated class, their wives, and family members. This policy was changed in 1923 when all entry was prohibited, with just a few exceptions.

Until the 1960s, Chinese women could immigrate only as dependants of men. Because of the ambiguous definition of the merchant class, some Chinese women entered Canada as wives of merchants, and most ended up working for the men. Women in these families became an integral part of Chinese immigrant life, and their economic contributions were vital to the survival of their families. But there were very few women for many years, partly because of the Chinese tradition of keeping the wives at home in China to look after the in-laws, the children, and the graves of the ancestors. However, in 1947, when Chinese exclusion was repealed and the civil war was raging in China, many of the Chinese Canadian men began to sponsor their wives and dependent children to come to Canada. This gradually transformed the bachelor societies and marks the beginning of my oral history research.

Since the majority of Chinese immigrants were from South China and Hong Kong until the latter part of the 1990s, my twenty-eight interviewees were Cantonese and Szeyup speakers. Based on their reminiscences, learning about their lives and the societies in which they lived before emigration and then hearing of their separation, their suffering and longing, their reasons for immigration to Canada, and their settlement experiences here, as well as their joy at reunification with their families. Along the way, I also learned of the latitude that Canadian immigration officers had in the decision-making process. The voices of these women bring to life the social and political backgrounds of China, Hong Kong, and Canada over the last half of the twentieth century.

With regard to the issues of patriarchy and racial and gender discrimination, my informants have all found their own agency in fighting for their rights, which proves that the view of Chinese women as victims is only partially true. Today, as in Imperial China, education remains the key to women's agency. Some of my informants have shown that those with higher education were able to use their own personal efforts as well as entering the public domain in their fight against discrimination. They are the women who have integrated well into mainstream Canadian society.

The fact that Chinese women were victims of patriarchy because of Chinese traditions raises the question whether the separation of Chinese families was entirely due to Canadian government policies. Chinese traditions ruled the lives of the women in the villages in China but, surprisingly; they also seem to have applied to Rena, who was a well-educated young woman when she immigrated to Canada. She was a victim not only of patriarchy but also of the Canadian immigration system, because she was married.

Canada's immigration policy in the latter part of the twentieth century was a reflection of the need for human capital, and a new era in immigration emerged based on skills and education. When the points system for selecting immigrants was first put in place, the demand was high in various less-skilled and middle-skilled categories, such as nursing, teaching, and clerical and administrative services, as well as in construction and industry. Many Chinese women who entered Canada in the 1960s and 1970s under those categories were often better qualified than was required.[1] Their immigration to Canada was surprisingly quick, and some visitors who had the needed skills were persuaded by immigration officers to come as landed immigrants instead.

Points were awarded for the occupation of the principal applicant, with no points given to the dependant unless husband and wife were co-applicants. In the latter case, a woman might apply as head of household if her profession was in greater demand than her husband's, as occurred with Faith. Others, such as Heather, immigrated as dependants even though husband and wife were equally qualified professionally. They continued to work to provide for their families, often working two to three jobs so that the husband could have time for language and job training, even though the wife's economic contribution was not recognized by Canadian immigration authorities.[2]

Most of my interviewees who immigrated from the 1960s on were independent immigrants under the points system. In the interviews, I learned about their settlement experiences and how well or badly the system worked. Some were able to find work similar to what they had done in their home society or work that was related to their training, while others had great difficulty because of differences in work environment or job description, as well as a lack of fluency in one of the official languages.

Some of these women talked about gender and race discrimination in their settlement experience. They believe it was because they are women and belong to an ethnic minority. I learned how they overcame the difficult situations in their lives and turned them to their advantage. Other informants expected that there would be discrimination because they were Chinese but were pleasantly surprised.

While Canada continued to need immigrants with skills, family-class immigrants were those emphasized during the economic downturn of the late 1970s and early 1980s. By the end of the 1980s, Chinese Canadian communities were well established, to the extent that Chinese immigrants could feel very much at home in such cities as Toronto and Vancouver, where there were shopping malls similar to those in Hong Kong, along with Chinese-language media and entertainment, and a variety of restaurants catering to them, as well as social services to take care of the seniors. It was in this period that some of my informants were able to find work within the ethnic enclave.

The 1980s were the years when business immigration, which had begun in the 1950s, was officially established, with the Canadian government seeking immigrants for their wealth and human capital. Many of those immigrating under the business category were Asians, and some were Chinese businesswomen. A few of those I interviewed experienced racism but were able to overcome it, while others, such as Belinda, came across deeply ingrained racist attitudes in their work.[3] It is interesting to note that as early as the 1970s, the findings of the Department of Manpower and Immigration had already confirmed that Asians have a particularly high propensity for business.[4] Authors Wong and Netting believe that these studies foreshadowed the Asianization of business immigration that was put in place in the 1980s, with the Hong Kong Chinese as targets.[5]

The investor category placed great emphasis on capital in order to encourage its flow into Canada.[6] The fact that business immigrants have many qualities that are valued by Canadian capitalist society, in addition to the capital they bring into the country and the jobs they create, cannot be overemphasized. Their willingness to work hard, their perseverance through hardship, and their keen competitiveness are respected, even though, paradoxically, the competitiveness was also perceived as a threat by some Canadians.[7]

There are those who say the points system has an inherent class bias – that discrimination based on race has been replaced by that of class, since it is mostly those from middle- and upper-class backgrounds who qualify as independent immigrants; they are the ones who have had the opportunity to acquire the "appropriate" educational, vocational, language skills required by the Canadian government. But this is what the points system was meant to achieve in the case of independent immigrants. Because Canada needed skilled workers, immigration was administered by the Department of Manpower and Immigration.

Although the points system was supposed to remove racial bias, there are those who view Canadian Immigration in the 1980s and 1990s as discriminatory, as evidenced by the number of offices it set up in different geographic locations around the world. There were few in African countries, but in Hong Kong the number was increased in order to facilitate the active recruitment of entrepreneurs with lucrative portfolios. Between the mid-1980s and the mid-1990s, Hong Kong had twenty-four Canadian immigration officers, more than at any other post.[8]

Based on an overseas survey published in 1991, more than half of the Hong Kong respondents obtained their immigration status by virtue of their professional skills.[9] The most common reason for emigration was the fear of Hong Kong's instability after 1997 and the possible loss of individual freedom and the freedom to travel, but there was also the wish to have one's children educated in Canada. The initial adjustments in Canada were related to language, climate, workplace, social life, and transportation. Although 74 percent of the immigrants were able to get their first job in Canada within the first three months, 65.8 percent experienced a drop in rank or level. Nevertheless, 80.4 percent of the respondents rated their emigration decisions as good or excellent.[10]

Demographics have long been a major concern for policy makers in the Immigration Department. In the 1970s a large proportion of the population was of child-bearing age, so the population was expected to grow until 2026. However since the Canadian fertility rate was below the population replacement level, it was estimated that from 2026 on, the population would experience a slow decline to 25 million (the 1986 level) by 2086, and the decline would continue. Without immigration, the below-replacement fertility rates would eventually lead to Canada's disappearance, even though this would take a long time. Meanwhile, the Canadian population is living longer, so the future population will have a higher proportion in the older age group. Therefore, fertility is a major demographic force affecting not only the age structure but also the sustainability of our pension system.[11]

The government undertook a three-year demographic review, and in 1989 the report *Charting Canada's Future* was published, connecting the Canadian fertility rate with immigration. It indicated that immigration was not a good tool for meeting the demographic goals set out in earlier policy statements because the population growth path will peak, followed by a decline, before eventually stabilizing.[12] According to this review, immigration was not the solution for a naturally aging population.

Even though immigration may not solve our long-term population dilemma in the attainment of an optimal equilibrium, it is still justifiable to conclude that positive immigration rates are needed to ensure that Canada's population does not fall below a level that would make it infeasible to administer such a geographically dispersed country. It can

also be argued that a certain amount of "new blood" can provide benefits to the economy.[13] So the debates on our immigration policy continue, and no solution to the problem seems forthcoming.[14]

What is the significance of the above information in relation to the
ethnic Chinese population, the fastest-growing ethnic group in Canada?
In 1991, 69 percent of this group consisted of immigrants, and they were
slightly younger than the total Canadian population. With balanced immigration between ethnic Chinese men and women since the 1980s, this
group will be contributing to the population growth, even though the
proportion of children was the same as the overall Canadian population.[15]

Despite the demographic review, the class and gender biases of our
immigration system remain important for their impact on the immigration of women, especially for Chinese women, since ethnic Chinese
have been by far the largest immigrant group entering Canada in recent
decades. From an economic point of view, immigration from Hong
Kong remains important for capital investments in Canada. Taking economic, social, and cultural aspects together, the immigrants from Hong
Kong can also be seen as a bridge across the Pacific, linking Canada to
Asia, keeping in mind that today more than 250,000 Canadians live in
greater China, mostly in Hong Kong.

Another aspect of Chinese immigration of great importance to
Canada is the educational attainment of the immigrants and their children. Earlier, I referred to the education system in Hong Kong and the
importance of the availability of higher education in Canada, not only
in connection with my informants' own achievements but because of
their expectation of and pride in the success of the next generation.
Many of my informants told me that they did not mind the hardship
they endured as immigrants to Canada because of the satisfaction they
had in foreseeing the educational and job opportunities of their descendants.[16]

If indeed the "Chinese work ethic," the networks, and the traditional
stress on education are transferred to future generations, the result will
be greatly beneficial to Canadian society. The parliamentarians of the
1920s who argued against the immigration of Chinese women in order
to contain the growth of the ethnic Chinese population would have been
really surprised.

In terms of the Chinese Canadian community as a whole, its status
changed from a community that was excluded from the rights of citi-

zenship – and was looked upon as inferior – to one that is now envied by many mainstream Canadians. In 1990 Environics conducted a national survey for the Laurier Institute which revealed that 56 percent of Canadians supported the investment immigration program, a program that brought into Canada the largest number of immigrants from Hong Kong. The most important finding of this survey was that it showed that the most educated Canadians were also the most tolerant.[17]

Looking at the economic effects of Chinese immigration to Canada in the latter part of the twentieth century, Graham E. Johnson concludes that the business immigration program worked in favour of British Columbia, particularly Vancouver, until the end of the 1990s.[18] During the last part of the 1980s and throughout the 1990s, because of its deep involvement with activities of the Asia Pacific region, British Columbia had been insulated from the worst ravages of the recession that affected Central and Atlantic Canada.[19]

With the characteristics of many Chinese immigrants – their wealth, education, and skills – do we see changes in Canadian attitudes and behaviour towards them? From many media reports, such as CTV's "Campus Giveaway" aired in 1979 and mentioned in Rena's interview, one sees resentment instead of welcome. Asian immigrants, particularly the Chinese from Hong Kong, complain about the sensational treatment by the mainstream media, owned and dominated by Anglo-Canadians.[20]

As noted before, racial tensions were rampant throughout the 1980s and into the 1990s, particularly in Vancouver. What can Canadians expect in future? Wong and Netting maintain that antagonism towards business immigrants is unlikely to disappear among working-class Canadians but that it should diminish over time within the capitalist class because of mutual class interests. The children of the wealthy already attend the same schools and learn each other's languages. They belong to the same clubs, marry into one another's families, and are often involved in business together. As national borders become increasingly open to capital investment, whether Asian or non-Asian, members of the international capitalist class will increasingly be leading participants in a global economy that will determine the social structure of nations.[21]

Despite what has been said, racism again raised its head at the end of 2010 with the article "Too Asian" in *Maclean's* magazine, mentioned in Carol's interview.[22] Like "Campus Giveaway," it was an attack on Canadian university students who happen to look Asian (Chinese), regardless of the fact that the majority are Canadians. Undoubtedly, as long as there are people, there will be racial conflict, and it is up to the different levels of government to keep it in check.

It would be advantageous for the Canadian government to have a long-term strategy regarding the worldwide Chinese networks, which have a combined economic output in the hundreds of billions of dollars. In order to come to grips with these networks and be able to use them to the greatest advantage, the government must understand the ways in which its policy decisions affect them in the areas of taxation, foreign investments, immigration, citizenship, education, and access to public services.[23] Further complicating the issue are new technologies that challenge the capacity of governments to influence national identity and achieve social control.[24]

The rise of transnational communities and networks has received increasing attention in the media, and ethnic Chinese play a very important role. A good example is Rose, whose company spans the continents. Additionally, Amber and Carol have clients both in Canada and in Asia. From the 1980s on, many of the immigrants from Hong Kong have been transnational elites, and since many of the transnational networks straddle several continents, they challenge policy makers in a variety of ways by virtue of their wealth, their political power, and the human capital they embody. It is vitally important that the Canadian government formulate an effective global strategy.

As mentioned at the end of chapter 9, by 1998 the number of immigrants from the People's Republic of China exceeded the number from Hong Kong and Taiwan. And as the number of the former increased, so did the percentage of immigrants being admitted in the economic class, based on the points system. This increase has been driven largely by the well educated. Between 1995 and 2000, the number of Chinese immigrants with university degrees increased by 509 percent. However, this sizable pool of immigrants with high human capital will not continue if economic opportunities for university graduates improve in the People's Republic of China.[25]

Although the research for this book has been limited to immigrants from South China and Hong Kong, whose immigration numbers had dwindled by the year 2000, the more recent large intake of immigrants from Mainland China has made a huge impact on Chinese Canadian communities. The arrivals from the People's Republic of China since 1998, together with the immigrants from Hong Kong since the 1980s, have formed communities that reach across international borders, bridging the Asia Pacific and reaching around the world.

At the turn of the twenty-first century, the Chinese Canadian communities have a character of their own. They are not merely a reflection of China, Hong Kong, or Taiwan. Despite the anti-Chinese sentiment that has surfaced from time to time, the communities will continue to be fortified by an energetic entrepreneurial spirit, an emphasis on education, strong family values, and an attachment to the important Canadian values of equality and democracy, as evidenced in the policy of multiculturalism and the Charter of Rights and Freedoms.[26] In other words, this group has a unique Canadian identity that is most beneficial to Canada, both nationally and internationally.

Afterword

In many ways, this book reflects my life experiences as well as my observation of everything around me. Having grown up in China and Hong Kong and having spent the past fifty-four years in Canada as an active participant in the community, I have had the opportunity to live and experience the evolution of Chinese settlement in Canada.

I was born in Hong Kong in May 1941. The British government did not want to believe that Hong Kong would be invaded during the war, despite the fact that the Japanese army was already in south China, and it had not provided adequately for the colony's defence. When the attack began in early December, it lasted less than three weeks; Hong Kong was forced to surrender on Christmas Day. Owing to the lack of provisions in the colony, the Japanese government announced that the Chinese population could leave if it wished. My family went into China as refugees, just ahead of the invading Japanese imperial forces. We remained in China until the end of the Pacific War in 1945, when we returned home to Hong Kong, which had been reclaimed by the British government. Although I was just a small child, I have vivid memories of the war years in China and the difficult reconstruction period in postwar Hong Kong.

When the civil war ended in 1949 and the Chinese Communist Party established the People's Republic of China, refugees from the mainland flooded into Hong Kong. Some refugees arrived over land, while others came by boat; still others swam to Hong Kong. I met cousins I didn't know I had, as well as the children of my parents' friends from all over

China. I remember listening intently to the adults as they talked about the difficulties of life under the Communist government.

Being an observant child, I noticed how Hong Kong society was gradually being transformed before my eyes by the influx of refugees. It prospered because of the tens of thousands of people who entered the colony in order to build new lives there. Hong Kong soon turned from a refugee way station into a manufacturing hub. Over the years, it became a vibrant, creative, and increasingly wealthy metropolis and a major global financial centre.

I received my early education in Hong Kong before being sent to a boarding school in England, where I spent two years of high school. I didn't like boarding school, however, and returned to Hong Kong to complete my final year. In 1959 I came to Canada on a student visa to study at McGill University in Montreal. On arrival at the Vancouver airport, I saw many Chinese "picture brides" dressed up to meet their prospective Chinese Canadian husbands. Some of them brought gold jewellery as a form of dowry, which had to be declared to the customs officers. Little did I know that this was the only way that Chinese women could immigrate to Canada at that time – as dependants of men.

During my years at McGill, where I was studying towards an honours degree in history, the Chinatown in Montreal was very small and familiar. All the older generation spoke the Szeyup dialect, which the elders in my family also spoke. This was because all the early Chinese immigrants to Canada originated from the same part of South China where my family came from. It was not until after my graduation from McGill in the 1960s, when the Canadian immigration regulations began to change, that some of my former schoolmates in Hong Kong also immigrated to Canada. The introduction of the points system and the elimination of discriminatory selection based on nationality or race dramatically changed the face of Canadian immigration.

I met my husband at McGill, and we were married in 1962 upon my graduation. He had graduated from medical school in 1960. In 1967, with our young son, we moved from Montreal to Toronto because of the uncertain political situation in Quebec. The move was a bit of a cultural shock, as the two cities were so different. Our family grew, and by the late 1970s, once our three children were of school age, I went back to school myself to study fashion arts. Upon graduation, I opened my own fashion design business and I also became very involved with volunteering in the arts and cultural communities in Toronto.

The next decade saw tremendous changes in Canadian society, owing partly to the large influx of immigrants from Hong Kong as a result of the British government's decision to return sovereignty of Hong Kong to China. The citizens of Hong Kong, many of whom were refugees from Communist China, were worried about having to live under the Chinese government. At the same time, many Western democracies wished to attract these citizens as immigrants. As we have seen, Canada was one of them, establishing special business and investor programs for immigrants in an effort to attract dynamic entrepreneurs and business owners. Because of our multicultural policies, Canada became the number-one country of choice for immigration for the Hong Kong Chinese. Within just a few years, the numbers of ethnic Chinese and their businesses grew dramatically, particularly in Toronto and Vancouver. As a Cantonese from Hong Kong, I was fascinated to see these changes unfold. With the dramatic increase in immigration from many parts of the world, I saw Canadian society becoming increasingly diverse and Canada becoming the multicultural country it is today.

In the mid-1990s, I closed my fashion business in Toronto and returned to university to pursue graduate studies in history, obtaining first a master's degree and then a doctoral degree. I have always loved to learn about real events and real people from the past – and besides, I enjoyed doing research. While I was in the midst of my PhD program, in the fall of 1998, Prime Minister Jean Chrétien appointed me to the Senate of Canada. Although I was well known in Toronto through my voluntary activities in the community, I had little interest in politics, so my appointment came as a great surprise and an even greater honour. As the first Canadian of Asian heritage to receive a Senate appointment, I naturally assumed responsibility for issues that were relevant to the lives of Asian Canadians.

Since my appointment to the Senate, I have regularly spoken publicly to groups all across the country, from school-age children to retirees, about the benefits of living in a multicultural country and about the importance of integrating new Canadians. The moment my appointment was announced, I was "adopted" by many immigrants' and women's groups across Canada and welcomed by them. Over the years, I have visited all our provinces and territories and have got to know Canadians from every corner of the country, many of whom are immigrants who now call Canada home.

The experience of meeting so many new Canadians, whose life stories were transformed by their decision to immigrate, was a powerful reminder that history unfolds through the lives of individuals and the choices they make. For my doctoral research, I decided to record and analyze the life stories of more than two dozen Chinese women from South China and Hong Kong who came to Canada between the end of the Second World War and the early 1990s, as a way of exploring the historic patterns and everyday realities of immigration and integration into twentieth-century Canada.

When I began my research I was warned that the women whom I wished to interview might not be open to speaking their minds because of my position as a senator. In fact, I was humbled to discover that the women trusted me implicitly because I had grown up in China and Hong Kong, knew its history, and spoke Cantonese – like them. They knew that I could understand their stories because of our shared backgrounds in China and in Canada, and that I would empathize with them. Some referred to me as their "village cousin" and others as their compatriot from Hong Kong.

I found that the interviewees were happy to have someone interested in their stories, since women's experiences have often been dismissed or regarded as unimportant. After our conversations, several of the women told me that they felt that a load had been lifted from them. A few of them brought snacks or their own baking to share; others brought photos to illustrate their stories.

When I listened to these women, I heard echoes of the past. Although the details differed from case to case, the essence of each story felt familiar and personal, invoking memories of my own family's history and my own journey to becoming a Canadian. I feel privileged to have had the opportunity to preserve the oral histories of these remarkable women, and I thank them for their generosity and cooperation, which have made this book possible.

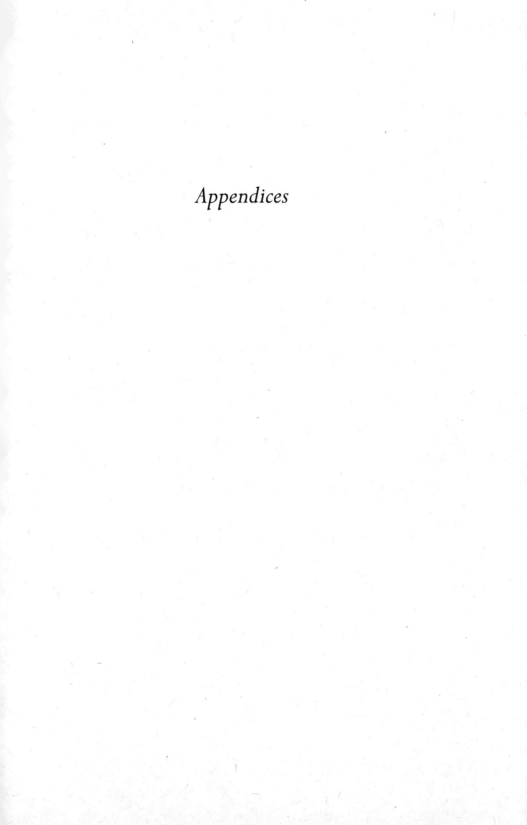

Appendices

Appendix 1

Interviewees

Chap.[1]	Name[2]	Marriage[3]	Emigration[4]	Age[5]	Criteria[6]	Occupation after emigration[7]
2	Chow	1930	1950	39	Dependant of husband	Worker in husband's restaurant
2	Kan	1928	1953	42	Dependant of husband	Farm labourer, factory worker
2	May	1947	1958	29	Dependant of husband	Salad maker
3	Gina	1961	1961	18	Dependant of husband	Sandwich and salad maker
4	Yee	1952	1952	22	Paper bride	Worker in husband's shoe repair
4	Lim	1966	1966	25	Dependant of husband	Worker in husband's restaurant

Chap.[1]	Name[2]	Marriage[3]	Emigration[4]	Age[5]	Criteria[6]	Occupation after emigration[7]
4	Irene	–	1967	5	Dependant of stepfather	Student, store clerk
4	Joyce	1956	1952	21	Paper daughter	Worker in husband's grocery store
5	Jean	1965	1964	24	Independent: secretary	Secretary
5	June	1967	1967	27	Independent: nurse	Nurse
5	Karen	1965	1968	27	Co-applicant: teacher	Schoolteacher
5	Iris	1973	1969	19	Dependant of father	Student, office worker, homemaker
6	Lucy	1968	1965* 1966	27	Independent: teacher	Schoolteacher

Chap.[1]	Name[2]	Marriage[3]	Emigration[4]	Age[5]	Criteria[6]	Occupation after emigration[7]
6	Hope	1968	1963* 1968	24	Independent: researcher	University tutor
6	Rena	1963	1963* 1968	27	Dependant of husband	Schoolteacher, homemaker, piano teacher, painter
6	Susan	1953	1970	35	Co-applicant: nurse	Seamtress, child caregiver, seniors' home caregiver, garment finisher
7	Nui	1946	1978	50	Dependant of husband	Farm worker, dish washer
7	Lily	1970	1977	28	Co-applicant: piano teacher	Piano teacher, concert pianist
8	Daisy	1978	1986	33	Principal applicant: garment distributor	garment distributor restaurant owner

Chap.[1]	Name[2]	Marriage[3]	Emigration[4]	Age[5]	Criteria[6]	Occupation after emigration[7]
8	Belinda	–	1989	26	Independent: investor	Insurance broker, real estate developer
8	Amber	1980	1974* 1983	30	Husband is Canadian citizen	Financial analyst, investment broker
8	Carol	1977	1972* 1977	23	Dependant of sister	Student, hospital technician, real estate broker
9	Faith	1979	1989	38	Principal applicant: university administrator	Administrator, PhD student
9	Rose	1977	1974* 1977	24	Husband is Canadian citizen	Ran travel agency with husband
9	Wing	1949	1974	48	Dependant of daughter	Homemaker

Chap.[1]	Name[2]	Marriage[3]	Emigration[4]	Age[5]	Criteria[6]	Occupation after emigration[7]
9	Heather	1976	1987	37	Dependant of husband	Media freelance writer
9	Han	1945	1980	53	Dependant of son	Factory worker, office clerk
9	Lee	1935	1968	55	Dependant of son	Homemaker

1 Chapter reference
2 Informant (pseudonym)
3 Year of marriage
4 Year of emigration or obtaining immigrant status (*entry on student visa)
5 Age at emigration
6 Criteria of emigration
7 Occupational profile after emigration

Appendix 2

The Points System

	1967	1974	1978	1986	1993	2001	2003	2010[1]
Education	20	20	12	12	15	25	25	25
Experience	–	–	8	8	8	21	21	21
Specific vocation	10	10	15	15	17			
Occupational demand	15	15	15	10	10			
Age	10	10	10	10	10	10	10	10
Arranged employment	10	10	10	10	10	10	10	10
Language	10	10	10	15	14	24	24	24
Personal suitability	15	15	10	10	10			
Levels	–	–	–	10	8			
Relative	0/3/5+	0/3/5		5	–			
Destination	5	5	5	–	–			
Adaptability (family in Canada; studied in Canada)						10	10	10
Total	100	100	100	100	100	100	100	100
Pass mark	50	50	50	70	67	75	67	67

1 In 2010 the points system was revised as follows: "According to Ministerial Instructions issued by Citizenship and Immigration Canada on 26 June 2010, skilled worker applications received after 26 June 2010 can only be processed if certain Citizenship and Immigration Canada (CIC) requirements are met. Only after these criteria are met does the points system apply. Firstly, an official language proficiency test must be taken at a CIC-designated agency. Secondly, an offer of arranged employment in Canada or one year of continuous full-time paid work experience (or part-time equivalent) in one of the CIC's eligible occupations is required. Work experience must have been within the last ten years in a managerial position (Skill Type 0), a professional occupation (Skill Level A), or a technical occupation or skilled trade which is listed on the Canadian National Occupational Classification (NOC) list."

Source: Department of Citizenship and Immigration, "Immigration and Refugee Protection Act: Updated Ministerial Instructions," *Canada Gazette*, 26 June, 2010. Online at http://gazette.gc.ca/rp-pr/p1/2010/2010-06-26/html/notice-avis-eng.html.

Appendix 3

Changes in Name of the Department of Immigration

1917	Department of Immigration and Colonization
1936–50	The portfolio was abolished. Immigration became part of the Department of Mines and Resources
1950	Department of Citizenship and Immigration
1966	Department of Manpower and Immigration
1977	Department of Employment and Immigration
1994	Department of Citizenship and Immigration
2008	Department of Citizenship and Immigration's portfolio was expanded to include multiculturalism.

Appendix 4

Legislation and Regulations Pertaining
to the Chinese, 1867–1990

1869
Immigration Act (assented 22 June 1869, proclaimed on 1 January 1870).
Act established immigration offices in Canada, the United Kingdom,
and Europe. A "head tax" of $1.00 or $1.50 imposed for every immigrant
above the age of one year. Act applied to everyone who entered the country. (SC 1869, c 10)

1885
Act to Restrict and Regulate Chinese Immigration into Canada (assented
20 July 1885). Head tax of $50 charged on every Chinese entering
Canada, with the exception of diplomats, merchants, and students. Vessels could carry only one Chinese immigrant for every fifty tons of cargo.
Chinese already resident in Canada had to obtain certificates of residence in order to remain in Canada. (RSC 1885, c 71)

1900
Act Respecting and Restricting Chinese Immigration (assented 1 January
1902). Head tax increased to $100. British Columbia received half of tax.
One Chinese immigrant allowed per fifty tons of cargo. (SC 1900, c 32)

1903
Act Respecting and Restricting Chinese Immigration (assented 10 July
1903). Head tax increased to $500. (SC 1903, c 8)

1906

Act Respecting Immigration and Immigrants (assented 13 July 1906). The Chinese fall under the "class liable to exclusion from Canada." Most important was the provision permitting passage of immigration regulations by order-in-council. (SC 1906, c 19)

1908

Order-in-Council PC 1908–27. Prohibited immigrants who did not come to Canada on a continuous journey. All Asian immigrants had to be in possession of $200 in addition to being able to pay head tax.

1908

Act to Amend the Chinese Immigration Act (assented 20 July 1908). List of prohibited persons expanded; classes of persons exempted from head tax narrowed. Teachers added as exempted from paying head tax. All those exempted had to substantiate their status. Bona fide students would have their head taxes refunded after being in Canada for one year. (SC 1908, c 14)

1910

Act Respecting Immigration (assented 4 May 1910). Prohibited immigrants who did not come to Canada on continuous journey and also those belonging to any race deemed unsuited to the climate or requirements of Canada. Chapter 79 applied to the Chinese specifically: "All provisions of this Act not repugnant to the provisions of The Chinese Immigration Act shall apply as well to persons of Chinese origin as the other persons." (SC 1910, c 27, s 38)

1910

Order-in-Council PC 1910-924. Required immigrants to be in possession of "landing money" of $25 or $50, depending on the season.

1910

Landing Money for Asians, PC 1910-926 (May 1910). Required immigrants of Asian origin to have $200 per person.

1914

Act Respecting British Nationality, Naturalization and Aliens (assented 12 June 1914). Gave district, county, or superior court judges authority to determine whether aliens seeking to be naturalized were qualified. Few Chinese were naturalized because of this discretionary power. (SC 1914, C 44)

1914

War Measures Act. Gave the government wide powers to arrest, detain, and deport. (SC 1914, C 2)

1917

Act to Amend the Chinese Immigration Act (assented 25 July 1917). Clergy and students exempted from paying head tax. (SC 1917, C 7)

1919

Amendment to the Naturalization Act. Added new grounds for denying entry and deportation. Section 38 allowed Cabinet to prohibit any race, nationality, or class of immigrants by reason of "economic, industrial, or other condition temporarily existing in Canada" (unemployment was high at the time) because of their unsuitability or because of their "peculiar habits, modes of life and methods of holding property." (SC 1919, C 38)

1920

Dominion Elections Act (assented 1 July 1920). Recognized that every eligible Canadian over twenty-one, male or female, could vote in federal elections. This did not include aboriginal peoples or anyone barred from a provincial voter's list, including Asians. (SC 1920, C 46)

1921

Act to Amend the Chinese Immigration Act (assented 4 June 1921). Extended period that the Chinese could leave the country from twelve months to two years. Every Chinese who did not register on leaving Canada would be subject to a $500 head tax upon return. (SC 1921, C 21)

1922

Amendment to the Opium and Narcotic Drug Act (June 1922). Provided for deportation of "domiciled aliens" (i.e., immigrants who had been in Canada five years or more) with drug-related convictions. This measure was particularly directed against the Chinese. In 1923–24, 35 percent of deportations by the Pacific Division were under these provisions. (SC 1922, C 36)

1923

Order-in-Council PC 1923–182 (31 January 1923). (Period of high unemployment in Canada.) Prohibition of immigrants of any Asiatic race, except for agriculturalists, farm labourers, female domestic servants, wives, and Canadian citizens' children under age eighteen. Monetary requirements for all immigrants were lifted, except for Asians, whose "landing money" was increased to $250 per person.

1923

Act Respecting Chinese Immigration (assented 30 June 1923). 1 July became known as Humiliation Day. Total exclusion of Chinese entry into the country, except for diplomats, students, children of Canadians born in Canada, and well-established merchants. All persons of Chinese origin, irrespective of allegiance or citizenship, were subject to the act. The act provided for re-registration of all persons of Chinese origin. Vessels restricted to carrying one Chinese immigrant for every 250 tons. (Act did note that a person should not be deemed to be of Chinese origin if mother or a female ancestor was of Chinese origin.) The only ports of entry were Victoria and Vancouver. (SC 1923, C 38)

1930

Landing in Canada of Immigrants of Any Asiatic Race Prohibited, PC 2115 (16 September 1930). Exceptions were "wife and unmarried child under age eighteen of Canadian citizen legally admitted to and resident in Canada, who is in a position to receive and care for his dependents."

1938

Dominion Elections Act, Amended (assented 1 July 1938). Those disqualified from voting in a provincial election because of race were barred from voting in federal elections. This meant that Canadian citizens of

Chinese, Japanese, or Indian descent could not participate in the democratic process. (SC 1938, c 46)

1946

Act Respecting Citizenship, Nationality, Naturalization, and Status of Aliens (assented 27 June 1946, proclaimed 1 January 1947). Created a separate Canadian citizenship, distinct from British citizenship (Canada was the first Commonwealth country to do so). (SC 1946, c 15)

1947

Act to Amend the Immigration Act and to Repeal the Chinese Immigration Act (assented 14 May 1947). The Chinese Immigration Act, chapter 95 of the Revised Statutes of Canada, 1927, was repealed. The Chinese were put under the same rules as other Asian immigrants (see PC 2115, 16 September 1930). (SC 1947, c 19)

1948

Repeal of Section 14(2)(i) of chapter 46 of the Dominion Elections Act (assented 30 June 1948). (SC 1948, c 46)

1950

Amendment to Immigration Act re: Landing of Immigrants in Canada, PC 1950-2856 (9 June 1950). Special preferences given to Europeans. The fact that the provisions did not apply to the Asiatic race was especially mentioned. In consideration of political upheaval in China, the age of children of admissible Chinese Canadians was raised from eighteen to twenty-one. This rule was interpreted very liberally, so in some cases unmarried children up to age twenty-five were admitted. (SOR/50-232, *Canada Gazette*, 28 June 1950, 765)

1952

Immigration Act (proclaimed 1 June 1953). Every person seeking to come to Canada was presumed to be an immigrant unless the immigration officer was satisfied otherwise. Regulations passed concurrent with the act limited the landing in Canada of any Asian to nationals of a country with which the Government of Canada had entered into an agreement. Countries with previous agreements were China, Japan, India, Pakistan, and Sri Lanka. Regulations authorized special inquiry officers to bar entry on grounds of peculiar customs, habits, modes of life, or methods of holding property, as well as inability to become readily assimilated. The act provided for immigration appeal boards, made up of department officials, to hear appeals from deportation. (SC 1952, c 42)

1954

Immigration Regulations (Norms of Admissibility), PC 1954-1351 (17 September 1954). Asians who were Canadian citizens could sponsor wives, husbands, or unmarried children under the age of twenty-one, as well as fathers over the age of sixty-five and mothers over the age of sixty. Landing of immigrants was limited to nationals of a country with which Canada had entered into an agreement.

1955

Order-in-Council PC 1955-1551 (26 October 1955). Asians who were landed immigrants could now sponsor immediate family members. This was a very important change for the Chinese because many who immigrated after 1950 had not yet acquired citizenship.

1956

Order-in-Council PC 1956-785 (24 May 1956). Divided countries into categories of preferred status. In the same year, PC 2115 was abandoned.

1960

Chinese Adjustment Statement Program announced by Ellen Fairclough, Minister of Immigration, 9 June 1960. Included measures to curtail illegal entry of Chinese and to land Chinese in Canada without legal status. This initiative followed a crackdown on a large-scale immigration scheme involving "paper families." The amnesty program continued through the 1960s. By July 1970, 11,569 Chinese had normalized their status. (*House of Commons Debates*, 3rd sess., 24th Parl., vol. 4, 1960)

1962

Immigration Regulations Part 1 (Landing Requirements), PC 1962-86 (18 January 1962). Those with skills given rights of landing. Family class expanded to include sons-in-law and daughters-in-law, as well as unmarried grandchildren under the age of twenty-one. Extended family members could be sponsored only by immigrants who were citizens of

Europe (including Turkey), North, Central, and South America, Egypt, Israel, or Lebanon. Unsponsored immigrants with education, skills, and other special qualifications were admitted. SOR/62-36, *Canada Gazette*, 14 February 1962, 138)

1967

Immigration Regulations, Part 1, Amended, Admissible Classes, PC 1967-1616 (16 August 1967). Abolished all forms of discrimination in respect to immigration on the basis of race or nationality. Points system introduced for unsponsored immigrants as well as nominated relatives. New category of nominated relatives created. Specific provisions made for visitors to apply for landing (as immigrants) while in Canada. (SOR/67-434, *Canada Gazette*, II, 13 September 1967, 1350)

1970

Diplomatic relations between Canada and China established, 1971–74. Family reunification followed.

1972

Order-in-Council PC 1972-2502 (6 November 1972). Students and visitors in Canada could no longer apply for landed immigrant status from within Canada, as had been allowed previously. Immigrant Settlement and Adaptation Program (ISAP) launched by the federal government to fund settlement services.

1976

Immigration Act, 1976–77 (came into force in 1978). Established three classes of immigrants: 1) family class, 2) refugees, 3) independents based on points system. Established Canada's commitment to fulfill its international obligations towards refugees and to uphold its humanitarian tradition with respect to the displaced and the persecuted. Moved towards population policy, recognizing that immigration must be a central variable in this policy. Business immigrants were admitted under points system, but their business skills were the primary entry criteria. Two subcategories: 1) entrepreneurs, 2) self-employed persons. The discriminatory provision of the 1910 act – to "prohibit ... the landing in Canada ... of immigrants belonging to any race unsuited to the climate or requirements of Canada" – was finally removed. (RSC 1985, c 52)

1977

Immigration Act (assented 5 August 1977, proclaimed 4 April 1978.) Points system incorporated into Immigration Regulations. Last element of racial discrimination eliminated. Sponsored family class reduced. Objectives were "to support the attainment of demographic goals of Canada from time to time; to enrich and strengthen the cultural and social fabric of Canada; facilitate the reunion in Canada of Canadian citizens and permanent residents; no discrimination on grounds of race, nationality, ethnic origin, colour, religion, or sex; to fulfill Canada's international obligations with respect to refugees and its humanitarian traditions." Since 1967, the selection of skilled workers has been based on finding immigrants who hold occupations that are in demand. This has required officials to identify labour shortages and then bring in workers who have both the right occupation and sufficient points under the points system. (RSC 1985, c 52)

1989

Immigration Exemption Regulations No.7, PC 1989-1090 (8 June 1989). Following the Tiananmen Square massacre, the government relaxed requirements for Chinese in Canada. About eight thousand acquired permanent residence.

Notes

CHAPTER ONE

1 Wickberg, *From China to Canada*, 42.

2 Mohanty, Russo, and Lourdes, *Third World Women*, 23–4.

3 With respect to economic contributions by the women in South China, particularly in the silk production area of the Pearl River Delta such as Shun-te hsien, there existed a marriage resistance culture among the women because of their involvement in the silk industry. These women worked outside of the home and did not bind their feet. They experienced much greater freedom than their sisters in other areas of China. Marriage resistance was often encouraged by the parents of young girls because of their economic contribution to the natal family. Similarly, married women were encouraged by their in-laws to stay away from the husbands' family for a period of time in order to work and contribute to the support of their husbands' families. (Topley, "Marriage Resistance," 67–88). In 1941 the male to female ratio was 5:1 in Vancouver and Victoria, 8:1 in Toronto, and as high as 17:1 in Winnipeg (Canada Census data cited in Wickberg, *From China to Canada*, 307).

4 Li and Bolaria, *Racial Oppression in Canada*, 118.

5 *Act Respecting Chinese Immigration*, SC 1923, c 38, s5. "Chinese Immigrant" means any person of Chinese origin or descent entering Canada for the purpose of acquiring Canadian domicile.

6 Szeyup: village dialect from the four counties in South China: Hoiping, Sunwui, Toisan, and Yunping.

7 In 1997, 18,530 came from the People's Republic of China (PRC), and 22,242 came from Hong Kong. In 1998, 19,749 came from the PRC, and 8,083 came from Hong Kong. In 1998, for the first time, Mainland China overtook the Hong Kong Special Administrative Region as the top source country of immigrants to

Canada; they are Mandarin speakers (Citizenship and Immigration Canada, "Permanent Residents by Country of Last Permanent Residence, 1980–2011," statistics prepared for author by Research and Evaluation Unit, 2012).

8 Overseas Chinese associations formed by early immigrants from the Pearl River Delta, which mostly comprised the four counties (Szeyup – Hoiping, Yunping, Sunwui and Toisan).

9 Hoiping and Sunwui.

10 Their husbands would settle them and their children in Canada and then go back to Hong Kong to work because of better opportunities. They would make trips back to Canada whenever they could. I believe they belong to a different category of immigrants, and scholarly studies have already been done on them.

11 The period was extended from twelve months to two years in 1921.

12 Chan, *Smoke and Fire*, 32–3.

13 The total population of Chinese origin in 1991 was 652,650, of whom 69 percent were immigrants (Statistics Canada, Catalogue 11-008E, "Canadian Social Trends: Special Edition 2007, Immigrants' Perspectives on Their First Four Years in Canada," online at http://publications.gc.ca/collections/collection_2007/ statcan/11-008-X/11-008-XIE20070009627.pdf). This comprised 11 percent of the population in Vancouver and 7 percent of the population in Toronto (Costa and Renaud, "The Chinese in Canada," 23–4). In 2001 the immigrants from China numbered 40,296, or 16.1 percent of total immigration; China was the top source country (Citizenship and Immigration Canada, "Permanent Residents by Country of Last Permanent Residence, 1980–2011").

14 Chinese includes Cantonese, Mandarin, and other dialects, e.g., Hakka, Toishan (Statistics Canada data cited in the *Globe and Mail*, 11 December 2002).

15 *House of Commons Debates*, 4th Parl., 1st sess., vol. 2 (8 April–15 May 1879) at 1255. The senator appointed in 1998, is the author of this book; the governor general is Adrienne Clarkson, appointed in 1999.

CHAPTER TWO

1 Toisan, Sunwui, Hoiping, Yunping.

2 Peterson, "Socialist China," 310.

3 Ibid., 330.

4 Ibid., 310–12.

5 Ibid., 309–31; Johnson, "Chinese Family and Community in Canada," 363.

6 *House of Commons Debates*, 20th Parl., 3rd sess., vol. 3 (1 May 1947) at 2645.

7 Ibid.

8 Assented to on 27 June 1946, effective on 1 January 1947.

9 Davis and Krauter, *The Other Canadians*, 56.

10 Dawson and Dawson, *Moon Cakes in Gold Mountain*, 140.

11 Tan and Roy, *The Chinese in Canada*, 15.

12 The Chinese Canadian members included Dr S.K. Ngai, a local surgeon; Chong Ying of the *Shing Wah Daily News*; Wong Yick, editor of the CKT (Chee Kung Tong – Chinese Freemason society) publication *Hung Chung She Po*; Professor C.C. Shih of the University of Toronto; and Dock Yip, who in 1945 was the first Chinese Canadian to be called to the bar. (Chinese Canadian National Council, "Historical Information" section, http://www.ccnc.ca/toronto/history/info/info.html).

13 Ibid.

14 In the House of Commons, J.A. Glen, minister of mines and resources, moved third reading of Bill 10 to amend the Immigration Act and repeal the Chinese Immigration Act. The motion passed, the bill was read for the third time and passed (*House of Commons Debates*, 20th Parl., 3rd sess., vol. 3 [1 May 1947] at 2798). In the Senate, A.B. Copp moved the bill to be read a second time. The bill was, on division, read the second time and, when read the third time, on division again, passed without amendment on division. (*Senate Debates*, 20th Parl., 3rd sess., vol. 1 [9 May 1947] at 337–42. It is important also to note the repeal of the Chinese exclusion act in the United States in 1943, granting a quota of 105 immigrants a year from China, and allowing Chinese Americans to become naturalized on the same terms as other aliens (Daniels, "Chinese and Japanese in North America," 184).

15 Troper, "Canada's Immigration Policy," 255–6.

16 Assented to on 14 May 1947. (*House of Commons Debates*, 20th Parl., 3rd sess., vol. 3 [1 May 1947] at 2646).

17 *Act to Amend the Immigration Act and to Repeal the Chinese Immigration Act*, SC 1947, C 19.

18 *Order-in-Council* PC 2115, passed on 16 September 1930, prohibited the landing of "any immigrant of any Asiatic race," except wives and minor children of Canadian citizens (*Amendment to Landing in Canada of Immigrants of Any Asiatic Race Prohibited*, PC 2115, 16 September 1930, in Consolidation, 1949, 2185).

19 In reference to PC 2115, "Minutes of Evidence, Standing Committee," 10 May 1948, cited in Adilman, "Preliminary Sketch," 331.

20 According to the census of 1911, of the total Chinese population, no one was naturalized. In the census of 1921, only 4.78 percent of the Chinese (a total of 1,766 persons) were naturalized, compared with 50 percent of all other nationalities. In the census of 1931, the number had increased to 2,173, which represented 5.27 percent, compared with 53.46 percent of other nationalities. By 1941, the number had grown to 2,272.

21 Based on Census of Canada information, cited in Davidson, "Analysis of the Significant Factors," 14.

22 Corbett, *Canada's Immigration Policy*, 45.

23 Out of a total Chinese population of 82,369, many of whom immigrated

between 1886 and 1924, approximately 34,000 were left at the end of the Second World War. Following the repeal of the Chinese Immigration Act, 24,000 family members immigrated between 1947 and 1962 (Wickberg, *From China to Canada*, 211–17).

24 Thompson, *Toronto's Chinatown*, 92.

25 "Address by the Prime Minister on the Chinese Head Tax Redress: Notes for an Address by the Right Honourable Stephen Harper, Prime Minister of Canada," Ottawa, 22 June 2006, http://pm.gc.ca/eng/media.asp?id=1220.

26 According to the act, students could have their head tax refunded. And if they could not produce the required certificate, the teachers of their schools or colleges could certify that they had been bona fide students for at least one year. This had to be done within eighteen months of the date of arrival in Canada. Thus, the head tax was not an issue for him.

27 Yee, "The Chinese in British Columbia's Salmon Canning Industry," 9–11.

28 In the 1950s, it became more and more difficult for the Chinese in the People's Republic of China (Peterson, "Socialist China," 309–10). The problem was ultimately resolved by the visit of Pierre Trudeau to China: the agreement with the Chinese government for the reunification of their citizens with their families in Canada was formalized on 24 October 1973.

29 It is likely that she was being shielded from the authorities by a person or persons in the village.

30 This was made possible because after 1954, parents of Asians were included in the admissible category: mother over the age of 60 and father over the age of 65 (*Immigration Regulations* [norms of admissibility], PC 1954–1351, 17 September 1954; in *Consolidation*, 1955, 1865.

31 She asked for permission to leave Hong Kong to get married, although she was already married.

32 Corbett, *Canada's Immigration Policy*, 27–37.

33 Ibid., 196.

CHAPTER THREE

1 Chan, "Chinese Canada," 7–8.

2 Wickberg, *From China to Canada*, 149–52.

3 Lock and Nipp, "From Ontario to 'Oblivion,'" 32.

4 Wong, *The Dragon and the Maple Leaf*, 80.

5 Ibid., 19.

6 Obituary of Douglas Jung, *Vancouver Sun*, 2 January 2002.

7 Lock and Nipp, "From Ontario to 'Oblivion,'" 32.

8 Douglas Sam was able to use his looks and the French he had learned in high school to disguise himself as an Indochinese student stranded in France during

the war, in order to help the French Resistance movement (Trevor Sam, draft of biography of Douglas Sam, 2000).

9 Ibid., 40–4.

10 Ibid., 44–5.

11 The order-in-council stated: "From and after the 16th August, 1930, and until otherwise ordered, the landing in Canada of any Asiatic race is hereby prohibited, except as hereinafter provided: the wife or unmarried child under 18 years of age, of any Canadian citizen legally admitted to and resident of Canada, who is in a position to receive and care for his dependents" (Wickberg, *From China to Canada*, 212–13).

12 Ng, *The Chinese in Vancouver*, 21–3.

13 The Chinese Consolidated Benevolent Association (CCBA) was in Victoria only because of its connection to the CCBA in California. In other Canadian cities, they are known just as the Chinese Benevolent Association (CBA).

14 In Wan Chai, named after Wilfred Thomas Southorn, colonial secretary of Hong Kong, 1925–36.

15 Lumb was born in Nanaimo, BC, in 1919.

16 Her father taught her how to read and write Chinese. As a teenager, he took her to work when he was running a hotel, and every day she had to copy names in the registration book to practise her Chinese. During this time she became very close to her father, and his teaching influenced her for the rest of her life (Chan, *Spirit of the Dragon*, 10–11).

17 Chan, *Spirit of the Dragon*, 19.

18 Ibid., 18; *Order-in-Council* PC 1955–1551 (26 October 1955).

19 Informal conversation with Jean Lumb, spring 2000.

20 *Shing Wah Daily News*, 13 March 1962.

21 Ibid., 12 May 1962, 4 April 1964. Unfortunately, English newspapers before 1970 are not indexed in the Library of Parliament, so it is extremely difficult to cross-check the above references.

22 Chan, *Spirit of the Dragon*, 19; *Shing Wah Daily News*, 23, 26 March 1963.

23 Chan, *Smoke and Fire*, 237.

24 Perhaps they just happened to be the ones asked, and also perhaps those who ended up in a poor situation would not feel comfortable to be interviewed, so there is a certain built-in bias in the interviews.

25 Chan, *Smoke and Fire*, 237.

26 Ibid., 39–40.

27 Thompson, *Toronto's Chinatown*, 104.

28 Ng, *The Chinese in Vancouver*, 25–6.

29 Ibid., 25–31.

30 Ibid., 39.

31 Ng, *The Chinese in Vancouver*, 48–9. The Vancouver-based biweekly publication was run by its founding editor, Roy Mah, a first-generation *tusheng* and a member of the Chinese Veterans' organization. The publication claimed to represent local-born English-speaking Chinese. It reported extensively on the activities of both the older and the younger *tusheng*, who were seldom covered by the Chinese-language press or the mainstream media. It was instrumental in reclaiming a cultural space for the *tusheng* as a group. This publication lasted until 1995.

32 Ibid., 55.

33 Thompson, *Toronto's Chinatown*, 102–3.

34 *Shing Wah Daily News*, 15 February 1960.

35 Ibid., 25 May 1960.

36 Ibid., 27 May 1960.

37 Ibid., 16 May 1960.

38 Ibid., 30 May 1960.

39 Ibid., 25 May 1960.

40 Ibid., 28 May 1960.

41 Member of the Liberal Party, MP for Bonavista-Twillingate (*House of Commons Debates*, 24th Parl., 3rd sess., vol. 4 [25 May 1960] at 4221–2).

42 Ibid., 4222.

43 *Shing Wah Daily News*, 25 May 1960.

44 *House of Commons Debates*, 24th Parl., 3rd sess., vol. 4 (25 May 1960) at 4222.

45 Chou T'ien-lu was consul general of the Republic of China (Taiwan).

46 This was the Canadian Trade Commission, which was renamed High Commission in 1971 and became a consulate general on 1 July 1997 (*Shing Wah Daily News*, 26 May 1960).

47 *Shing Wah Daily News*, 30 May 1960; 11 June 1960.

48 One of the few Chinese community newspapers.

49 It consisted of fifteen questions (*Shing Wah Daily News*, 11 June 1960).

50 *Shing Wah Daily News*, 18, 21, 23, 28, 29 June 1960.

51 *House of Commons Debates*, 24th Parl., 3rd sess., vol. 4 (9 June 1960) at 4722. Nineteen fifty-seven was an important year for the Chinese community in Canada. Douglas Jung, a Vancouver lawyer, became the first ethnic Chinese to be elected to the federal parliament. As a Progressive Conservative, he held his seat from 1957 to 1962. His election meant that the Chinese community had come of age, having a political representative in the federal government, and in fact, he became its mouthpiece in Parliament.

52 *Shing Wah Daily News*, 30 June, 4, 6 July 1960.

53 By "cultural heritage," Diefenbaker was also referring to his own heritage, which was Scottish and German. While previous prime ministers had concerned

themselves with the reconciliation of Canada's French and English cultures, he
aspired to include those of other ethnic extractions in the national identity.
As he said on 29 March 1958, "I am the first prime minister of this country of
neither altogether English or French origin. So I determined to bring about a
Canadian citizenship that knew no hyphenated consideration ... I'm very happy
to be able to say that in the House of Commons today in my party we have
members of Italian, Dutch, German, Scandinavian, Chinese and Ukrainian
origin – and they are all Canadians," (*House of Commons Debates*, 24th Parl.,
3rd sess., vol. 6 (7 July 1960) at 5939-40).

54 *Shing Wah Daily News*, 7 July 1960.
55 This controversy over illegal immigration cost Douglas Jung his seat in the next
election.
56 *Shing Wah Daily News*, 3 July 1960.
57 Ibid., 4, 20 July 1960.
58 Ibid., 29 July 1960. Paper families were those whose papers had been obtained
illegally. For an explanation, see chapter 4.
59 Ibid., 24 October 1960.
60 Ibid., 27 March, 17, 18, 19 April 1960.
61 Ibid., 20 July 1961.
62 Ibid., 29 August 1961.
63 Ibid., 12 September 1961.
64 Ibid., 27 October 1961.
65 Ibid., 1 November 1961.
66 Thompson, *Toronto's Chinatown*, 103.
67 *Shing Wah Daily News*, 28 November 1961.
68 He was well aware of the Chinese immigration situation, because in his private
law practice he had handled many immigration cases for his Chinese clients
(*Shing Wah Daily News*, 4, 6 July 1960).
69 *Immigration Regulations, Pt. 1 (Landing Requirements)*, PC 1962–86 (18 January
1962), SOR/62-36, *Canada Gazette*, 14 February 1962, 138.
70 Ibid.; Hawkins, *Critical Years*, 38–9.
71 *Shing Wah Daily News*, 24 July 1963; 4 April 1964.
72 Ibid., 20 August 1964.
73 Ibid., 19 August 1964.
74 Ibid., 25 September 1965.
75 Hawkins, *Canada and Immigration*, 133.
76 Ng, *The Chinese in Vancouver*, 57.
77 People of Chinese origin who are acculturated in the Canadian way of life and
in the official languages of the country (Ng, "Becoming 'Chinese Canadian,'"
206).

CHAPTER FOUR

1 Thompson, *Toronto's Chinatown*, 104–5.

2 Woon, *The Excluded Wife*, 47.

3 Ibid., 55–6.

4 Ng, *The Chinese in Vancouver*, 56.

5 These conditions were similar in both the United States and in Canada. Because of the US and Canadian exclusion acts and the discrimination against Chinese immigrants, in order to have family reunification some Chinese men resorted to claiming births of children in China fraudulently. Papers were sold for a tidy profit as well. This caused a great furor in Canadian Immigration, as detailed in the previous chapter.

6 She would have had exposure to English during her years in Hong Kong, especially when she was attending school part-time.

7 Ng, *The Chinese in Vancouver*, 56–7.

8 It would be more than an admission of failure. She would feel she could not face her friends and relatives in Hong Kong. The *Report of the Royal Commission on the Status of Women*, published in 1970, did not deal with violence against women; it was considered too controversial a topic even to mention. This was the year that Irene's grandmother immigrated to Canada.

9 These were the prosperous years before the Asian financial crisis, which started in Thailand soon after 1 July 1997.

10 Luk, *History of Education in Hong Kong*.

11 The travel, or head tax, documents were stamped on the back with the date a Chinese individual left Canada and when he or she returned. The births of children were reported, which was sometimes used as a loophole for immigration purposes.

12 Conversation with Paul Chan, former president of CCBA, spring 2001. This was common knowledge among the old Chinese in Victoria's Chinatown.

13 "Paper families" were a way in which Chinese Canadian men circumvented the discriminatory Canadian immigration policy, making them agents instead of victims of immigration into Canada. Also, the reporting of births was not common in China, particularly that of girls. Even where births of sons were recorded in the villages, the dates of birth would not correlate with the Western calendar. The reporting of births to the state is a feature of modern societies. In China it started in the 1950s, and it was not universal in Hong Kong until the late 1950s.

14 Thompson, *Toronto's Chinatown*, 104.

15 The Marco Polo Bridge incident (Spence, *The Search for Modern China*, 445).

16 Letter from Ellen L. Fairclough, minister of citizenship and immigration, to Mr W.A. Lee, secretary of the Chinese Benevolent Association, Vancouver, read in the House of Commons by Fairclough: "I should like to repeat to you what I

have already said on a number of occasions … the government … [is] just as anxious as the Chinese … caught in this position, to regularize their status under the laws of Canada … [I]ndividuals … who decide to come forward and give to the officers of my department a true account of their identity, and the circumstances under which they entered Canada, will be given the utmost consideration and every possible help in regularizing their status in this country" (*House of Commons Debates*, 24th Parl., 3rd sess., vol. 4 [9 June 1960] at 4723).

17 Thompson, *Toronto's Chinatown*, 105.

18 For the process of acculturation, see Ng, *The Chinese in Vancouver*, 59.

19 Alan Phillips, "The Criminal Society that Dominates the Chinese in Canada," *Maclean's*, 7 April 1962, 43–8. By the beginning of the 1960s, Canadian immigration policy was beginning to stress education and skills as requirements for independent immigrants. This article was written in anticipation of the new policy and the expected business immigration from Hong Kong.

20 *House of Commons Debates*, 24th Parl., 3rd sess., vol. 4 (9 June 1960) at 4717.

21 Avery, *Reluctant Host*, 213–14.

22 *House of Commons Debates*, 24th Parl., 3rd sess., vol. 4 (9 June 1960) at 4720–2.

23 *Immigration Regulations, Pt. 1 (Landing Requirements)*, PC 1962-86 (18 January 1962), SOR/62-36, *Canada Gazette*, 14 February 1962, 138. Applicants with skills were given rights of landing; family class was expanded to include sons-in-law and daughters-in-law as well as grandchildren who were unmarried and under the age of twenty-one.

24 Chinese Canadian Military Museum, "Biography of Douglas Jung."

25 House of Commons *Debates*, 24th Parl., 3rd sess., vol. 4 (9 June 1960) at 4721–2.

26 Ng, *The Chinese in Vancouver*, 95.

CHAPTER FIVE

1 Morton, *Short History of Canada*, 282–9.

2 Quoted in ibid., 269.

3 Weinfeld and Wilkinson, "Immigration, Diversity, and Minority Communities," 59–60.

4 Troper, "Canada's Immigration Policy," 267–8.

5 In 1961 there were only 71,689 immigrants (Saywell, *Canadian Annual Review*, 203).

6 *Globe and Mail*, 21 November 1962; Saywell, *Canadian Annual Review*, 204.

7 From the end of the Second World War to 1971, approximately 4 million immigrants entered Canada, but by 1971 approximately 1,200,000 had either died or emigrated (Burnet and Palmer, *Coming Canadians*, 39).

8 Ibid., 203–4.

9 Avery, *Reluctant Host*, 177–8.

10 Between 1961 and 1970, 21 percent of immigrants came from Britain. By 1983,

38.3 percent came from the Asia Pacific region, while 27 percent came from Europe, including the United Kingdom. (Hawkins, *Critical Years*, 260–1).

11 Immigration Regulations, PC 1962-86. Ibid., 38–9.

12 Saywell, *Canadian Annual Review*, 205.

13 D'Costa, "Canadian Immigration Policy," 13.

14 Saywell, *Canadian Annual Review*, 206.

15 *Hill Times*, 25 October 2010. John Diefenbaker said on 19 January 1962, "There will always be discrimination in the heart, but when discrimination is translated into law or national policy, then it's frightening."

16 Avery, *Reluctant Host*, 179.

17 Jean Marchand, introduction to the Department of Manpower and Immigration's *White Paper on Immigration*, 5–6.

18 Ibid., 7–16.

19 Ibid., 17.

20 Ibid., 39.

21 *Immigration Regulations, Pt. 1, Amended, Admissible Classes*, PC 1967-1616 (16 August 1967), SOR/67-434, *Canada Gazette*, 13 September 1967, 1350.

22 Marchand, *White Paper*, 39. Australia's immigrant selection system was based partly on the Canadian points system.

23 Ibid., 52–3.

24 Thompson, *Toronto's Chinatown*, 93–5.

25 This was the difference between Australian and Canadian immigration policies at that time. The "white Australia" policy did not end until the beginning of the 1970s (Hawkins, *Critical Years*, 8–41).

26 *Immigration Regulations, Pt. 1, Amended, Admissible Classes.*

CHAPTER SIX

1 The per capita gross domestic product put Hong Kong among the wealthiest in the world by the mid-1990s (Luk, *History of Education in Hong Kong*, 86–148).

2 Siu, "Hong Kong: Cultural Kaleidoscope on a World Landscape," 105–6.

3 Ibid., 110.

4 Ibid., 110–11.

5 Luk, *History of Education in Hong Kong*, 86–148.

6 Started in 1964 as the first registered Chinese charity in Ontario.

7 CTV, "Campus Giveaway," W5, 30 September 1979. The implication was that "foreign" Chinese students were monopolizing university enrolment to the detriment of Canadian students. What were shown were Chinese faces, some of whom were Canadian citizens, others landed immigrants, while a few were visa students. The most important objection of the Chinese community was that if one looked Chinese, one was regarded as foreign, and it did not matter whether one was Canadian or not. The other point implied in the program was that

Canadian universities should accept students on the basis of the colour of their skin and not on academic standing. These conclusions could easily be drawn from viewing "Campus Giveaway."

8 The controversy divided the Chinese communities. One view was to make a quiet telephone call to the president of CTV to have the producer fired. The other was to launch a big campaign, with demonstrations in the streets across Canada. The latter led to the eventual formation of the Chinese Canadian National Council (Olive, "Breaching the Chinese Wall," 79).

9 As a dependant, if the husband broke the law and was deported, the wife would be deported with him. It was not until 1974 that a bill, introduced in the House of Commons by Health Minister Marc Lalonde, conformed that either a husband or a wife could apply as the main breadwinner in the family when seeking landed immigrant status. In addition, the woman would be permitted to stay if her husband were deported. (Boyd, "The Status of Immigrant Women in Canada," 4). In 1973 the word "spouse" replaced "wife" in immigration statistics.

10 Activist movements in Hong Kong in the 1970s included the Chinese-language movement, in which students went on strike to have Hong Kong made into a bilingual colony, using both Cantonese and English for public, administrative, and political purposes; the Diaoyutai movement that demanded the return of the island to China; the anti-corruption movement; the labour protests and primary teachers' strike. All these events empowered the people who grew up in Hong Kong (Luk, *History of Education in Hong Kong*, 104–48).

11 By 1974, the number of immigrants from Hong Kong reached 12,704, compared with 379 from the People's Republic of China and 1,382 from Taiwan. Chinese immigration to Canada that year was 6.62 percent of total immigration (Luk and Lee, "The Chinese Communities of Toronto," 14–36).

12 Luk, *History of Education in Hong Kong*, 86–148.

13 Ibid., 99–103.

14 A home for Chinese seniors. It was established in 1964 and was the first Chinese charity in Ontario. The need for social services for Chinese seniors increased as time went by, not only with the aging of earlier immigrants but also with the immigration of parents of Canadian residents as family-class immigrants. By 1971, the total number of Chinese in Toronto was 26,285; in Ontario, the total was 39,325. This charity was founded, run, and used mainly by Hong Kong Torontonians; it is distinguished by the use of the Cantonese dialect in its everyday operations (Luk and Lee, "Chinese Communities of Toronto," 14–36).

15 An English-speaking seniors' home.

16 Hawkins, *Critical Years*, 45.

17 Ibid., 46.

18 The Adjustment Status Program lasted from 15 August to 15 October 1973 (Hawkins, *Critical Years*, 46–8).

19 Ibid., 48–9.

20 The number of Chinese immigrants who entered Canada in 1974 was 14,465, and in 1977 it was 8,068 (Thompson, *Toronto's Chinatown*, 148–50; Luk and Lee, "Chinese Communities of Toronto," 14–36).

21 Hawkins, *Critical Years*, 53–4.

22 Assented to on 5 August 1977 and proclaimed on 4 April 1978. The discriminatory provision in the act of 1910, to "prohibit the landing in Canada … [of] immigrants belonging to any race unsuited to the climate or requirements of Canada," was removed (Ungerleider, "Immigration, Multiculturalism, and Citizenship," 7–22).

23 See "Canadian Immigration Policy, Objectives," *Immigration Act 1976*, pt. I, no. 3, SC 1976-77, C 52.

24 In July 1988 the family class was expanded to include all unmarried sons and daughters of Canadian citizens and landed immigrants. In July 1992 the regulations were narrowed, restricting children admitted under family class to those under nineteen and still dependent on the parents (Young, "Canada's Immigration Program," background paper, 29; D'Costa, "Canadian Immigration Policy," 15).

25 Troper, "Canada's Immigration Policy," 277.

26 Hawkins, *Critical Years*, 39, 76.

27 Until 1976, there were no more than a thousand Indo-Chinese immigrants in Canada, mainly students and trained professionals living in Quebec. After the fall of the Thieu regime in 1975, about six thousand Indo-Chinese refugees came to Canada via refugee transition camps in Hong Kong, Guam, and the United States. Most of them were formerly middle-class people who had worked in the government, the military, and the professions in Vietnam. About half of them had relatives who were former students and were already in Canada (Chan, *Smoke and Fire*, 251).

28 In October 1976, Canada agreed to accept 180 "boat people" and in August 1977 an additional 450. In January 1978, Ottawa established a program in which 50 "boat" families a month would be admitted. In August 1978, 20 refugee families from Thailand were added. In November 1978, 604 refugees stranded on the freighter *Hai Hong*, who had been refused landing in Malaysia, were airlifted to Canada (Hawkins, *Critical Years*, 173).

29 According to the census of 1981, 25 percent of the Indo-Chinese living in Quebec were of ethnic Chinese origin; this amounted to 15 percent of the total Chinese population of Quebec.

30 Young, "Canada's Immigration Program," 12.

31 Troper, "Canada's Immigration Policy," 274.

32 The maximum number of points for education dropped from 20 to 12, while

vocational training and job experience together accounted for a maximum of 23 points (Hawkins, *Critical Years*, 77).

33 Ibid., 77–8.

34 See Lam, "The Pursuit of Cultural Homogeneity and Social Cohesion," 97.

CHAPTER SEVEN

1 A Trudeau legacy that will be discussed in detail later in this chapter.

2 Ng, *The Chinese in Vancouver*, 298.

3 *House of Commons Debates*, 24th Parl., 3rd sess., vol. 6 (7 July 1960) at 5940.

4 Ng, *The Chinese in Vancouver*, 208–9.

5 Hawkins, *Critical Years*, 218–19.

6 *House of Commons Debates*, 28th Parl., 3rd sess., vol. 1 (8 October 1971) at 8545–6.

7 Ibid., 8546.

8 "The ultimate goal for multicultural education is 'good' citizenship. The concept … can be used advantageously to lay a sound foundation for a model of citizenship education for all members of society … [with] establishment of a framework … which minimizes the potential for the cultivation of different 'classes' of citizens" (Johnes, "Multiculturalism and Citizenship," 122).

9 Luk and Lee, "The Chinese Communities of Toronto," 14–36.

10 Ng, *The Chinese in Vancouver*, 119–20.

11 Canada started selling wheat to China in 1958 under Prime Minister Diefenbaker; it became a major export to China.

12 Frolic, "Canada and the People's Republic of China," 41.

13 The Chinese Cultural Centre was founded on 11 February 1973.

14 The conflict was between the earlier immigrants from the Pearl River Delta, who were Nationalist supporters, and the later immigrants from Hong Kong's civil society. This conflict was evident in the article written by David Olive, in which he said that diversity and disunity characterized the Chinese presence in Toronto (Olive, "Breaching the Chinese Wall," 76).

15 Both the CCC and the CBA applied for funding for cultural activities, and this led to the confrontation (Johnson, "Hong Kong Immigration," 127–8).

16 Ibid., 46.

17 *Exchange of Notes between the Government of Canada and the Government of the People's Republic of China Constituting an Understanding Concerning the Reunification of Families, Peking, 24 October 1973* (Ottawa: Department of Foreign Affairs, 1973).

18 Thompson, *Toronto's Chinatown*, 176–8.

19 Ng, *The Chinese in Vancouver*, 206–7.

20 Peterson, "Socialist China," 310.

21 Ibid., 311.

22 Ibid., 314–15.

23 1 catty = 0.60 kg (1.33 lb).

24 The overseas Chinese households not only had the right to receive remittances but also to rely on them as a sole source of livelihood and to dispose of them freely, without official interference, even for such "feudal" purposes as weddings, funerals, and ancestral worship (Peterson, "Socialist China," 315).

25 Johnson, "Hong Kong Immigration," 125–7.

26 Larson, "Expert Reflections and Enriched Literature," 44.

27 Ng, *The Chinese in Vancouver*, 124.

28 One of the colleges of the Chinese University of Hong Kong.

29 Wigs and hairpieces were very fashionable in the 1960s.

30 Thompson, *Toronto's Chinatown*, 155–6.

31 The Mon Sheong Foundation was established in 1964; the Yee Hong Foundation officially opened in October 1994.

32 Olive, "Breaching the Chinese Wall," 78–9. The 4 June protests take place annually to commemorate the Tiananmen Massacre of 4 June 1989.

33 Thompson, *Toronto's Chinatown*, 160.

34 In 1992, 38,910 immigrants came from Hong Kong, compared with 10,429 from the People's Republic of China and 7,456 from Taiwan. Various banks and businesses cater to the Hong Kong Chinese in the economic sphere. These include the Hong Kong Bank of Canada, with many branches across Canada; the Bank of East Asia Canada in Vancouver and in the Greater Toronto area; real estate companies that target Hong Kong clientele; and shopping malls and large grocery stores, restaurants, etc., that cater to Hong Kong tastes (Luk and Lee, "The Chinese Communities of Toronto," 28–34).

35 The real forces of Chinese capitalism are the household entrepreneurs who move to the places where money can be made. Although this type of capitalism was integrated and dependent on the global economy, it is independent of any political order (Hamilton, "Rise of Capitalism in Asia," 24; Johnson, "Hong Kong Immigration," 136).

36 Pierre Trudeau, "The Proclamation of Canada's Multiculturalism Policy," Statement by the prime minister, 8 October 1981.

37 Li, "The Multiculturalism Debate," 154.

38 Ibid., 155.

39 Ibid., 155–6.

40 Ibid., 156–7.

41 Mitchell, "Multiculturalism," 263–94.

42 Johnson, "Hong Kong Immigration," 132.

43 Li, "Unneighbourly Houses," 23.

44 Mitchell, "Multiculturalism," 263–94.

45 David Lam was born in Hong Kong in 1923, immigrated to Vancouver in 1967, and made a fortune in real estate. After his retirement he focused his energy on philanthropic endeavours related to Canadian institutions. He was the twenty-fifth lieutenant governor of British Columbia.

46 Li, "Unneighbourly Houses," 28–9.

47 Olive, "Breaching the Chinese Wall," 74.

48 Ibid., 78.

49 Mitchell, "Multiculturalism," 263–94.

50 Wong and Netting, "Business Immigration to Canada," 117.

51 Laquian, Laquian, and McGee, *The Silent Debate*, 53–5.

52 http://www.thelaurier.ca. Founded in 1989 by business and community leaders, it "is a national, non-profit membership-based, charitable organization. Its mission is to advance and disseminate knowledge about the economic and social implications of Canadian diversity" (Mitchell, "Multiculturalism," 263–94).

53 Avery, *Reluctant Host*, 238.

CHAPTER EIGHT

1 Luk, "The Rise of a Civil Society in Hong Kong," 1–4.

2 Ibid., 4-11; Luk, *A History of Education in Hong Kong*, 86–103.

3 Siu, "Hong Kong," 108.

4 Harrison, "Class, Citizenship, and Global Migration," 10.

5 Canada, Department of Manpower and Immigration, *White Paper on Immigration*, 1966.

6 Harrison, "Class, Citizenship, and Global Migration," 10–11.

7 Ibid., 11.

8 "People who have a net worth of at least half a million dollars and undertake to: invest $150,000, dollars [sic], for a minimum of three years, in a province which during the preceding year, received less than 3% of immigrants in the business class, or invest $250,000 dollars [sic] in Canada for a minimum of three years, or invest $500,000 for a minimum of five years – these persons must have a fortune of $700,000" (ibid., 12).

9 It is interesting to note that the total landing of immigrants from Hong Kong in 1988–89 was 23,286, out of which 13,739 were in the independent class, 3,872 in the entrepreneur class, 472 in the investor class, and 133 in the self-employed class. (Lary, "Immigration Statistics," 2–5; Harrison, "Class, Citizenship, and Global Migration," 7).

10 Wong, "Silent Voices," 59.

11 Chinatown in downtown Toronto.

12 Scarborough was a city northeast of Toronto (now amalgamated into the City of Toronto).

13 Harrison, "Class, Citizenship, and Global Migration," 7–9.

14 Mitchell, "Multiculturalism."

15 See Asia Pacific Foundation of Canada at, http://www.asiapacific.ca.

16 Mitchell, "Multiculturalism," 263-94.

17 On 1 November 1994, approval of new private funds was frozen pending development of a program which, after many delays, came into effect on 1 April 1999. The tiered system was eliminated, the investment amount was increased to $400,000, and the net worth was raised to $700,000–$800,000. All investor money would be channelled through Citizenship and Immigration Canada acting as agent for the provinces (Young, "Canada's Immigration Program," 16).

18 Harrison, "Class, Citizenship, and Global Migration," 12–13.

19 Ibid., 16-17.

20 Concerns in Hong Kong about the projected 1997 handover to China were greatly exacerbated by the Tiananmen Massacres in Beijing in 1989 (Henders and Pittis, "Hong Kong Capital Flows into Canada," 1–6).

21 Wong and Netting, "Business Immigration to Canada," 105, table 5.

22 Employment and Immigration Canada, *Immigration Statistics*, 1991; Citizenship and Immigration Canada, *Citizenship and Immigration Statistics*, 1998.

23 Wong and Netting, "Business Immigration to Canada," 97.

24 A term applied to business people, mostly men, who spend a lot of their time in airplanes, travelling between their adopted home, where they have left their spouses and children, and their businesses worldwide.

25 Wong and Netting, "Business Immigration to Canada," 103.

26 Li, "The Economic Cost of Racism to Chinese-Canadians," 102–13.

27 An example is section 27 of the act, used in the case of *R. v. Big M Drug Mart Ltd.* The Supreme Court held that it was unconstitutional to require that all stores close on Sunday as a day of rest because the majoritarian (Christian) practice may not be imposed on citizens who take a contrary view (Canadian Legal Information Institute, "Sunday Shopping Is Legal").

28 Magsino, Long, and Théberge, "Canadian Pluralism, the Charter, and Citizenship Education," 89–110.

29 *Employment Equity Act*, SC 1986, c 31, assented to on 27 June 1986. Its purpose was to correct the conditions of disadvantage in employment experienced by women, aboriginal peoples, persons with disabilities, and members of visible minorities by giving effect to the principle that employment equity means more than treating persons in the same way but also requires special measures and the accommodation of differences.

30 Section 15 (1) of the *Canadian Charter of Rights and Freedoms*. See Henry and Tator, "State Policies and Practices as Racialized Discourse," 101.

31 Section 28 of the *Canadian Charter of Rights and Freedoms*: "Notwithstanding anything in this Charter, the rights and freedoms referred to in it are guaranteed equally to male and female persons."

32 After the riots in 1967–68, the Government of Hong Kong paid much more attention to the needs of the community. This created a sense of belonging to Hong Kong. Also, the children of the refugees had grown up and begun to feel pride as Hong Kongers.

33 Luk and Lee, "Chinese Communities in Toronto," 14–36.

34 In Hong Kong the gender gap with students of higher education narrowed from the 1980s on. By the 1990s, the ratio was 1:1. In addition, with the increase in student activism and the growth of civil society in Hong Kong caused its emigrants to expect equality (Luk, *History of Education in Hong Kong*, 119–27).

35 Findlay and Kohler, "Too Asian," 76–81. The article insinuated that some Canadian universities had accepted too many Asian students, "Asian" meaning anyone who looked Asian, regardless of the fact that most of them were Canadians, and some were from families that had been in Canada for generations.

36 Henry and Tator, "State Policies and Practices," 88–115.

37 Canadian Human Rights Commission, *Annual Report, 1996*, 66–9.

38 Ibid., 316.

39 Based on Statistics Canada data. Hong Kong had been the top source country for immigrants from 1987 to 1993; cited in Lam, "The Pursuit of Cultural Homogeneity and Social Cohesion," 86.

CHAPTER NINE

1 Lary, "Immigration to Canada, 1990," 6–8.

2 Luk, *History of Education in Hong Kong*, 117–19.

3 Pearson and Leung, *Women in Hong Kong*, xiv–xv.

4 Ibid.

5 Ibid.

6 Free and compulsory education up to the age of fifteen was phased in between 1978 and 1981, and a grants and loan scheme was introduced as of 1969 for needy students for local universities (Luk, *History of Education in Hong Kong*, 88–9).

7 Hong Kong Women Christian Council, *Uncertain Times*, 98.

8 The first issue was published on 8 August 1988 (Lary, "Immigration to Canada," 9).

9 Hong Kong Women Christian Council, *Uncertain Times*, 77.

10 Government of Hong Kong, *White Paper: The Development of Representative Government: The Way Forward*, 3–9.

11 Lary, "Statistical Imponderables," 12-13.

12 Some 91 percent of applications for emigration from Hong Kong in 1989 were for immigration to Canada (Lary, "Changing Patterns of Immigration from Hong Kong," 8–9)

13 See chapter 8.

14 The largest group of immigrants to Canada is Chinese, and the second largest is

South Asian. In 2001, the immigrants from China numbered 40,365; from India, 27,902; from Pakistan, 15,350 (Citizenship and Immigration Canada, "Permanent Residents by Country of Last Permanent Residence, 1980–2011").

15 Wong and Netting, "Business Immigration to Canada," 104.

16 Mitchell, "Multiculturalism."

17 Ibid.

18 Ibid.

19 Henders, "Choosing to Stay Behind," 12–13.

20 Lary, "Statistical Imponderables," 12–13.

21 Johnson, "Hong Kong Immigration," 123–4.

22 Ibid., 124.

23 Ng, "Immigrant Women and Institutionalized Racism," 188.

24 See chapter 6.

25 Chan, "Coping with Aging and Managing Self-Identity," 49.

26 Ibid., 40.

27 Ibid., 48.

28 Not only restaurants, but shopping malls, grocery stores, theatres, hairdressers, dentists, and other services with Cantonese as the language of operation have made life very comfortable for seniors (Luk, "The Chinese Communities of Toronto," 14–36).

29 Carefirst was established in 1976 as a pilot project with Meals on Wheels for Chinese seniors and was known as the Chinese Seniors Support Services Association. Since 1997 it has offered services to a wider community, and in 2000 it was relaunched as Carefirst Senior and Community Services Association. CICS originated in 1968, when a group of Chinese students in Toronto volunteered to provide information and interpretation services to the Chinese residents under the University Recreation Centre. In 1974 it became the Chinese Interpreter and Information Services (CIIS), and in 1988 the name was changed to Chinese Information and Community Services (CICS). In 1998 it was changed to Centre for Information and Community Services of Ontario, serving immigrants from all ethnic backgrounds. Most of the Chinese immigration and community services set up between the 1970s and 1990s were by immigrant social workers from Hong Kong.

30 Luk, "The Chinese Communities of Toronto," 46–56.

31 It is now a university.

32 Lary, "Statistical Imponderables," 12–13.

33 After the 1970s, with the growth of the Chinese population, newspapers based in Hong Kong and Taiwan began to launch subsidiaries in eastern Canada, such as Sing Tao, Ming Pao, and World Journal. There were also numerous magazines, newsletters, and community publications, as well as two TV stations (CFMT

and Fairchild), and five radio stations that broadcast in Chinese, mainly in Cantonese (Luk, "The Chinese Communities of Toronto," 54–5).

34 Carol, chapter 8; Rose, chapter 9. See *Immigration Regulations, Pt. 1, Amended (Admissible Classes)*, P C 1967-1616 (16 August 1967), S O R/67-434, *Canada Gazette* 2 (13 September 1967), 1350, section 34 (1). In this section, "applicant in Canada" means a person who has been allowed to enter and remain in Canada as a non-immigrant under subsection (1) of section 7 of the act.

35 Centre for Chinese seniors.

36 Citizenship and Immigration Canada, "Permanent Residents by Country of Last Permanent Residence, 1980–2011" (statistics prepared for author by Research and Evaluation Unit, 2012).

37 Ibid. In 1998 there were 8,087 from Hong Kong; 19,789 from the People's Republic of China. The highest year for Mainland China was 2005, at 42,292, when the number from Hong Kong was only 1,783.

38 Citizenship and Immigration Canada, "Immigration Overview: Permanent and Temporary Residents – Canada – Permanent Residents by Source Country," http://www.cic.gc.ca/english/resources/statistics/facts2008/permanent/10.asp.

CHAPTER TEN

1 Laquian, Lacquian, and McGee, *Silent Debate*, 34.

2 Ibid.; Ng, "Immigrant Women," 184–97.

3 Wong and Netting, "Business Immigration to Canada," 93–5.

4 Both positive and negative stereotyping. These beliefs were no doubt fuelled by statements such as "I had learned that Hong Kong is a place of stupendous wealth created by a remarkably industrious people" and "The new Hong Kong immigrants are going to be making money eighteen hours a day" (Cannon, *China Tide*, 10, 26).

5 Wong and Netting, "Business Immigration to Canada," 109.

6 Ibid., 94–5.

7 Ibid., 115.

8 Since the 1990s, a few immigration officers from Hong Kong have been transferred to Beijing, but the Hong Kong consulate still has a large number of officers who also handle applicants from South China and Taiwan.

9 Tang, "Hong Kong Emigrants in Canada," 1991.

10 Ibid., 2–3. All the above statistics, which include both men and women, have to be viewed within the context of the economic climate of Canada at the time of the survey, which was concluded in 1991. The economic recession in the early 1990s would have produced very different results.

11 Between 1976 and 1986, Canada's rate of natural increase was 0.81 percent per year, and Canada's total fertility rate was 1.6 in 1985, way below the replacement

level of 2.1. One-fifth of Canada's annual population growth is from immigration. The aging of the Canadian population is another factor. Statistics Canada projected that the median age would rise to 37 years by the year 2000, which prompted some to suggest that "every effort should be made to consider using immigration policy to smooth out the current age imbalance in the Canadian population" (Laquian, Laquian, and McGee, *Silent Debate*, 14–15).

12 Assuming the fertility rate stays the same at 1.7, the review showed that, even with immigration of large inflows and 50 percent of the inflow under age fifteen, there would not be a substantial impact on the age structure of Canada.

13 In the early 1990s, the government's rhetoric directed more attention to the economic component of the inflow (Laquian, Laquian, and McGee, *Silent Debate*, 25).

14 According to Margaret Young (of Canada's Immigration Program, Law, and Government Division), the replacement level of Canada's population is considered to be 2.1 children per woman, but the last year this level was achieved was 1971. At the same time, the population is aging. At the beginning of 2001, approximately 12 percent of the population was over 65 years of age. By 2020, the figure will have risen to approximately 20 percent. Based on these figures, there were arguments for and against increased immigration, the latter being that the demographic problems could not be solved by immigration (Young, "Canada's Immigration Program," 5–6).

15 Tan and Roy, *The Chinese in Canada*, 9; based on Statistics Canada data, cited in Costa and Renaud, "The Chinese in Canada," 24.

16 Statistics Canada gave the following figures for the 25–44 age group in 1991: 30 percent of Chinese immigrants and 53 percent of Canadian-born Chinese had at least some university education, compared with 27 percent of the total Canadian population; 32 percent of Chinese women immigrants and 52 percent of Canadian-born Chinese women had at least some university education, compared with 26 percent of the women in the general population (Costa and Renaud, "The Chinese in Canada," 25) It is interesting to note that Canadian-born Chinese women were more likely than all other women to have participated in the workforce: in the 25–44 age group, 88 percent of Canadian-born Chinese women were participating in it, compared with 78 percent of immigrant Chinese women and 79 percent of women in general. Canadian-born Chinese women (35 percent) were slightly more likely than women in general (32 percent) to be employed in managerial and professional occupations. In terms of unemployment rates, Canadian-born Chinese women were at 6 percent, compared with immigrant Chinese women and women overall, both at 10 percent. In the older age group, 45–64, the unemployment rate among Canadian-born Chinese women was 5 percent, half that of Chinese immigrant women (10 percent); among the total population it was 8 percent (ibid., 26).

17 Wong and Netting, "Business Immigration to Canada," 118.

18 At this time, many business immigrants pulled out of Canada, anticipating new rules on reporting worldwide assets.

19 Johnson, "Hong Kong Immigration," 123.

20 Laquian, Laquian, and McGee, *Silent Debate*, 9–11.

21 Wong and Netting, "Business Immigration to Canada," 121.

22 Findlay and Kohler, "Too Asian," 76–81.

23 Hoffman, "Report on Business," *Globe and Mail*, 31 July 2010; Richard Blackwell, *Globe and Mail*, 13 December 2010.

24 Laquian, Lacquian, and McGee, *Silent Debate*, 71.

25 Li, "Immigration from China to Canada in the Age of Globalization," 217–39.

26 Chan, "Chinese Canada," 9–10.

Bibliography

GOVERNMENT DOCUMENTS

"Address by the Prime Minister on the Chinese Head Tax Redress: Notes for an address by the Right Honourable Stephen Harper, Prime Minister of Canada." Ottawa, 22 June 2006, http://pm.gc.ca/eng/media.asp?id=1220.

Canada. Department of External Affairs. "Exchange of Notes between the Government of Canada and the Government of the People's Republic of China Constituting an Understanding Concerning the Reunification of Families." Peking, 24 October 1973; in force 24 October 1973

– Department of Manpower and Immigration. *White Paper on Immigration.* Ottawa: Queen's Printer, 1966

Canadian Human Rights Commission. *Annual Report, 1996.* Ottawa: Minister of Public Works and Government Services Canada, 1997

Citizenship and Immigration Canada, *Citizenship and Immigration Statistics.* Ottawa: Minister of Public Works and Government Services Canada, 1998

– *Immigration Statistics.* Ottawa: Supply and Services Canada, 1991

– "Permanent Residents by Country of Last Permanent Residence, 1980–2011." Statistics prepared for author by Research and Evaluation Unit, 2012

Hong Kong. *White Paper. The Development of Representative Government: The Way Forward.* Hong Kong: Government Printer, 1988

Report of the Royal Commission on the Status of Women. Ottawa: Information Canada, 1970

Statistics Canada. "Canadian Social Trends: Immigrants Impressions on their First Four Years in Canada, Special Edition: 2007." Catalogue 11-008E. Online at http://publications.gc.ca/collections/collection_2007/statcan/11-008-x/ 11-008-xIE20070009627.pdf

Trudeau, Pierre. "The Proclamation of Canada's Multiculturalism Policy." Statement by the Prime Minister, 8 October 1981. Copy in Library of Parliament

Young, Margaret. "Canada's Immigration Program." Background paper. Ottawa: Parliamentary Research Branch, Library of Parliament, 2001

PERIODICALS AND NEWSPAPERS

Chinatown News (Vancouver)

Hill Times (Ottawa)

Shing Wah Daily News (Toronto)

Globe and Mail

Vancouver Sun

BOOKS AND ARTICLES

Adilman, Tamara. "A Preliminary Sketch of Chinese Women and Work in British Columbia, 1858–1950." In *British Columbia Reconsidered: Essays on Women*, edited by Gillian Creese and Veronica Strong-Boag, 309–39. Vancouver: Press Gang Publishers, 1992

Asia Pacific Foundation of Canada. http://www.asiapacific.ca

Avery, Donald. *Reluctant Host: Canada's Response to Immigrant Workers, 1896–1994*. Toronto: McClelland & Stewart, 1995

Blackwell, Richard. "Solar Firm Making Return to Its Canadian Roots." *Globe and Mail*, 13 December 2010, B11

Boyd, Monica. "The Status of Immigrant Women in Canada." Paper presented at the meeting of the Canadian Sociology and Anthropology Association, Edmonton, Alberta. Ottawa: Carleton University, 1975

Burnet, Jean R., and Howard Palmer. *Coming Canadians: An Introduction to a History of Canada's People.* Toronto: McClelland & Stewart, 1988

Canadian Legal Information Institute. http://chatt.hdsb.ca/~ClarkSte/FOV1
-000F0650/FOV1-000F59C8/ca_03_blm_06_bigm.pdf

Cannon, Margaret. *China Tide: The Revealing Story of the Hong Kong Exodus to Canada.* Toronto: HarperCollins, 1989

Chan, Anthony B. "Chinese Canada: Reflections on Historical Eras and Watersheds." *Polyphony* 15 (2000): 1–12

Chan, Arlene. *Spirit of the Dragon: The Story of Jean Lumb.* Toronto: Umbrella Press, 1997

Chan, Kwok Bun. "Coping with Aging and Managing Self-Identity: The Social World of the Elderly Chinese Women." *Canadian Ethnic Studies* 15, no. 3 (1983): 36–50

– *Smoke and Fire: The Chinese in Montreal.* Hong Kong: Chinese University Press, 1991

Chinese Canadian Military Museum. "Biography of Douglas Jung." Vancouver, January 2002

Chinese Canadian National Council. "Historical Information" section. http://www.ccnc.ca/toronto/history/info/info.html

Chu, Garrick, ed. *Inalienable Rice: A Chinese and Japanese Canadian Anthology.* Vancouver: Powell Street Revue and the Chinese Canadian Writers Workshop, 1979

Corbett, D.C. *Canada's Immigration Policy.* Toronto: University of Toronto Press, 1957

Costa, Rosalinda, and Viviane Renaud. "The Chinese in Canada." *Canadian Social Trends*, Winter 1995, 22–5

Daniels, Roger. "Chinese and Japanese in North America: The Canadian and American Experiences Compared." *Canadian Review of American Studies* 17, no. 2 (1986): 173–87

Davidson, Anne. "An Analysis of the Significant Factors in the Patterns of Toronto Chinese Family Life as a Result of the Recent Changes in Immigration Laws Which Permitted the Wives of Canadian Citizens to Enter Canada." MSW dissertation, University of Toronto, 1952 (microfiche)

Davis, Morris, and Joseph F. Krauter. *The Other Canadians: Profiles of Six Minorities.* Toronto: Methuen, 1971

Dawson, J. Brian, and Patricia M. Dawson. *Moon Cakes in Gold Mountain: From China to the Canadian Plains.* Calgary: J. Detselig Enterprises, 1991

D'Costa, Ronald. "Canadian Immigration Policy: A Chronological Review with Particular Reference to Discrimination." Paper presented at the Canadian Political Science Association annual meeting, McMaster University, Hamilton, 6–8 June 1987

Findlay, Stephanie, and Nicholas Kohler. "Too Asian." *Maclean's*, 10 November 2010

Frolic, Michael. "Canada and the People's Republic of China: Twenty Years of a Bilateral Relationship, 1970–1990." In *Canada and the Growing Presence of Asia*, edited by Frank Langdon, 41–62. Occasional Paper no. 9. Vancouver: Institute of Asian Research, 1990

Hamilton, Gary G. "Rise of Capitalism in Asia." In *Cosmopolitan Capitalist: Hong Kong and the Chinese Diaspora at the End of the 20th Century*, edited by Gary G. Hamilton, 24. Seattle: University of Washington Press, 1999

Harrison, Trevor. "Class, Citizen, and Global Migration: The Case of the Canadian Business Immigration Program, 1978–1992." *Canadian Public Policy* 22 (March 1996): 7–23.

Hawkins, Freda. *Canada and Immigration: Public Policy and Public Concern.* 2nd ed. Montreal & Kingston: McGill-Queen's University Press, 1988

– *Critical Years in Immigration: Canada and Australia Compared.* 2nd edn. Montreal & Kingston: McGill-Queen's University Press, 1991

Henders, Susan. "Choosing to Stay Behind." *Canada and Hong Kong Update,* Fall 1991

Henders, Susan, and Don Pittis. "Hong Kong Capital Flows into Canada." *Canada and Hong Kong Update* (Toronto), Summer 1993

Henry, Frances, and Carol Tator. "State Policies and Practices as Racialized Discourse: Multiculturalism, the Charter of Rights and Freedoms, and Employment Equity." In *Race and Ethnic Relations in Canada,* 2nd edn., edited by Peter S. Li, 88–115. Oxford University Press, 1999

Hoffman, Andy. "A Canadian Key Drives a Chinese Success." *Globe and Mail,* 31 July 2010

Hong Kong Women Christian Council. *Uncertain Times, Hong Kong Women Facing 1997.* Women and Faith Book no. 2. Hong Kong: Hong Kong Women Christian Council, 1995

Johnson, Graham E. "Chinese Family and Community in Canada: Tradition and Change." In *Two Nations, Many Cultures,* edited by Jean Leonard Elliot, 358–71. Scarborough: Prentice-Hall, 1979

– "Hong Kong Immigration and the Chinese Community in Vancouver." In *Reluctant Exiles? Migration from Hong Kong and the New Overseas Chinese,* edited by Ronald Skeldon, 120–38. Armonk, NY: Sharpe, 1994

Johnes, Beryle Mae. "Multiculturalism and Citizenship: The Status of 'Visible Minorities' in Canada." *Canadian Ethnic Studies* 32, no. 1 (special issue, 2000): 111–25

Lam, Fiona Tinwei. "The Pursuit of Cultural Homogeneity and Social Cohesion in Immigration and Naturalization Policy: The Example of the Chinese in Canada." LL M thesis, Faculty of Law, University of Toronto, 1994 (microform)

Laquian, Eleanor, Aprodicio Laquian, and Terry McGee, eds. *The Silent Debate: Asian Immigration and Racism in Canada.* Vancouver: Institute of Asian Research, University of British Columbia, 1998

Larson, Laura. "Expert Reflections and Enriched Literature: A Review of Chinese Canadian Women's Narratives." *New Scholars – New Visions in Canadian Studies* 2 (Fall 1987): 40–5

Lary, Diana. "Changing Patterns of Immigration from Hong Kong." *Canada and Hong Kong Update* (Toronto), Fall 1992

– "Immigration Statistics." *Canada and Hong Kong Update* (Toronto), Spring 1990

– "Immigration to Canada, 1990." *Canada and Hong Kong Update* (Toronto), Winter 1991

– "Statistical Imponderables: What We Do Not Know." *Canada and Hong Kong Update* (Toronto), Winter 1991

Li, Peter S. "The Economic Cost of Racism to Chinese-Canadians." *Canadian Ethnic Studies* 19 (1987): 102–13

– "Immigration from China to Canada in the Age of Globalization: Issues of Brain Gain and Brain Loss." *Pacific Affairs* 81 (Summer 2008): 217–39

– "The Multiculturalism Debate." In *Race and Ethnic Relations in Canada*, 2nd edn., edited by Peter S. Li, 147–76. Toronto: Oxford University Press, 1999.

– "Unneighbourly Houses or Unwelcome Chinese: The Social Construction of Race in the Battle over Monster Homes in Vancouver, Canada." *International Journal of Comparative Race and Ethnic Studies* 1, no. 1 (1994): 14–33

Li, Peter S., and Singh Bolaria. "Capitalist Expansion and Immigrant Labour: Chinese in Canada." In *Racial Oppression in Canada*, edited by Peter S. Li and Singh Bolaria, 101–26. Toronto: Garamond Press, 1988

Lock, Keith, and Dora Nipp. "From Ontario to 'Oblivion': War Veterans." *Polyphony* 15 (2000): 32–5

Luk, Bernard Hung-kay. "The Chinese Communities of Toronto: Their Languages and Mass Media." *Polyphony* 15 (2000): 46–56

– *A History of Education in Hong Kong.* Report submitted to Lord Wilson Heritage Trust, 2000

– "The Rise of a Civil Society in Hong Kong." Paper presented at the Human Rights and Democracy in Asia Conference, Joint Centre for Asia Pacific Studies, 16–17 May 1997

Luk, Bernard H.K., and Fatima Lee. "The Chinese Communities in Toronto." *Proceedings of an International Symposium, The Chinese Expansion and the World Today*, 14–36. Tokyo: Centre for Area Studies, Keio University, 1996

Magsino, Romulo F., John C. Long, and Raymond G. Théberge. "Canadian Pluralism, the Charter, and Citizenship Education." *Canadian Ethnic Studies* 32 (special issue, 2000): 89–110

Mitchell, Katharyne. "Multiculturalism, or the United Colors of Capitalism." *Antipode* 25, no. 4 (1993): 263–94

Mohanty, Chandra Talpade, Ann Russo, and Lourdes Torres, eds. *Third World Women and the Politics of Feminism.* Bloomington: Indiana University Press, 1991

Morton, Desmond. *A Short History of Canada.* 3rd edn. Toronto: McClelland & Stewart, 1997

Ng, Roxana. "Immigrant Women and Institutionalized Racism." In *Changing Patterns: Women in Canada*, edited by Sandra Burt et al. Toronto: McClelland & Stewart, 1988

Ng, Wing Chung. "Becoming 'Chinese Canadian': The Genesis of a Cultural Category." In *The Last Half Century of Chinese Overseas*, edited by Elizabeth Sinn, 203–15. Hong Kong: Hong Kong University Press, 1998

– *The Chinese in Vancouver, 1945–1980: The Pursuit of Identity and Power.* Vancouver: University of British Columbia Press, 1999

Olive, David. "Breaching the Chinese Wall." *Toronto Life*, November 1990

Pearson, Veronica, and Benjamin K.P. Leung. *Women in Hong Kong.* Oxford: Oxford University Press, 1995

Peterson, Glen D. "Socialist China and the Huaqiao: The Transition to Socialism in the Overseas Chinese Areas of Rural Guangdong, 1949–1956." *Modern China* 14 (July 1988): 309–35

Sam, Trevor. Draft of biography of Douglas Sam. 2000

Saywell, John T., ed. *Canadian Annual Review for 1962.* Toronto: University of Toronto Press, 1962

Siu, Helen F. "Hong Kong: Cultural Kaleidoscope on a World Landscape." In *Cosmopolitan Capitalists: Hong Kong and the Chinese Diaspora at the End of the Twentieth Century*, edited by Gary G. Hamilton, 100–17. Seattle and London: University of Washington Press, 1999

Spence, Jonathan D. *The Search for Modern China.* New York and London: W.W. Norton, 1991

Sun, Wanning. "'Monster Houses,' 'Yacht Immigrants,' and the Politics of Being Chinese: Media and Ethnicity in Canada." *Australian-Canadian Studies* 15, no. 2 (1997): 143–57

Tan, Jin, and Patricia Roy. *The Chinese in Canada.* Saint John, NB: Canadian Historical Association, 1985

Tang, Sarah F.Y. *Hong Kong Emigrants in Canada: Overseas Survey.* Hong Kong: Hong Kong Institute of Personnel Management, 1991

Thompson, Richard H. *Toronto's Chinatown: The Changing Social Organization of an Ethnic Community.* New York: AMS Press, 1989

Topley, Margery. "Marriage Resistance in Rural Kwangtung." In *Women in Chinese Society*, edited by Margery Wolfe and Roxanne Witke, 67–88. Stanford: Stanford University Press, 1975

Troper, H. "Canada's Immigration Policy since 1945." *International Journal* 48, no. 2 (1993): 255–81

Ungerleider, Charles S. "Immigration, Multiculturalism, and Citizenship: The Development of the Canadian Social Justice Infrastructure." *Canadian Ethnic Studies* 24, no. 3 (1992): 7–22

Weinfeld, M., and L.A. Wilkinson. "Immigration, Diversity, and Minority Communities." In *Race and Ethnicity in Canada*, edited by Peter Li, 55-87. Toronto: Oxford University Press, 1999

Wickberg, Edward. *From China to Canada*. Toronto: McClelland & Stewart, 1982

Wong, L.L., and N.S. Netting. "Business Immigration to Canada: Social Impact and Racism." In *Deconstructing a Nation: Immigration, Multiculturalism, and Racism in '90s Canada*, edited by V. Satzewich, 93–121. Halifax: Fernwood, 1992

Wong, Marjorie. *The Dragon and the Maple Leaf: Chinese Canadians in World War II*. London: Pirie Publishing, 1994

Wong, Oye-Nam Christine. "Silent Voices: Help-seeking Patterns of Recent Immigrant Chinese Women from Hong Kong to Canada." ED D thesis, University of Toronto, 1998

Woon, Yuen-Fong. *The Excluded Wife*. Montreal & Kingston: McGill-Queen's University Press, 1998

Yee, Paul. "The Chinese in British Columbia's Salmon Canning Industry." In *Inalienable Rice: A Chinese and Japanese Canadian Anthology*, edited by Garrick Chu, 9–11. Vancouver: Powell Street Revue and the Chinese Canadian Writers Workshop, 1979

Index

tion patterns, 198–9; strengths of, 198–9; Wing's story, 178–9. *See also* family reunification; media, Chinese language; Toronto; Vancouver; Victoria

Chinese Canadian National Council, 109, 137

Chinese Consolidated Benevolent Association, Victoria, 7, 21, 227n13

Chinese Cultural Centre, Vancouver, 126, 136, 235n15

Chinese Immigration Act, 13, 14, 30. *See also* Immigration Act; Immigration Regulations

Chinese language, 6, 7, 10, 223n6, 224n14

Chinese University of Hong Kong, 112

Ching, Wong Wai, 40

Chow, Olivia, 10

Chow's story, 9, 16–20, 23–4, 31, 207

chronology of legislation (1867 to 1990), 215–22

citizenship: judges, 109; legislation for naturalization (1946), 13, 219; legislation on powers of judges (1914), 217; and multiculturalism, 235n8; process, 14, 99; statistics on naturalization, 13, 15, 225n20

Clarkson, Adrienne, 224n15

college students. *See* student immigration

Committee for the Repeal of the Chinese Immigration Act, 13

Commonwealth: importance of relationships between, 175; recognition of qualifications, 94–5, 155

Communist China. *See* People's Republic of China

communities, Chinese. *See* Chinese Canadian communities

concubinage, 146, 177

Council of Chinese Canadians in Ontario, 108–9

Daisy's story, 145–51, 163, 209

Davidson, George E., 43–4, 74

Department of Immigration, history of names for, 214

Diefenbaker, John, 36, 42–3, 45, 124, 144, 228n53, 232n15

discrimination: Canadian survey on (1990), 197; Charter rights, 157; class bias, 151, 194; Diefenbaker on, 124, 232n15; employment equity, 157, 165–6, 238n29; government departments, 164; legislation to abolish discrimination in immigration, 79–80, 194, 221, 222; reports on, 165; white paper statement on, 79, 144

– gender: birth records, 53–4; Carol's story, 163–5; Charter rights, 157, 238n31; employment equity, 157, 165–6, 238n29; expectations, 10, 193; Hope's story, 100–1; immigration (1960s), 105; paper families, 53–4, 65–7; pay equity, 100, 165–6; preference for males to emigrate, 23; settlement services, 177; statistics on male to female ratios (1941), 223n3; university students in Hong Kong, 104. *See also* patriarchy

– racial: employment equity, 165–6, 238n29; expectations, 193; housing issues, 139–41, 154, 166, 239n40; immigration policies before 1960s, 191; impact on Canada's international image, 74, 81; increase in 1980s, 139–40; legislation to abolish discrimination in immigration, 79–80, 194, 221, 222; racist magazine articles, 152, 197–8

– stories of: Amber, 159; Belinda, 154, 194; Carol, 163–5, 197–8; Hope, 100–1; Jean's husband, 77; Karen, 84; Rena's husband, 136; Yee's husband, 51

– stories of no discrimination: Iris, 91, 92; May, 27; Rena's husband, 106; Yee, 51

Dominion Elections Act (1920; 1938; 1948), 217, 218, 219

England. *See* Great Britain

entrepreneur category: Daisy's story, 147–8; legislation (1976), 120–1, 144–5, 221; overview, 145; points system (chart), 212–13; requirements, 145,

147; statistics, 144, 167, 237n9. *See also* business immigration; points system

European immigrants: immigration advantages, 5, 13, 15, 45, 74; legislation, 45, 215, 219, 220–1; and multiculturalism, 138; statistics, 73, 156, 166, 231n10

The Excluded Wife (Tin-Shaang), 48–9

"Exclusion Act" (1923), 4, 13, 29, 218, 223n5

Fairclough, Ellen, 41, 42, 70, 74, 220, 230n16

Faith's story, 168–71, 210

family reunification, 1947 to late 1950s: benefits of, 37–8; community identity of newcomers, 39, 46–7; illegal immigration investigations (1950s), 40–5, 69–71; immigration policy changes (1950s), 7, 31; impact of separation on bachelor husbands, 37–8; impact on communities, 39, 46–7; intergenerational relations, 24, 38–9; landed immigrants as sponsors, 16; legislation (1947), 13–14; legislation (1955), 36; legislation (1962), 45–6; overview, 14–16, 31, 37–8; statistics, 15, 16, 27, 225n23. *See also* amnesty programs; paper sons and daughters

– stories: Chow, 16–20; Gina, 31–5; Kan, 20–4; May, 24–7

family reunification in 1970s: agreement (1973), 173; diplomatic relations with PRC, 126–7, 128, 221, 226n28; legislation (1976; 1977), 120–1, 221–2; Nui's story, 128–31; PRC's emigration processes, 130–1; student-sponsored family members, 186–7

firsts for Chinese Canadians: Chinatown in a Canadian city, 3; female executive councillor, 167; female legislative councillor, 167; female to be awarded Order of Canada, 126; lawyer called to bar, 225n12; Member of Parliament, 228n51; Senator, 202

French immigrants, 73

French language, official bilingualism, 124, 125, 138

Fulton, E.D., 41

gender discrimination. *See* discrimination, gender

German business emigration (1981), 156

Gina's story, 31–5, 54, 207

globalization of capital: Hong Kong entrepreneurs and investors, 156, 176–7; increase in 1980s and 1990s, 140–1, 145; independence of elites, 155, 156, 166, 236n35; Mulroney on multiculturalism and, 151–2; recent immigration patterns, 198–9; transnational capitalist elites, 151, 166, 175, 198. *See also* business immigration; investor category

Gold Mountain (*Gum San*): myth of wealth, 17, 35, 60, 64; song on, 48–9

Great Britain, statistics: business emigration to Canada, 156; immigrants, 73, 166, 231n10

Green Paper on Immigration (1975), 120–1

Gum San. See Gold Mountain

Han's story, 186–8, 211

head tax: Chow's husband's story, 16, 19–20; documents, 230n11; history of, 4, 20, 191; Kan's husband's story, 21, 226n26; landing money orders-in-council (1908; 1910; 1923), 216, 218; legislation on amounts (1869; 1885; 1900; 1903), 215; legislation on exemptions (1908; 1917), 216, 217; legislation on leaving without registering (1921), 217; refunds for students, 226n26

Heather's story, 181–6, 193, 211

Himel, Irving, 13

history of immigration: appeal boards, 119–20, 219–20; chronology of legislation (1867 to 1990), 215–22; "Exclusion Act" (1923), 4, 13, 29, 218, 223n5; green paper on (1975), 120; lobbying for reform, 30–1, 36, 40–5, 69; overview, 3–5, 12–14, 45–6, 72–3, 142, 191–9; white paper on (1988), 79, 144;

"white" policies, 5, 121, 142, 166, 191. *See also* business immigration; citizenship; family reunification; head tax; points system; student immigration; voting rights

Hong Kong (British): activist movements (1970s), 137, 233n10; brides from (1950s and 1960s), 31, 53, 55; Canadian businesses for entrepreneurs from, 236n34; cultural identity, 39, 93–4, 136–7, 143, 190; culture and living conditions (1970s to 1990s), 137, 239n32; entrepreneurs and investors, 176–7; history of, 143–4, 194; human rights, 157, 167; illegal immigration, 40–4; immigrants in 1950s and 1960s, 39, 111–13; immigrants in 1970s and 1980s, 136–8; medical system, 87, 91; process for immigration, 167; racial discrimination, 155, 181; recognition of qualifications, 94, 114; return of immigrants to, 160–1, 166, 170, 175–6, 185–6; riots (1967), 82, 83, 88, 239n32; tax system, 155, 160; transnational elites, 175–7

– education system: overview, 33, 112, 167–8, 196, 239n6, 239n34; as push factor, 115, 118; stories, 75, 87, 94, 98, 103, 104, 115. *See also* University of Hong Kong

– relationship with PRC: impact of return to PRC (1997), 147, 151, 153, 162–3, 168–9, 195, 202; refugees from PRC, 56, 74, 133, 172, 200–1; smuggling of immigrants from PRC, 32–3, 130

– statistics: business immigrants, 156, 176, 237n9; Canadians in, 196; immigrants (1974), 233n11; immigrants (1987–93), 237n9, 239n12, 239n39; immigrants (1991–92), 141, 236n34; immigrants (1997–98), 189, 223n7, 241n37; immigrants (2005; 2008), 189, 241n37; immigration officers, 194, 241n8; time to process immigration applications, 167

– stories: Carol, 171–2; Faith, 168–9; Heather, 181–3

Hope's story, 97–102, 209

human rights: in Hong Kong, 157, 167; human rights movement (1960s), 72–3; reports on, 165–6. *See also* Canadian Charter of Rights and Freedoms

illegal drugs, legislation (1922), 217–18

illegal immigration investigations (1950s), 40–5, 69–71. *See also* amnesty programs; paper sons and daughters

Immigration, Department of. *See* Department of Immigration

immigration, history of. *See* history of immigration

Immigration Act: (1869), 215; (1952), 219–20; (1976–77), 120–1, 144–5, 221–2; (1988; 1992), 234n24

Immigration Appeal Board (1967), 119–20

Immigration Department, history of names for, 214

immigration officers: discretionary powers, 50, 51, 75–6, 81, 130, 178, 192; legislation on powers (1914), 217

Immigration Regulations: (1954), 220, 226n30; (1962), PC 86, 45, 77–8, 220–1; (1967), 119–20, 221

independent category: gender issues, 74; legislation (1962; 1967), 45–6, 77–8, 221; points system (chart), 212–13; statistics on immigrants, 167. *See also* points system

– stories: Hope, 97–102; Jean, 75–6; Karen, 83

Indian immigrants, 240n14

Indo-Chinese refugees, 121, 234nn27–8

interviewees. *See* research on immigrant women

investor category: administration of investor funds, 153, 155–6, 238n17; "astronaut" families, 8, 141, 157, 224n10, 238n24; Belinda's story, 152–5; financial requirements, 153, 176, 237n8, 238n17; Hong Kong investors, 176–7, 237n9; loyalty to Canada, 156; overview, 145, 194; points system (chart), 212–13; process, 153; recruitment of, 152; statistics on funds invested (1961–91), 156; survey of Canadian support for, 197. *See also* business immigration; globalization of capital; points system

Irene's story, 58–65, 208

Iris's story, 88–92, 208

Japan. *See* Sino-Japanese War

Jean's story, 74–9, 208

Johnson, Graham E., 197

Joyce's story, 65–9, 208

June's story, 80–2, 208

Jung, Douglas, 31, 42, 43, 44, 70–1, 72, 228n51, 229n55

Kan's story, 9, 20–4, 31, 38, 207

Karen's story, 83–8, 112, 115, 208

King, William Lyon Mackenzie, 12, 13–14

Lam, Andrew, 124

Lam, David, 140, 165, 237n45

landing money orders-in-council (1908; 1910; 1923), 216, 218

Laotian refugees, 121, 234n27

Larson, Laura, 132

Laurier Institute, 142, 197, 237n52

Lee, Cindy, 10

Lee, W.A., 230n16

Lee's story, 188–9, 211

legislation: chronology of (1867 to 1990), 215–22; order-in-council in place of (1906), 216

Leung, Sophia, 10

Li, Ellen, 167

Lily's story, 133–6, 209

Lim's story, 53–7, 207

Lo, Anna, 175–6

Lowe, Allan, 3

Lucy's story, 94–7, 208

Lumb, Jean: community activism, 132; her life, 35–6, 111, 227nn15–16; immigration reform activism, 31, 35–7, 43–5; meetings with Diefenbaker, 36, 42; Order of Canada, 126

Macao, 31, 32, 53, 145–6, 186–7, 188

magazines. *See* media

Mah, Roy, 228n31

Mandarin speakers, 6, 103, 189, 223n7

Manitoba, lobbying for reform, 44

Mark, E.C., 13

marriage: concubinage, 146, 177; divorce, 62, 150; domestic abuse, 61–4; in-law relationships, 9, 17, 24, 25, 83, 85, 105; loss of face, 62, 64; marital breakdown, 115–16, 149–50; marital separation by immigration restrictions, 37–8; marriage resistance in South China, 223n3; traditional roles, 83. *See also* arranged marriages; picture brides

May's story, 24–7, 207

media, Chinese-language: availability, 179–81, 240n33; film co-production treaty with PRC, 110; Heather's story, 181–6; reports on illegal immigration investigations (1950s), 42; support for amnesty program, 44; support for immigration reform, 36–7

– mainstream: anti-Chinese rhetoric, 139–41; magazine articles, 152; magazine article ("Too Asian"), 165, 197–8, 239n35; reports on illegal immigration investigations, 43, 44, 69–70; support for amnesty program, 44–5; support for immigration reform, 36–7; treatment of Asians, 197; TV program ("Campus Giveaway"), 108, 137, 197–8, 232n7, 233n8; Vancouver housing controversies, 139–41, 166, 239n40

military service: lobbying by veterans, 5, 13, 30–1; and voting rights, 29–30

Mitchell, Katharyne, 152

Mon Sheong Foundation, 117, 136, 180, 233n14, 236n31

Montreal: Chinese community, 201; illegal immigration investigations, 40

Mulroney, Brian, 151–2

multiculturalism: and assimilation, 125–6; conferences, 108; cultural retention, 138; and economics, 151–2; education for citizenship, 235n8; equality for visible minorities, 138;

Faith's story, 169; government support, 138–9; impact of government policies, 107, 123–4; impact on immigration, 202; legislation, 138; Mulroney on, 151–2; official languages, 123–4, 125, 138; and Quebec, 123–4; Rena's story, 107; royal commission on, 124; support for Chinese organizations, 180; and Trudeau, 72, 125
Multiculturalism Act, 138

naturalization. *See* citizenship
Netting, N.S., 157, 194, 197
newspapers. *See* media
Ngai, S.K., 225n12
Nui's story, 128–33, 209

Ontario: naturalization rate (1930s), 29; teaching in, 84–5, 94–5. *See also* Ottawa; Sudbury, ON; Toronto
Order-in-Council: (1910) PC 1908–27, 216; (1923) PC 1923-182, 218; (1930) PC 2115, 14, 31, 225n18, 227n11; (1955), 36, 220; (1956), 220; (1972), 221; (1974), 120
Ottawa, location of interviews, 7, 16
overseas Chinese: countries of immigrants, 137, 189–90; Jamaica, 75–6, 77; Philippines, 32, 35, 49. *See also* remittances

Pakistani immigrants, 240n14
paper sons and daughters: agency of men, 230n13; birth records, 53–4, 65–7; costs, 66–7; gender differences, 53–4, 65–7; inheritance issues, 43, 65; Iris's husband's story, 89; Joyce's story, 66–9; overview, 65. *See also* amnesty programs; family reunification (1947 to late 1950s)
patriarchy: agency of women, 4–5, 192; education of girls, 146; Karen's story, 83, 85; Rena's story, 105, 107–9, 192. *See also* arranged marriages; discrimination, gender; paper sons and daughters; traditional Chinese culture; violence against women
People's Republic of China: cultural identity, 190; Cultural Revolution, 12, 52, 82, 187; diplomatic relations with, 126–7, 221, 226n28; education system, 6; emigration, recent, 190, 198–9; emigration after Tiananmen Square, 190, 222, 236n32, 238n20; emigration by economic class, 22, 23, 25–6, 32, 50, 89, 102–3, 129; emigration push factors, 5, 17–18, 22–3, 25–6, 98, 102, 172; family reunification, 126–7; land reform, 12, 18, 128–9; living conditions, 128–9; Mandarin speakers, 6; remittance policies, 11–12, 25–6, 102–3, 127–8, 131; Rose's story, 172; Susan's story, 113–14; tourism industry, 173–5
– statistics: Canadians in, 196; immigrants (1946–62), 16, 27, 80, 226n23; immigrants (1971–77), 127, 233n11, 234n20; immigrants (1992–93), 190, 236n34; immigrants (1997–98), 198, 223n7, 241n37; immigrants (2001), 224n13; immigrants (2005), 190, 241n37; immigrants with university degrees (1995–2000), 198; overseas households in, 11–12
Philippines, 32, 35, 49, 54
Pickersgill, Jack W., 41, 70
picture brides: age differences, 48; deposits and dowries, 50, 201; impact of immigration policies, 49; overview, 48–9, 58; prevalence, 49, 89–90, 201; stepmother roles, 48, 49–50, 51; Yee's story, 49–52. *See also* arranged marriages; marriage
points system: advantages of Hong Kong immigrants, 93; class and racial bias issues, 194; co-applications, 115, 169, 193; education points, 234n32; legislation (1967), 79–80, 221; legislation (1976–78), 121, 221, 222; legislation (1985), 121; occupational issues, 135, 170, 184; overview (1967), 10, 45, 79–80; overview (1978; 1985), 121, 144, 192–3; overview (chart), 212–13; revision (2010), 213; white paper on, 79, 144. *See also* entrepreneur category; independent category; investor category; self-employed category

- stories: Faith, 169–70; Heather, 182, 184; June, 80, 88; Karen, 88
population. *See* Canada
Poy, Vivienne: appointment as senator, 10, 202–3, 224n15; her life, 7–8, 200–3
PRC. *See* People's Republic of China

qualifications, recognition of: from British Commonwealth countries, 94–5, 155; doctors and nurses, stories, 82, 99, 116; in Hong Kong, 94, 114; job title differences, 170; teachers, stories, 84–5, 88
Quebec: Indo-Chinese refugees, 234n27, 234n29; language issues, 147–8; official bilingualism, 124, 125, 138; political culture, 100, 104, 123–4, 125, 138, 201. *See also* Montreal

race and ethnicity: Diefenbaker's comments on, 42–3, 124; human rights movement (1960s), 72–3; impact of Second World War on attitudes, 12; white paper statement on, 79, 144. *See also* discrimination, racial
radio. *See* media
refugees in Canada: after Tiananmen Square, 190, 222, 236n32, 238n20; history of policies, 74; legislation (1976), 120–1, 221; Southeast Asians, 121, 234nn27–9
refugees in Hong Kong. *See* Hong Kong (British)
Reitz, Jeffrey, 142
religion: ancestral traditions, 35, 54, 191; increase in churches and temples, 136; significance of, 101, 183; stories of Catholics, 86, 101, 103, 104, 187–8; stories of Christians, 68, 82, 95, 97, 133, 135, 183, 185; white paper statement on, 79
remittances: Chinese Communist policies, 11–12, 25–6, 102–3, 127–8, 131; Chow's husband's story, 9, 17, 20; cultural institutions, 9–10, 236n24; husbands and brothers as sources, 9, 17; impact of war, 22, 53; impact on Canadian economy, 44; impact on

Chinese economy, 131; Kan's husband's story, 22; statistics on, 11
Rena's story, 102–11, 136, 192, 209
Republic of China, People's. *See* People's Republic of China
Republic of China (Taiwan). *See* Taiwan
research on immigrant women: agency of women, 6–7, 8; author's background, 7–8, 10, 200–3, 224n15; fictitious names, 9; impact of immigration policies on interviewees, 191–7; impact of research on interviewees, 8–9, 203; interviewees, 7–9, 203, 227n24; interview periods, 5, 7; languages spoken, 6, 7–8, 192; location of interviews, 7; overview, 5–6; period of immigration, 6, 7; privacy concerns, 9. *See also* names of individual interviewees.
reunification of families. *See* family reunification
Rose's story, 172–5, 198, 210

Sam, Douglas, 226n8
Second World War: impact on Canadian immigration policies, 13; impact on communications with China, 25; impact on racial discrimination, 12–13; impact on remittances, 22, 53. *See also* military service
self-employed category: immigrants from Hong Kong (1988–89), 237n9; legislation (1976), 120–1, 144–5, 221; points system (chart), 212–13. *See also* business immigration; points system
seniors: Chinese media, 179–80, 185; government pensions, 38, 119, 179, 189; housing, 117, 132, 177, 178–9, 189, 233n14; intergenerational relations, 179; personal outlook, 38, 118, 132, 151, 178–9; services, 240nn28–9; volunteer support, 188–9
settlement services: federal programs (1972), 221; federal programs (1976), 120–1; services for heads of households, 177; stories of, 177, 178

Shanghai, China: Rena's story, 102–3, 109–10
Shih, C.C., 225n12
Sien, Foon, 13, 31
Sinn, Elizabeth, 93
Sino-Japanese War, Second, 17, 113, 200
Siu-kuen, Angela Kwong, 168
Southeast Asian refugees, 121, 234nn27–9
Stanfield, Robert, 125
student immigration: after Tiananmen Square, 190, 222, 236n32, 238n20; applications for landed immigrant status, 94; children of transnational elites, 175; Hong Kong immigrants, 94; legislation (1903), 21; legislation (1972), 221; prevalence (1960s), 97; residence qualifications for university years, 97, 99, 105–6; sponsorship of parents, 186–7
– stories: Amber, 157–9; Carol, 161; Han, 186–8; Hope, 98; Kan's husband, 21; Lucy, 94–5, 97
students, university. *See* university students
Sudbury, ON, 18–19
Sung, Goh Jung, 41
Susan's story, 112–19, 177, 209
Symons, Joyce, 167
Szeyup speakers, 6, 7, 16, 21, 128, 192, 223n6

Taiwan: Canadian pro-Taiwan associations, 126; cultural identity, 190; statistics (1974; 1992), 233n11, 236n34
television. *See* media
Thai refugees, 121, 234n28
Tiananmen Square, 190, 222, 236n32, 238n20
T'ien-lu, Chou, 40, 41, 228n45
Tin-Shaang, 48–9
Toisan dialect, 201
"Too Asian," 165, 197–8, 239n35
Toronto: Chinatown, 132, 149; cultural centres, 136; cultural conflicts, 235n14; Hong Kong immigrants, 140–1, 149, 163; housing and racial issues, 139–41, 154; illegal immigration

investigations, 44; location of interviews, 7; statistics, 223n3, 224n13; Wing's story, 178–80
traditional Chinese culture: adoption, 112; concubinage, 146, 177; in-law relationships, 9, 17, 24, 25, 83, 85, 105, 191; intergenerational relations, 179; loss of face, 62, 63, 64; marriage resistance, 223n3; May's story of a foster mother, 25–7; religious ancestral traditions, 4, 35, 54, 191; stepmothers, 49–50. *See also* arranged marriages; Chinese Canadian communities; marriage; patriarchy; picture brides; remittances
transnationals. *See* globalization of capital
Trudeau, Pierre, 72, 125, 126–7, 226n28
tusheng (born in Canada): and assimilation, 124; identity, 39, 46–7, 127; lobbying for immigration reform, 30–1, 40–5, 69; and multiculturalism, 124; publications, 228n31; relationship with new immigrants, 35–6, 39; statistics on literacy, 29; as term, 28; wives for new immigrants, 49, 53, 57–8. *See also* Lumb, Jean

United Kingdom. *See* Great Britain
United States: Canadian emigration to (1960s), 73; diplomatic relations with PRC, 126; legislation on immigration, 225n14, 230n5; statistics, 156, 166; worldwide taxation rule, 152
University of Hong Kong: English-language instruction, 103–4, 158; overview, 112, 158, 239n34; student experiences, 104
university students: magazine article ("Too Asian"), 165, 197–8, 239n35; TV program ("Campus Giveaway"), 108, 137, 197–8, 232n7, 233n8. *See also* student immigration

Vancouver: Chinatown, 132; community solidarity, 39; cultural centres, 126, 136, 235n15; Hong Kong entrepreneurs, 139–40, 176–7; housing and